Practical IPv6 for Windows Administrators

Edward Horley

Apress

Practical IPv6 for Windows Administrators

ISBN-13 (pbk): 978-1-4302-6370-8

ISBN-13 (electronic): 978-1-4302-6371-5

President and Publisher: Paul Manning
Lead Editor: Jonathan Gennick
Technical Reviewer: Richard Hicks, Jason Jones
Editorial Board: Steve Anglin, Mark Beckner, Ewan Buckingham, Gary Cornell, Louise Corrigan, James T. DeWolf, Jonathan Gennick, Jonathan Hassell, Robert Hutchinson, Michelle Lowman, James Markham, Matthew Moodie, Jeff Olson, Jeffrey Pepper, Douglas Pundick, Ben Renow-Clarke, Dominic Shakeshaft, Gwenan Spearing, Matt Wade, Steve Weiss
Coordinating Editor: Anamika Panchoo
Copy Editor: Lori Jacobs
Compositor: SPi Global
Indexer: SPi Global
Artist: SPi Global
Cover Designer: Anna Ishchenko

Distributed to the book trade worldwide by Springer Science+Business Media New York, 233 Spring Street, 6th Floor, New York, NY 10013. Phone 1-800-SPRINGER, fax (201) 348-4505, e-mail orders-ny@springer-sbm.com, or visit www.springeronline.com. Apress Media, LLC is a California LLC and the sole member (owner) is Springer Science + Business Media Finance Inc (SSBM Finance Inc). SSBM Finance Inc is a Delaware corporation.

For information on translations, please e-mail rights@apress.com, or visit www.apress.com.

Apress and friends of ED books may be purchased in bulk for academic, corporate, or promotional use. eBook versions and licenses are also available for most titles. For more information, reference our Special Bulk Sales–eBook Licensing web page at www.apress.com/bulk-sales.

Any source code or other supplementary material referenced by the author in this text is available to readers at www.apress.com/9781430257882. For detailed information about how to locate your book's source code, go to www.apress.com/source-code/.

For my wife Krys and my daughters Briana and Aisha

Contents at a Glance

Contents

Forward

Much of the conversation around IPv6 has been based on the fear of IPv4 address exhaustion and the impending collapse of the Internet if we don't migrate. Customers will be unable to reach our sites and we will simply disappear from the electronic world. Fear, however, is a poor motivator; it does not build a business case.

The last IPv4 /8 range was allocated in June 2013. So many companies started asking questions: "Should I move now? If I don't will my costs go up? Will my web sites be disrupted? Are we ready to make the move? Are our competitors moving over?" These are all valid questions.

It was also at this time that I was the Senior Product Marketing Manager for the Windows Commercial Team. My focus was on readiness for IT professionals, and on delivering content via The Springboard Series on TechNet (windows.com/itpro) where there was a huge gap in user-friendly content around learning and mastering IPv6. Hey, I have been in IT since 1998, and I am still terrified of IPv4 subnetting, never mind doing it with IPv6!

It was at this time I reached out to Ed to leverage his IPv6 for Beginners decks and content, both externally and on occasion internally. He had a great way of taking complex concepts and making them easy enough for anyone to grasp and eventually master IPv6 networking,

I cannot recommend Ed's book enough. After hours of struggling with IPv6 when I was younger, I would have killed to have a book this friendly and concise to help me along.

Have you been scratching your head wondering what this IPv6 thing is all about and how it might impact you? Have you seen an IPv6 address and wondered, "How in the world do I subnet that?" Then this is the book for you.

—Stephen L. Rose
Sr Product Marketing Manager -
Windows- US M&O Microsoft.

About the Author

Edward Horley is a Principal Solutions Architect at Groupware Technology in the San Francisco Bay Area. He is actively involved in IPv6 serving on the North American IPv6 Task Force (http://www.nav6tf.org/) and is the co-chair of the California IPv6 Task Force (http://www.cav6tf.org/).

Ed presents on IPv6 regularly and is still amazed that people want to listen to what he has to say about it. Some of the previous conferences he has presented at are the Rocky Mountain IPv6 Summit, the North American IPv6 Summit, and the Texas IPv6 Summit, in addition to co-chairing and presenting at the annual gogoNETLive IPv6 conference in Silicon Valley. He has also presented at both Microsoft TechEd North America and Europe in 2012 and presented at TechMentor conferences in Redmond, Orlando, and Las Vegas. In all his spare time he co-chairs the IT professional conference TechDays in San Francisco which happens annually in the spring.

Ed is a ten-time Microsoft MVP (Most Valuable Professional) awardee (first awarded back in 2004) and has spent the last 18+ years working in networking as an IT professional. He is actively involved in the Pacific IT Professionals users group (http://www.pacitpros.org/) located in Northern California. He also enjoys umpiring Women's Lacrosse when he isn't playing around on IPv6 networks and maintains a blog at http://www.howfunky.com/, where he covers technical topics of interest to him. He is also on twitter at @ehorley. He received a BS in Civil Engineering from the University of the Pacific. Go Tigers! You can reach him at ed@howfunky.com. He currently lives in Walnut Creek, California and grew up in the Bay Area. Ed is married to Krys and has two wonderful daughters, Briana and Aisha.

About the Technical Reviewers

Richard Hicks (MCP, MCSE, MCTS, and MCITP Enterprise Administrator) is a network and information security expert specializing in Microsoft technologies. As a five-time Microsoft MVP, he has traveled around the world speaking to network engineers, security administrators, and IT professionals about Microsoft edge security and remote access solutions. Richard has nearly two decades of experience working in large-scale corporate computing environments and has designed and deployed perimeter defense and secure remote access solutions for some of the largest companies in the world.

He blogs extensively about Microsoft edge security and remote access solutions, and is a contributing author at popular sites such as CloudComputingAdmin.com, WindowsSecurity.com, ISAserver.org, and the Petri IT Knowledgebase. In addition, he is a Pluralsight author and has served as the technical reviewer on several Windows server and network security books.

Richard is the Director of Sales Engineering for Iron Networks, a Microsoft OEM partner developing secure remote access, network virtualization, and converged cloud infrastructure solutions. He's an avid fan of Major League Baseball, and in particular the Los Angeles Angels (of Anaheim!), and also enjoys craft beer and single malt Scotch whisky. Born and raised in beautiful, sunny Southern California, he still resides there with Anne, the love of his life and wife of 27 years, along with their four children and one grandchild. You can keep up with Richard by visiting http://www.richardhicks.com/.

Jason Jones is a Senior Security Consultant with Microsoft Consulting Services (MCS) in the UK and a former Microsoft MVP (five years). He holds a Bachelor of Science degree in Applied Mathematics.

Jason's role at Microsoft encompasses providing design, architectural, and technical consulting to provide the highest levels of customer and partner experience. Jason specializes in several technology areas including Microsoft Security, Identity and Access space with in-depth knowledge of technologies like Active Directory Certificate Services (PKI), DirectAccess, VPN, Forefront Edge (TMG/UAG), and other Remote Access technologies. Given Jason's infrastructure, firewall, and remote access background networking has always been a fundamental part of his skillset, with a strong focus on the networking aspects of the Windows ecosystem. This has been strengthened further over recent years with direct exposure to IPv6 while working within the DirectAccess field.

Prior to joining Microsoft, Jason worked for a highly respected Microsoft Partner for 15 years as security practice lead, helping to define vision and strategy and to provide technical design authority on all aspects of Microsoft security infrastructure. Jason is a long-time community contributor, especially within the Microsoft secure access space, and is author of several industry renowned technical blogs including the current "The Microsoft Security Guy" blog available at http://blogs.technet.com/b/jasonjones/.

Acknowledgments

I want to extend my personal thanks to the technical reviewers for this book. First up is fellow Microsoft MVP Richard Hicks whose advice is always welcome regarding Microsoft technologies and DirectAccess in particular. Next is Jason Jones, former Microsoft MVP and now a Microsoft employee, for his engaging and interesting discussions around IPv6 and DirectAccess which partially motivated the idea for doing this book. Without your valuable input and time this book would not be what it is, so thank you.

Most important, I need to thank my family for allowing me to take time to write this. They have lived with all the missed time of my presenting, speaking, and attending events around the world related to IPv6. So to my family; Krys, my wonderful wife, deserves a huge thank you for getting "why" user group and IPv6 are so important to me or at least humoring me to make me think you understand why. To Briana and Aisha, my daughters, as soon as you can hack the home router you are free to surf the Internet freely (IPv4 and IPv6) as much as you want; until then, my house, my router, my rules! To my father, Dr. Albert Horley, for letting me play with computers and networking equipment from a young age and for always letting me know that engineering is a wonderful profession. To my mother, Jeanette Horley, for showing me how important libraries are and the value of information and reading. To my sister, Kathleen Loia, for tolerating me as a brother and all my quirks. And finally to my in-laws, Don and Iretta Hunter, thank you for letting me date and marry your daughter and for having me along to all the Hunter abalone camping trips—they are epic!

There are many others who need to be thanked for supporting me in all different ways over the years:

In the Microsoft camp, Jennelle Crothers, a former Microsoft MVP, who is my user group colleague of over 16 years and the person who always keeps me grounded in reality, both personally and professionally, your opinion is, and will always be, valued. Stephen Rose (another former Microsoft MVP) for the years of support, mentorship and championship! Joseph Davies, who honored me by asking me to technically review his *Understanding IPv6, Third Edition* (Microsoft Press, 2012) from which I learned so much in that process. Christopher Palmer for putting up with all my e-mails and in-person questions about IPv6 in Windows, your patience is appreciated. Dave Thaler for taking the time to let me ask lots of questions about the history of IPv6 at Microsoft and for answering questions about networking in general in the Windows OS.

A big thank you to all my fellow (current and former) Microsoft MVPs who have encouraged, tolerated, and listened over the years as I have talked about IPv6: Ed Bott, Alan Burchill, Jessica Deen, Jessica DeVita, Steve Evans, Ed Gallagher, Alun Jones, Mark Minasi, Doug Spindler, plus so many more . . .

From the IPv6 Task Force community: Scott Hogg, Chair Emeritus of the Rocky Mountain IPv6 Task Force and co-author of *IPv6 Security* (Cisco Press, 2011) for being such an open and sharing friend. Bruce Sinclair, Chair of the gogoNET Live! IPv6 Conference and fellow California IPv6 Task Force member for pushing me to do more by example. Shannon McFarland, co-author of *IPv6 in Enterprise Networks* (Cisco Press, 2011) for showing me that being engaging while presenting really is important and that only having one narrow technical topic won't keep folks interested. Jeff Doyle who authored the definitive CCIE study book, *Routing TCP/IP* Volumes 1 and 2 (Cisco Press, 1998, 2001) for being kind enough to think of me as someone with the right Microsoft IPv6 knowledge to interview and have some great discussions. Silvia Hagen who authored *IPv6 Essentials, Third Edition* (O'Reilly, forthcoming) which I was lucky enough to technically review and pushed me (in that polite European way) to author a book—well here it is! Tom Coffeen, Chief IPv6 Evangelist at Infoblox, for the many wonderful conversations and musing about what should be happening with IPv6. There are many people in the IPv6 community who as colleagues and friends over the years have helped me grow as an individual. To each of and every one of you a heartfelt thank you. Let's keep evangelizing the IPv6 story!

I need to extend a personal thank you to Ashley McNamara who took my photo for the book. She is a wonderful photographer and managed to somehow make me appear presentable and approachable, which is not easy.

Finally, a huge thank you to my editorial team Jonathan Gennick and Ana Panchoo with Apress who kept the faith and helped me in so many ways to complete the book.

Introduction

The idea for this book came about after discussions with many IT professional colleagues in the networking, systems, and developer communities. There was a lot of frustration with the IPv6 materials available being a bit biblical in size and breadth and therefore requiring a huge investment of time. Specifically, I was asked time and again for a fast "get me up to speed quickly" guide. So, here it is, my short list of what I think Microsoft Windows administrators need to know about IPv6 and how to get it operationally working in their environment quickly and in the best way. When you need to learn more in-depth IPv6 material you can go pick one of the other books listed as additional reference materials in Chapter 1.

Who should read this book

This book is ideal for those working with the Microsoft Windows operating systems (OS). It is designed for Microsoft Windows administrators but can be useful for those who do architecture of Windows solutions, developers, network engineers, and storage administrators too. Basically, if you work with Windows this book should be useful to you.

What you should know before reading this book

I assume the reader has a working knowledge of IPv4 and the Microsoft Windows OS, both client and server. There is no assumed previous knowledge of IPv6. The reader should be comfortable doing IPv4 subnetting, building DNS (Domain Name System) forward and reverse entries, knowing how to build a DHCP (Dynamic Host Configuration Protocol) scope with options, and knowing how basic routing works. You should also be familiar with netsh, AD (Active Directory), Group Policy, and PowerShell.

How to read this book

I know it might seem odd to tell people how to read a book, but in this case I want to be clear what I was trying to do while writing the book. I want the reader to feel comfortable opening the book and just using part(s) of it. I want it to be practical, so you might use some of the PowerShell examples to get one aspect of your job done and set the book aside or hand it off to a colleague for some other purpose. The goal is not to have a book you will sit down and read cover to cover and put up on a shelf. You can certainly do that, but it wasn't designed that way. I try to provide cross-references in the book for you when possible and I try and give you the RFCs too so you don't spend forever trying to look for things.

I hope the book ends up with sticky notes all inside it marking pages of interest plus scribbled notes and comments in the margins. The book should have a broken spine with coffee rings from late night lab hacking and perhaps a pizza stain or two. I really hope it is one of the go to books that you keep on your desk and not the bookshelf of "knowledge" where big volumes go to die. I will tell you now, the book has errors, and every technical book does. By the time this book goes to print I am sure something in IPv6 will have changed and something I wrote about is either incorrect or no longer best practice. It happens.

Why you should read this book

I really believe that IPv6 is one of the keystone technologies that will be the foundation of the next generation of the Internet. Not knowing it will hurt your career. Maybe not today and maybe not tomorrow but eventually, if you try too long to avoid it, it will hurt you not to know it. This book allows those who already know Windows well to jump into using IPv6 without a lot of pain (I hope) and to leverage all the skills they already have with running production Windows environments. What is important is I am getting you jump-started on your journey with IPv6. Even if you only build an IPv6 lab you are better off and you can answer those IPv6 questions on the Microsoft or Cisco exams too perhaps.

Finally, if you design or architect Microsoft solutions I hope Chapter 4 gives you some of the best practice recommendations that you can leverage in your discussions with colleagues. Remember, these are not hard and fast rules and if your design calls for doing something else that is fine. The goal was to give guidance for those who don't have any operational experience with IPv6 in their environment.

Disclaimers and Support

While I have put effort into the example netsh scripts and PowerShell to make sure they are accurate I do not recommend executing them against your production network. Please make sure to build a lab or test environment and use that to validate everything you plan to do with IPv6. Test and then test again.

Errata

Any errors and omissions are not intentional. Please provide feedback and corrections to ed@howfunky.com and I will do my best to get future content updated.

■ ■ ■

## CHAPTER 1

IPv6 the Big Picture

This chapter is an overview of the "Big Picture" of where IPv6 is at now. Its goal is to bring you up to speed on the current status of IPv6; it is not a rehash of all the old iterations IPv6 has gone through. Additionally, it will provide a very short summary of why IPv6 is important to Microsoft.

I feel it is important to have some background and framework of IPv6 before you dive into the inner workings of IPv6 on Windows. I feel this way because the most common questions I get asked about IPv6 are rarely technical ones. The questions are typically around the big picture such as "Why IPv6 now?" and "Why do we have to do all this work to support IPv6?" or "What business driver can I use to sell management on deploying IPv6?" and not "What PowerShell cmdlets do I use to disable Teredo?" Clearly, depending on your knowledge level, discipline, and practice area this chapter may or may not be as useful for you, but I still think if you are considering deploying IPv6 in your Windows environment it is worth the time to read. So let's jump right in and talk about what is happening with IPv6 right now.

IPv6 Now

For many involved in information technology (IT) the evolution of the Internet and its associated technologies are easy enough to learn (Wikipedia and other resources are available online), so I will skip over the history of IPv6 and provide a more current snapshot of what is happening now and how it impacts Microsoft Windows and the Internet at large.

The current general consensus is that IPv6 adoption has been slow in most of the world due to a fundamental lack of a financial business driver forcing IT to adopt it. Overall, the global statistics for IPv6 adoption in 2013 are deplorably low (when measured against IPv4). While many large Internet companies such as Google, Yahoo!, Facebook, Comcast, Akamai, Microsoft, and others have actively attempted to drive adoption, the penetration of IPv6 for end users has been pathetically small with a few exceptions in Europe.

Granted, IPv6 has a bit of a chicken-and-egg problem. No customers will use IPv6 if their service provider does not make it available and no service provider is willing to invest to expand IPv6 on its network (as it is an expense) if the customer is not asking for that service. Something needs to happen to break this stalemate. The good news is that it finally appears to be happening.

Market Drivers

There have been a few market drivers that have been changing the landscape as of late. Specifically they are

- Depletion of address space

- Support in major operating systems

- Rise of cloud-based computing

- Ubiquity of mobile computing

- Access to reference materials

The subsections to follow describe each of these drivers in more detail.

Depletion of Address Space

Far more devices are being connected to the Internet than were ever envisioned when IPv4 addressing was conceived. Everything from cars to refrigerators to phones is being connected. As a result, we are facing

- The global depletion of IPv4 address allocations by the Internet Assigned Numbers Authority (IANA). IANA maintains the global pool of available IPv4 addresses, and that pool is now completely allocated.

- The global depletion of IPv4 address allocations in APNIC (the first regional Internet registry to run out).

- The global depletion of IPv4 address allocations in RIPE (the second regional Internet registry to run out).

- The coming depletion of IPv4 address allocations in ARIN (forecasted to happen in January 2014).

■ **Note** You can view a projection of when IPv4 addresses are expected to run out. Just visit
`http://www.potaroo.net/tools/ipv4/index.html`.

The impact of the depletion event is that the first Regional Internet Registry (RIR) to run out influences everyone else. The combined RIRs have effectively run out of IPv4 address space, and can really only give out IPv6 addresses. Their ability to give out only IPv6 addresses means that you *will* be seeing a more rapid adoption rate of IPv6 in that geography. As a result, if you want to continue doing business with entities in that geography, you also have to run IPv6. This means that businesses in other regions will start asking for IPv6 address blocks, so that they are able to communicate with those that have only IPv6 available to them.

For example, if you are trying to partner with a business or even market to a customer base in APNIC (which covers all of Asia plus Australia and New Zealand) and you do not have an IPv6 presence, you are likely missing a certain population in that market. Additionally, that market of users will only grow over time.

Even if all of those customers had a transition solution to connect to you via IPv4 do you really want some other company proxying your relationship? Do you trust the Internet service provider (ISP) (either in that region or closer to you) to do the right thing? Perhaps the ISP decides that because these translation services cost a lot of money to maintain it will inject advertisements in your web content to offset that cost or have another method to compensate for its operational cost to provide that service.

You can simply avoid all of that by obtaining your own IPv6 address space or setting up your services on dual-stacked servers to have a direct relationship with your partners and potential customers. From a business perspective it just makes sense.

Support in Major Operating Systems

All major operating system (OS) manufacturers have managed to implement IPv6 into their OS. Not only do they support IPv6, but that support is on by default. This means that for most people IPv6 is possible to use with any modern OS. Indeed, IPv6 support can be found in the following:

- Microsoft Windows since Windows Vista (January 30, 2007) and Server 2008 (February 4, 2008)

- Apple OS X since 10.2 Jaguar (May 2002). The caveat here is that OS X has had variable behavior until 10.6.7 Snow Leopard

- Linux since kernel 2.6.12 (2005)

Windows XP did NOT have IPv6 on by default. XP required IPv6 support to be installed by the end user, so I don't consider it a valid OS for IPv6 by default. However, XP is not really an issue. The pending end of support on April 8, 2014, ensures that companies will be moving to Windows 8 or 8.1 for their client deployments anyway.

For reference, a current comparison of IPv6 support across OSs can be found at http://en.wikipedia.org/wiki/Comparison_of_IPv6_support_in_operating_systems.

There is also good information about IPv6 deployment at the following URL: http://en.wikipedia.org/wiki/IPv6_deployment.

The bottom line is that IPv6 is supported by current iterations of all the widely used OSs. Not only is IPv6 supported, but that support tends to be enabled by default. In the case of Windows, IPv6 is, for the most part, preferred and it is enabled by default. Understanding how IPv6 interacts with Windows and your network will be an important skill to master.

Rise of Cloud-Based Computing

When considering cloud solutions, IPv6 is important as it solves some key constraints that many service providers have today. Some items to consider around IPv6 and the cloud are the following:

- Rapid adoption of cloud services brings the expectation that they will be able to accommodate large scalable workloads and be elastic in capabilities.

- Amazon.com provides public IPv6 support with their Elastic Load Balancer (ELB) service that points to IPv4 resources running on Elastic Compute Cloud (EC2) servers. My understanding is that Amazon.com currently provides limited IPv6 support on internal cloud infrastructure. See: http://aws.amazon.com/about-aws/whats-new/2011/05/24/elb-ipv6-zoneapex-securitygroups/

- Azure supports IPv6 within its cloud offering (with future external IPv6 support planned).

- Many virtualized networking software solutions support IPv6 but might have limited functionality at this point.

- All major networking hardware manufacturers have support for IPv6.

- All major OS and Hypervisor manufacturers have support for IPv6.

- All major cloud management platforms have or soon will have IPv6 support in some fashion.

When you think about the impact that cloud services are having on the industry today, it is easy to see why IPv6 will become an important factor. IPv6 allows for building elastic and scalable infrastructure without the constraints or problems of managing Network Address Translation (NAT) and Internet protocol (IP) address range conflicts. While it will take a while for IPv6 support to be pushed to all cloud platforms, it logically makes sense to have IPv6 as a key foundation for cloud functions. Just imagine having as many IP addresses as you want for your infrastructure, and that they are globally unique! No more conflicts, no more managing overlapping address spaces, no concerns about number of hosts in a subnet, because the number you can have is effectively limitless.

Ubiquity of Mobile Computing

The rapid expansion of mobile handsets along with 3G and 4G cellular capabilities being able to provide increasingly faster and faster data speeds has led to an explosion in IP address requirements for mobile operators. In fact, the LTE specification that Verizon adopted for its 4G services deployment requires IPv6. Many other service providers have done similar IPv6 specification requirements. At this point, it just makes sense to utilize IPv6, as it is the ONLY way to address the huge adoption rate of smartphones, mobile hotspots, and embedded 4G devices that are flooding the market.

Mobile solutions also have the opportunity to leverage Mobile IPv6 if desired by the mobile provider. While Microsoft Windows does not support Mobile IPv6, it does not mean that other devices won't. At this point, I do not think Microsoft will do any development on Mobile IPv6, because no other mobile OS is going in that direction. There just is not enough incentive to invest to make Mobile IPv6 happen at this point.

■ **Note**   If you are interested in learning more about Mobile IPv6, please see *Understanding IPv6, Third Edition* by Joseph Davies (Microsoft Press, 2012) or *IPv6 Essentials, Second Edition* by Silvia Hagen (O'Reilly Media, 2006).

Access to Reference Materials

A principal hurdle in adoption for IPv6 was (until recently) the lack of reference materials on how to properly deploy IPv6 in enterprise networks. That situation has changed. There is finally enough practical IPv6 deployment, planning, and operations guides for IT professionals to follow.

In addition, there are enough manufacturers supporting IPv6 in their software and hardware for people to feel confident in doing a trial or production deployment. Almost every major network manufacturer has specific guidance for deploying IPv6 with its products, and that guidance is growing. Every major OS platform has had IPv6 integrated long enough that there are plenty of platform recommendations and many blogs and articles about how to properly deploy. In addition to what is available online, following is a list of some reading materials that are useful:

- *Understanding IPv6 Third Edition* by Joseph Davies (Microsoft Press, 2012)

- *IPv6 in Enterprise Networks* by Shannon McFarland, Muninder Sambi, Nikhil Sharma, and Sanjay Hooda (Cisco Press, 2011)

- *IPv6 Security* by Scott Hogg and Eric Vyncke (Cisco Press, 2008)

- *Planning for IPv6* by Silvia Hagen (O'Reilly Press, 2011)

- *IPv6 Essentials, Second Edition* by Silva Hagen (O'Reilly Press, 2006)

- *IPv6 Fundamentals: A Straightforward Approach to Understanding IPv6* by Rick Graziani (Cisco Press, 2012)

- *DNS and BIND on IPv6* by Cricket Liu (O'Reilly Press, 2006)

- *Day One: Exploring IPv6* by Chris Grundermann (Juniper Networking Technologies Series, 2011)

- *IPv6 Network Administration* by Niall Richard Murphy and David Malone (O'Reilly Press, 2009)

- *Running IPv6* by Iljitsch van Beijnum (Apress, 2005) (an older book but a great reference)

- *Global IPv6 Strategies: From Business Analysis to Operational Planning* by Patrick Grossetete, Ciprian Popoviciu, and Fred Wettling (Cisco Press, 2004)

- *Deploying IPv6 Networks* by Ciprian Popoviciu, Eric Levy-Abegnoli, Patrick Grossetete (Cisco Press, 2006)

At this point, some of the best online content for IPv6 deployment and operation is from the Internet Society. Its *Deploy 360 Programme* is focused on IPv6, DNSSEC, and Routing. More information can be found at http://www.internetsociety.org/deploy360/. Also consider reading Wikipedia articles, as those have been kept reasonably current. You can start at http://en.wikipedia.org/wiki/IPv6 and then follow the appropriate links from there.

Business Drivers

The current (but not only) business driver that is helping to push adoption by enterprise organizations is the need for business continuity. This is specifically dealing with businesses in APNIC (Asia Pacific region), which includes China, India, Japan, Australia, and many other significant Asian economies. There are many parts of that region that are now *only* getting IPv6 address blocks assigned due to the depletion issue.

For many businesses (traditionally only doing IPv4) the challenge becomes doing business with a company that only has IPv6 available to it. This is especially true for international businesses that have manufacturing, design, or operations in these geographic areas. It can have just as great an impact for businesses without an international footprint but which partner extensively with companies in that geography.

This issue has caused a large interest in IPv6 Internet edge transition technologies. These will be covered later in more detail in Chapter 4, but in summary many enterprises are getting IPv6 services enabled at their Internet edge and using an application delivery controller (ADC) or a content delivery network (CDN) to translate from an IPv6 request to an IPv4 resource. The use case looks no different than providing large-scale load-balanced IPv4 services, but in this case there is an additional step of translating between IPv6 and IPv4. It is very cost-effective and relatively easy to deploy once the IPv6 Internet services have been procured; however, these solutions do have their challenges and pitfalls too, which companies need to keep in mind as they design and deploy solutions.

So with this simple solution in hand some of the largest Internet properties have been able to make their content available via IPv6. The next logical question is, Can their customers access that content if they do not have IPv6 available from their service provider? The answer is a bit more complex than would be expected due to the variety of OSs available today. Mobile devices, smartphones, tablets, laptops, and any other Internet-enabled device can all potentially behave differently.

To address the vast array of access options available to OSs plus all the different provider networks that are at different stages of deploying IPv6, there have been several proposed standards to improve the end user experience of those that have IPv4 and IPv6, which is referred to as dual-stack. Specifically, RFC 6555, which started out as "Happy Eyeballs," was written to address some shortcomings in OS implementations of selecting the right networking protocol. Microsoft implemented this solution in a specific way; Chapter 10 discusses this implementation in detail.

■ **Note** Microsoft chose to leverage an existing tool within the Windows OS called Network Connection Status Indicator (NCSI) to determine if a Windows 8 or Server 2012 host has native IPv6 access to the Internet. This solution gives partial behavior specified in Windows RFC 6555 to the OS, with a more predictable outcome in traffic sourcing. This behavior change was back-ported to Windows 7 and Server 2008R2 with the following IPv6 Readiness Update, http://support.microsoft.com/kb/2750841, and if you continue to run Windows 7 or Server 2008R2 it is recommended that you install these updates. Do note that this means Windows is technically not RFC 6555 compliant, but for all practical purposes the end result is the same.

Service Providers

The global depletion of the available IPv4 address pool has had a significant effect on ISPs. Service providers in general are in the unique position that they have no service to sell if they are unable to provide IP addresses (IPv4 traditionally) to their customers. Now that no more IPv4 addresses are available to procure, there is the business challenge of how the service providers can continue to grow.

There are two ways the service providers can proceed. They can deploy solutions that preserve IPv4 address space and deploy methods that conserve IPv4 addresses used in their networks. Often these methods have undesirable side effects. The predominant solution today is Carrier Grade NAT (CGN) or Large Scale NAT (LSN) which is covered in Chapter 10.

Alternately, some service providers are deploying IPv6 for client devices and then making use of protocol conversion. There are several options available, such as 6rd or NAT64, and ready to deploy immediately and then longer-term eventual solutions like DS-Lite. Chapter 2 discusses 6rd and DS-Lite and Chapter 3 covers NAT64. These solutions could consume an entire book itself (and they do), so I will leave that topic to others. If you would like a nice summary of these transition mechanisms please refer to http://en.wikipedia.org/wiki/IPv6_transition_mechanisms.

Why Is IPv6 Important to Microsoft

The growth of the Internet is driving sales of new platforms, devices, and consumption of services around the world. The continued uninhibited growth of the Internet is key to a software company's growth strategy. This is why Microsoft, Google, Yahoo!, Facebook, Amazon, Apple, and other major Internet players are interested in having a smooth transition to IPv6. The potential for a poor-performing Internet grows dramatically with the use of CGNs within ISP networks and the suppression of innovative software solutions that could leverage the unique unencumbered Internet access that was once available in a world without NAT.

IPv6 gives ISPs unconstrained growth to expand their offerings (cloud, access, network, etc.) and it gives software companies the ability to innovate on top of that ubiquitous access. IPv6 can provide all companies the ability to work directly with their customers in an unconstrained way never before possible.

Software is becoming the next frontier of innovation and Microsoft *is* and always has been at its core a software company. Microsoft, like every software company, wants a direct relationship with its customers and wants to allow its software to have the most extensible and flexible networking model available. Microsoft realized to achieve this goal it needed to adopt IPv6 to avoid the constraints that IPv4 has on it today—specifically, the lack of address space and the brokenness that NAT subjects its applications to.

Microsoft invested heavily to make IPv6 just work within its OS platform. In many ways it could be argued that Microsoft has some of the best IPv6 support out there. (I make this argument repeatedly.) Microsoft certainly has the most widely deployed IPv6 client and server OS in the market today. In fact, since 2008 Microsoft no longer tests its software in IPv4-only environments. This means that those companies that disable IPv6 in their network are running their networks in an unsupported and untested configuration. For many this comes as a surprise; however, with the release of Server 2008, which had IPv6 enabled and preferred by default, it makes complete sense why this is the case.

Overall, Microsoft has made significant investments within its own IT infrastructure to run IPv6 for its enterprise and in addition for Microsoft's external properties. As of this publication, Bing, Microsoft Update, Office 365, and Azure all have some sort of public IPv6 capabilities and more Microsoft Internet properties are being IPv6 enabled. It is important to know that not all Microsoft software is IPv6 capable and some may never become so due to planned end of life or end of support. To determine what Microsoft software and services have current IPv6 support, please see http://technet.microsoft.com/en-us/network/hh994905.aspx.

So there you have it, a very quick summary on how and why IPv6 got added to the Microsoft OS platform and why IPv6 is important to Microsoft.

CHAPTER 2

▪ ▪ ▪

IPv6 Support in Windows

This chapter starts with a history of how IPv6 was added to Microsoft Windows and explains the current IPv6 support in Windows. Its goal is to show how to implement IPv6 in Windows so those designing, deploying, and operating Windows will understand its impact in different versions of Windows.

Microsoft IPv6 History

I have done my best to document the history of IPv6 at Microsoft with the information and resources I have available. Given I was not on the teams or directly involved with the work, and thus this is not a first-person account, there will naturally be errors and omissions. For this I apologize in advance, but I felt it was an important story to tell to help put IPv6 support in Windows in proper context.

The Early Days

Microsoft's earliest experimentation with developing IPv6 support for Windows evolved around building an IPv6 stack for developers to use at Microsoft Research. The initial developers of that IPv6 stack were Richard Draves and Brian Zill who at the time were in the Microsoft Research group. The first public developer release of an IPv6 stack was actually made available around late 1999 for Windows NT 4.0. Much of the early work is outlined on the Microsoft Research web site at http://research.microsoft.com/en-us/projects/msripv6/default.aspx.

Around 2000 Microsoft made some significant changes in technology investments due to the dotcom bust. Dave Thaler, who at the time was working on Routing and Remote Access Service (RRAS) for Microsoft, was told no significant investments in RRAS for Windows would be made in the foreseeable future. At this point Dave decided to continue working on networking and wanted an interesting project to spearhead. It turns out that Dave was also serving on the Internet Engineering Task Force (IETF). He decided it made sense to ask some key questions at the IETF. So he asked:

What is the biggest problem for the Internet?

And the answer was that Network Address Translation (NAT) and firewalls were making it harder and harder for developers to write applications (remember, this is late 1999 to early 2000, when firewalls and NAT were becoming more common but applications were not necessarily being developed to work around them).

Dave's next question was the following:

What is the correct way to address this?

The obvious answer here was to switch over to using IPv6.

And his final question was

What is the biggest technical blocker to the adoption of IPv6?

Answer: It is not in Windows. The largest roadblock to IPv6 adoption is that the most-used client operating system (OS) of the day lacked support for the new technology.

So Dave now had a specific technical problem from the IETF that he could actually work on and solve within Microsoft's Windows Core Operating System Division (COSD) team. Dave decided to leverage the work already done and put together a virtual team to start building out IPv6 support for the Windows platform. His virtual development team was made up of Richard Draves (from Microsoft Research), Brian Zill (from Microsoft Research), Mohit Talwar (developer in Windows COSD), and himself (lead IPv6 developer in Windows COSD). Later it was expanded to include Aaron Schrader (tester in Windows COSD) and Joseph Davies (documentation in Windows COSD). At this point Dave had gotten management buy-in to do two things: (1) develop a production-ready IPv6 network stack and (2) a longer-term goal, rewrite the networking stack for Windows.

Henry Sanders (a Distinguished Engineer at Microsoft) wrote much of the networking stack for Windows 3.x and NT. Maintenance of that code had been passed to several different teams as many networking protocol changes had occurred over time including IPX, AppleTalk, and TCP/IP (Transmission Control Protocol/Internet Protocol) along with newer LAN (local area network) protocols and VPN (virtual private network) technologies. To address code maintenance and performance issues with the existing network stack implementation plus some of the requirements within IPv6 it made sense to eventually rebuild the networking stack for Windows.

Windows XP and Windows 2000 Server

Microsoft developed an add-on IPv6 stack for Windows XP and Windows 2000 Server. This release was a technical preview of IPv6 for Windows Server and was included with Windows XP but had to be manually installed. At this point the team had expanded to include Christian Huitema (technical advisor and author of one of the earliest books on IPv6, *IPv6: The New Internet Protocol* (Prentice Hall, 1996) and Tony Hain (Program Manager for IPv6), along with much of the existing team that was doing the IPv4 networking stack development in COSD.

At the time, Dave pushed for the release of an IPv6 protocol stack for Windows XP to start testing functionality and compatibility of IPv6 within Microsoft. In addition, the work on Windows Vista had begun and it was time to start working to integrate IPv6 as a protocol in a meaningful way into Windows. This meant changing how IPv6 and IPv4 were implemented as two separate networking stacks called *dual-stack*.

■ **Note** The common definition for dual-stack is to run both IPv4 and IPv6 on the host at the same time. The reference in the preceding paragraph is strictly to a Microsoft definition of that term used to distinguish the difference between the older networking stack and the newer one.

Previously, to keep IPv6 from breaking any IPv4 functionality for existing networks the team decided to keep the two protocols completely separate and for them to operate like ships in the night. This reduced potential bugs and problems for functional IPv4 networks, but it also meant that IPv6 lacked some features that were defined in the Request for Comments (RFCs). With the pending development happening for Windows Vista and Windows Server 2008 it was decided to build a unified IP stack which is called a dual IP layer architecture.

■ **Note**   I really recommend picking up *Understanding IPv6, Third Edition* by Joseph Davies (Microsoft Press, 2012) if you need an in-depth look at how the IPv6 protocol is implemented in Microsoft Windows. This book is not an attempt to redo all the wonderful work Joe has done; it is an attempt to bridge the divide between a comprehensive knowledge reference which *Understanding IPv6, Third Edition* is at 674 pages and a practical guide that most information technology (IT) professionals seem to require when trying to learn and deploy IPv6. Full disclosure: I was the technical reviewer of *Understanding IPv6, Third Edition*. It really is the best technical knowledge reference on IPv6 and Windows, so go pick it up (a recommendation from someone who actually read the book cover to cover).

IPv6 continued to be carried forward into Windows Server 2003 and enhanced more in Windows XP Service Pack2, but the real changes happened when Microsoft released Windows Vista. The team at that point included Abolade Gbadegesin (developer in Windows COSD) and Dmitry Anipko (developer in Windows COSD) and went through several program managers, including (not in order) Dr. Stewart Tansley (Program Manager IPv6), Chris Mitchell (Group Program Manager for TCP/IP), and Sean Siler (Program Manager IPv6). The team had many additional developers working on networking and related functions within COSD.

While Windows Vista did not enjoy the admiration of industry pundits, as an OS it had significant breakthroughs in the networking stack especially with regard to IPv6. So, regardless of the unfortunate reputation (deserved or not) that Windows Vista may have, it was a very important OS for the adoption and use of IPv6 within Microsoft.

■ **Note**   IPv6 is not unique to Microsoft Windows. Other major operating systems such as Linux, Apple's OSX, and BSD all support and run IPv6. This book does not cover those other operating systems and how to set up and use IPv6 on them. If you need information on how to do that than *Running IPv6* by Iljitsch van Beijnum (Apress, 2005) is the book you need. While the book is a bit older now, it still has a lot of relevant IPv6 information. My hope is that it will be updated soon to reflect some of the newer RFCs that have been published along with some significant changes in addressing that have occurred. The book also covers network routing protocols, which is very useful.

Current IPv6 Networking Stack Implementation

It is important to know that the TCP/IP protocol stack since Windows Server 2008 and Windows Vista is a dual IP layer architecture implementation. This is different from older versions of Windows and is also different from how many other OS manufacturers implement IPv6. Figure 2-1 shows how the current networking stack is architecturally built for Windows compared to the old version.

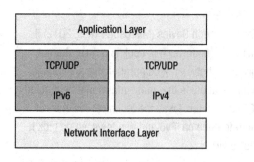

Older TCP/IP Networking Stack (Dual-Stack)   New TCP/IP Networking Stack (Dual IP Layer)

Figure 2-1. *TCP/IP networking stack for Windows*

■ **Tip**   While Figure 2-1 does not show them, the new TCP/IP networking stack supports several transition technologies to help transition from IPv4 to IPv6. Specifically, Windows has support for 6to4, ISATAP, and Teredo built in natively to the OS. The section "Transition Technologies" provides an overview and more details on these transition technologies can be found in Chapter 3.

As Figure 2-1 illustrates, it is not technically possible to remove IPv6 from the networking stack (or Tcpip.sys). Many IT professionals think it is possible to "turn off" IPv6 within the Microsoft OS. While it is possible to technically limit (severely so) the capabilities of IPv6 within the networking stack you cannot actually fully disable the protocol. Even after applying all the instructions from Microsoft TechNet knowledgebase articles (e.g., http://support.microsoft.com/kb/929852) on disabling IPv6 you are still able to ping localhost (::1) because the core OS needs to be able to make that call for certain functions regardless of what is made available to external (non-local) network resources. IPv4 and IPv6 are combined in Tcpip.sys and the only way to totally turn off IPv6 is to remove TCP/IP.

For some odd reason, some IT professionals find it upsetting that the protocol cannot be turned off. It is as if somehow IPv6 is an affront to what they do and how they functionally run their environments. "If I want to disable IPv6, then it should be disabled!" is a common refrain I have heard at conferences and workshops. I believe this view to be misguided due to the lack of understanding around IPv6 and how it now operates in Windows. Many security professionals will argue that you should disable services to help reduce attack surfaces, which is an appropriate answer, but in the case of IPv6 I would argue that they likely do not understand the new Tcpip.sys architecture and need to reconsider their position.

Perhaps a different view can be considered? I believe the fact that the protocol cannot be turned off shows how critical IPv6 and TCP/IP are to the core OS functionality of Windows, and perhaps everyone should be learning a whole lot more about IPv6. Many seem to think learning something new like IPv6 is a waste of their time—that IPv4 functions just fine as is and that if we all continue to use NAT we can avoid this new networking protocol all together. I hope that with the knowledge of how deeply coupled IPv6 and Windows OS are, more people will come to realize that their hopes of avoiding IPv6 are unrealistic. I have heard more than one IT professional say that he hopes to retire before he has to learn IPv6; I'm just curious why? I think fear of the unknown is getting the upper hand in many cases. I hope we can overcome your fear and objections in this book and get you rapidly deploying IPv6 with confidence.

More recently, the IPv6 team at Microsoft is now under the networking umbrella, originally led by Scott Roberts (Principal Program Manager Lead—Windows Networking). Today, Christopher Palmer (Program Manager—Windows Networking and Devices) is at the IPv6 helm.

Features and Functions of the Stack

So what features and functions did Microsoft include in its IPv6 TCP/IP networking stack? It is far easier to actually list what Microsoft chose NOT to implement in Windows rather than the other way around. The items that follow are ones I felt were significant enough to mention. So, for the sake of brevity (even though it looks more negative listing what some would interpret as shortcomings), here is a short list of what was left out.

> **Mobile IPv6:** allows your host to keep an IPv6 address while moving from one network to another.
>
> **RFC 6106—IPv6 Router Advertisement Options for DNS Configuration:** allows a router to advertise Domain Name System (DNS) information in a router advertisement.
>
> **DS-Lite–dual-stack lite:** allows service providers to reduce their IPv4 needs when deployed on an IPv6 network.
>
> **6in4:** was replaced with 6to4, which is more flexible. This is because the IPv4 endpoint information is embedded dynamically into the 6to4 address, unlike 6in4 which was all statically configured.
>
> **6rd:** helps with rapid deployment of IPv6 across IPv4 networks.
>
> **SEND (SEcure Neighbor Discovery):** provides a secure method for neighbor discovery in IPv6.

This list outlines what was left out of the actual networking stack (Tcpip.sys) in Windows. However, that doesn't necessarily mean the capability is excluded from Windows because third parties can develop extensions. For instance, there is an open source version of SEND available to run on Windows because Microsoft, as an OS manufacturer, is not specifically supporting SEND at this time. It is my personal opinion there will be little to no adoption of SEND in the near future (much to my IPv6 colleague Jeremy Duncan's dismay) until companies start operating IPv6-only networks.

There are also security, third-party firewall, and application impacts that are not reflected in this list. For instance, IPv6 hosts can be susceptible to security attacks like router advertisement (RA) floods, RA spoofing, and other exploits due to how the actual IPv6 protocol works. Sam Bowne, a security researcher and professor, has done some wonderful work documenting these and testing them. You can find his work and that of his students online at YouTube (you can use your favorite search engine to find them) or at his blog `http://samsclass.info/`.

Mobile IPv6

Mobile IPv6 allows a host to retain its IPv6 address while moving to other networks. It does this through a registration process to the IPv6 router that is providing that Mobile IPv6 service; therefore, the host OS must natively support Mobile IPv6 or it is not possible to register to have traffic forwarded or sent directly to the host. There are advantages to being able to retain your IPv6 address while moving around on different networks—specifically, for things like Skype, Lync, or other voice and video services so you do not drop your call or video chat even if you moved from your corporate wifi onto your cellular data plan. Your session should (in theory) not drop due to changing networks.

Mobile IPv6 was not implemented in Windows and likely will not make it into the standard client or server version anytime soon (this is my personal opinion and should not be interpreted as anything other than such). It is possible that Microsoft might feel it is important to add Mobile IPv6 to its Window Phone OS in the future. If you are interested in more details about Mobile IPv6 please refer to *Understanding IPv6, Third Edition* by Joseph Davies (Microsoft Press, 2012) or *IPv6 Essentials, Second Edition* by Silvia Hagen (O'Reilly Media, 2006), which both have explanations of how Mobile IPv6 works. Because Windows does not support Mobile IPv6 and there are very few Mobile IPv6 platforms deployed (if any), your time is better invested learning other IPv6 technologies. If you are using the Windows Server or Client OS today you just don't need to know Mobile IPv6 at this point.

RFC 6106-IPv6 Router Advertisement Options for DNS Configuration

Due to how the IPv6 protocol works, there is no mechanism to allow a host that has automatically configured its IPv6 address (through a process known as StateLess Address AutoConfiguration, or SLAAC, which is covered in Chapter 3) to also automatically obtain information about a DNS server. This is actually no different from IPv4. RFC 6106 was developed to allow that host to obtain DNS server IP addresses from the local router in an Router Advertisement (RA). The vast majority of networks today make use of Dynamic Host Configuration Protocol (DHCP) to provide this type of information to IPv4 hosts, and there is no reason you would not continue to do this in IPv6.

Microsoft has publicly stated that it does not intend to develop any support for RFC 6106 into Windows. It is my understanding that Microsoft feels that any organization that wishes to publish DNS information will use either DHCPv6 Stateful or Stateless (more information on DHCPv6 is covered in Chapter 9) to provide that function. Use of RFC 6106 is a bit of an IPv6 religious war requiring more time and space to explain than what is allowed here. At this point, you should not anticipate any support for this feature. If you have clients in your environment that require this feature you will have to find a different solution to support this function. Some network hardware manufacturers have started supporting RFC 6106 for this reason. At this point in time, the main OS platform that does not have DHCPv6 support is Android. If Android adds support for DHCPv6, then the need for RFC 6106 effectively goes away.

DS-Lite

DS-Lite or dual-stack lite is a transition technology that allows service providers that have transitioned or deployed IPv6 networks to run IPv4 services at their customer edge. The IPv4 traffic is encapsulated in IPv6 and tunneled to a transition device that allows the remote IPv4 address to talk natively to the IPv4 services that the service provider exposes. This greatly reduces the number of IPv4 addresses a service provider has to use in its network, which helps it conserve the IPv4 address pools it has currently.

Because DS-Lite is designed for service providers it doesn't make a lot of sense to include DS-Lite as a transition technology in the Windows OS. DS-Lite is really a technology that a service provider would utilize and have operating in the customer premise equipment (CPE). It is unlikely you will see support for DS-Lite make it into Windows unless a third party implements it as an open source or commercial product.

6in4

6in4 is a transition technology that was a predecessor to 6to4 and provided the same functionality but was a manual and static configuration. It allows a host that has a public IPv4 address to have a tunnel and encapsulate its IPv6 traffic in an IPv4 tunnel.

6in4 as a result does not have wide adoption and was replaced with 6to4 as an alternate method due to the fact that 6in4 was a manual process. Microsoft logically chose to adopt 6to4 instead as a transition technology. If you find any references to Microsoft supporting 6in4 they are outdated. Microsoft had 6in4 support in early experimental code, but as stated previously, it was replaced with 6to4.

6rd

6rd allows service providers to rapidly deploy IPv6 for their customers without having to dual-stack their entire network (which can be a long and potentially costly process). 6rd makes use of tunnels to encapsulate its IPv6 traffic in an IPv4 tunnel.

Like DS-Lite, 6rd is a transition technology that service providers would utilizing in deploying IPv6. It uses many of the same processes as 6to4 to implement IPv6 but allows the service provider to use its own IPv6 address range (in IPv6 vernacular an address range is called a prefix) instead of the 6to4 standardized prefix of 2002::/16. At this point I do not anticipate Microsoft adding any 6rd support to the Windows OS.

SEND

SEcure Neighbor Discovery (SEND) is a method of validating the neighbor discovery process in IPv6 for hosts. Microsoft has publicly stated that at this time it does not intend to develop native SEND support in the Windows OS, principally because SEND is an IPv6-only solution and most networks for the foreseeable future will be dual-stacked. Not until networks are IPv6-only will SEND provide a beneficial security service.

While open source SEND clients are available today for Windows we are unlikely to see widespread adoption. SEND is available for other OS platforms and you may see some secure IPv6-only networks choose to deploy this solution, but they will likely utilize third-party tools to do so.

Tools Available to Manage IPv6 in Windows

The great news is that IPv6 is just as manageable and easy to operate as IPv4 in Windows. In fact, IPv6 forces a few changes in managing networks that will actually benefit most organizations.

First, you can use Active Directory Domain Services (AD DS), PowerShell, netsh, and the registry to manage the majority of IPv6 parameters within Windows. Every current native tool Microsoft has released to manage the OS or to manage related software systems and components properly supports IPv6 and if required has the correct fields and attributes. Tools such as System Center, Server Manager, PowerShell, and even Microsoft's cloud platform Azure all have the appropriate changes to accommodate IPv6.

It is important to point out how critical this change by Microsoft was to its tools because of the impact it has in the big picture of IPv6 adoption. Both adoption rates and operational environments would suffer from a lack of implementing IPv6 if ubiquitous support of IPv6 was not available in the tools that IT professionals use to build and run data centers, enterprise networks, or even home networks. No one would bother deploying IPv6 if they had to keep adding features and functions over and over again because Microsoft had chosen to ignore IPv6 support and overlooked building the tools directly into the Windows platform.

Tools Available to Migrate to IPv6 in Windows

Microsoft realized that most organizations would not rush to adopt IPv6 and many would try and avoid it. To help with the transition to IPv6 Microsoft developed a specific migration plan and then went about utilizing available transition technologies (and in one case even inventing one) to help solve some specific problems it felt were important to help in migration.

Realize that migrating to IPv6 typically follows a pretty standard formula. Many IPv4-only networks first start with a transition technology to allow them to deploy islands of IPv6 hosts to start testing (basically lab build-outs and proof of concepts.) In many early Microsoft Infrastructure Planning and Design (IPD) Guides it was recommended to utilize ISATAP (Intra-Site Automatic Tunnel Addressing Protocol) to build out Proof of Concept (POC) IPv6 networks, mainly around DirectAccess solutions. ISATAP is one of the three main transition technologies in Windows, so let's go ahead and list all of them now.

Transition Technologies

Since Windows Vista and Windows Server 2008, Microsoft has included IPv6 transition technologies to help accelerate the adoption of IPv6. The goal of transition technologies is to allow those that are still utilizing IPv4 to have a method to start utilizing IPv6 with a low barrier to adoption. Microsoft chose three transition technologies to include in its OS: 6to4, ISATAP, and Teredo. The following sections give a brief overview of each transition technology (Chapter 3 provides details and Chapter 4 gives best practice recommendations).

6to4 Transition Technology

6to4 is a native transition technology available from the Windows Vista and Server 2008 release onward. It is designed to allow a host that has a public IPv4 address to be able to automatically assign and build itself an IPv6 address it can utilize to talk to the IPv6 Internet. 6to4 IPv6 addresses always use the following IPv6 prefix:

```
2002::/16
```

6to4 makes use of public 6to4 routers that connect the IPv6 and IPv4 Internet and allow 6to4 hosts to connect to the IPv6 Internet. One of the challenges with 6to4 is that you are relying on others in the IPv6 and IPv4 community to maintain and run these 6to4 routers. An additional problem is the asymmetrical nature of 6to4 traffic which can introduce very high latency due to suboptimal routing. Chapter 3 provides details regarding how 6to4 works.

That is the very quick overview of 6to4. 6to4 is also enabled by default. If you are lucky enough to have public IPv4 address readily available you can test this out in a lab very quickly by simply giving your Windows client a public IPv4 address then trying to connect to an IPv6-enabled Internet resource such as http://www.cav6tf.org (if you have IPv6 working, then the turtle on the web site should be swimming) or http://www.bing.com. You will likely need to use a browser plug-in like IPvFox for Firefox or IPvFoo for Chrome to help you determine if you are using IPv6 to connect to those resources. Another wonderful site to test IPv6 availability is http://test-ipv6.com, which displays exactly how you are connecting and rates your IPv6 connectivity.

ISATAP Transition Technology

ISATAP is a native transition technology available from the Windows Vista release onward. It is designed to allow a host that has an IPv4 address to be able to automatically assign and build itself an IPv6 address it can utilize to talk to the IPv6 Intranet or Internet. ISTAP utilizes DNS to determine what gateway to use.

In practice, ISATAP is an IPv6 overlay tunnel network that runs on top of your IPv4 network. The ISATAP server assigns the IPv6 prefix and may or may not provide IPv6 routing.

That is the very quick overview of ISATAP. ISATAP is also enabled by default. ISATAP is only utilized if a published DNS record exists. This record will utilize the Fully Qualified Domain Name (FQDN) along with the host record ISATAP in the following syntax ISATAP < FQDN > (i.e., isatap.example.com). If there is no entry, then the host does not attempt to use ISATAP unless it is manually configured using netsh or PowerShell or centrally configured through Group Policy.

Teredo Transition Technology

Teredo is a native transition technology available from the Windows Vista release onward. It was developed by Microsoft and designed to allow a client behind a NAT device with a private IPv4 address to be able to automatically assign and build itself an IPv6 address it can utilize to talk to the Teredo server and other Teredo clients connected to that Teredo server.

A Teredo client uses DNS to determine which Teredo server to utilize, and that Teredo server assigns an IPv6 prefix for the client Teredo host to build an IPv6 Teredo address. The Teredo server may also operate as a Teredo relay, meaning it is capable of forwarding Teredo client traffic to the IPv6 Internet.

That is the very quick overview of Teredo. Teredo is also enabled by default, meaning an application can make an application programming interface (API) call to Teredo to turn it on. Teredo is not technically on by default but has to be activated via that application request in order for the OS to build out a Teredo IPv6 address. This can also be done via the command line or PowerShell. Microsoft does put in a default DNS entry for a Teredo server of teredo.ipv6.microsoft.com. Teredo is commonly used in DirectAccess deployments.

Microsoft's Long-Term Goals with IPv6

This section is entirely my personal opinion, so take it with a grain of salt. I believe Microsoft has long wanted to enable the Internet of Things (IoT) and to allow its OS to not be restricted by NAT and Port Address Translation (PAT) solutions. Additionally, IPv6 removes the barrier for application developers to have to do extra work in their code to avoid problems with NAT/PAT and stateless firewalls. Microsoft has allowed application developers utilizing IPv6 to bypass all the headaches of not having a direct, nonproxied, or address-translated connection with its customers. Microsoft itself benefits from this for services it provides, such as Microsoft's Xbox gaming network or Office 365.

In fact, it is not possible to have the IoT without IPv6. What does the IoT really encompass? The IoT includes sensor devices (many that are developed with only IPv6 networking stacks), remote instrumentation, and controlled devices like light bulbs. These devices require low power but have value from being on the network. They provide information like the temperature of each specific room where a sensor is located, or perhaps the humidity or carbon monoxide levels in a room, by reporting in real-time back to a central controller. Many of these devices do not run as well on IPv4 networks due to the need for the protocol stack to do NAT/PAT keep alive packets to stay connected to their central controller. They also consume more power in order to do this NAT/PAT keep alive work. With IPv6 the devices can be superefficient in the IPv6 address headers. There is also reduced power draw due tto the fact that keep alive payloads no longer need be sent. Devices send data only when they need to push it or when they are queried.

In addition, there are practical reasons you want this direct relationship with your customers when you are providing services like Xbox games. Many of the multiplayer games make use of peer-to-peer gaming. IPv4 with NAT/PAT can break the ability of these gaming platforms to allow efficient multiplayer experiences. Even with the workaround in place today for NAT/PAT, they will not continue to work when Internet service providers (ISPs) start to deploy Carrier Grade NAT (CGN) within their environments. CGNs basically use PAT to hide customer CPE devices behind another layer of NAT. So instead of your home router having a public IPv4 address, it may now have an RFC 1918 address and the real public IPv4 address is running on the ISP's router in its network. You no longer have the ability to provide a peer-to-peer solution because your public IPv4 address is being shared with everyone in your ISP region.

Microsoft recognized early on what a problem this would be for games, music, photo, and video sharing services along with their ability to extend their service offerings directly to their customers. With that in mind, Microsoft strategically chose to implement IPv6 early and have robust support within the OS. In addition, Microsoft decided to put IPv6 transition technology services directly into the OS to help facilitate enabling more customers to utilize IPv6 and to ease the work developers would have to do to write applications to make use of IPv6.

Some Final IPv6 Support Thoughts

Often IT professionals argue that turning off IPv6 will make their Windows environment more secure and stable since they are under the impression IPv6 is not utilized in their network or is not explicitly utilized. Interestingly enough, Microsoft no longer tests its software in IPv4-only networks and has not done so since 2008. Microsoft considers IPv6 critical to the function of Windows. A Windows deployment where IPv6 was disabled can be considered an unsupported configuration, and when troubleshooting with customers Microsoft will often ask them to turn IPv6 back on. This is especially true when working on cluster solutions, active directory replication, and authentication problems. Thus, it may actually be more secure and stable to turn off IPv4! Microsoft has a published IPv6 FAQ for customers wanting to know more about IPv6 (available at http://technet.microsoft.com/en-us/network/cc987595.aspx).

So, clearly, turning off IPv6 does not help keep the environment more stable if Microsoft considers IPv6 an operational requirement. In regard to security, it is more than likely the same security exploits are available on IPv4 as on IPv6. Many try to argue that IPv4 is more secure than IPv6 and they use this rational to justify disabling IPv6. It turns out this is far from the truth. In fact, at Defcon in August 2013 an IPv6 exploit was demonstrated that works only if you are running an IPv4-only network. If IPv6 has already been properly implemented the exploit is not successful. The caveat is that hosts on the IPv4-only network were dual-stacked capable hosts. Given that all major OSs now have IPv6 enabled by default (making them dual-stack capable) it is almost impossible to insure all your hosts are IPv4-only with no IPv6 at all.

I think it is more likely that people simply do not want to learn a new networking protocol and use the excuse of security to deflect their lack of knowledge. In fact, the Windows Firewall with Advanced Security (WFAS) was written at the same time as the new network stack and is as robust in IPv6 as in IPv4 in protecting the OS. Furthermore, lacking understanding of IPv6 puts IT professionals at a huge disadvantage. They do not fundamentally understand how the OS is communicating for many of the common services that run on the network. IPv6 is on by default, and is preferred for link-local communications. This means that servers on the same subnet will potentially utilize IPv6 to communicate with each other before using IPv4. If you do not understand this simple fact you may have a difficult time debugging problems.

A clear example of this is Microsoft clustering. Clustering utilizes IPv6 when left with the default settings. If you did not know this, trying to understand why clustering may not be working with Hyper-V virtual networking and Network Virtualization with Generic Routing Encapsulation (NVGRE) could be difficult if you did not plan on supporting IPv6 in your virtual network.

In summary, you should learn as much about IPv6 as is practical for your job. Then encourage your colleagues who do networking, storage, security, applications, databases, helpdesk, and even management to learn it as well. All of the Internet will eventually have to move to IPv6, so there is no time like the present to learn something as important as IPv6.

CHAPTER 3

■ ■ ■

IPv6 Addressing

IPv6 addressing is not unique to the Microsoft Windows operating system (OS). This chapter covers the basics about IPv6 addresses and then jumps into the types of IPv6 addresses, how Windows behaves when using IPv6 (including transition technologies), and finally how to do some address planning and routing. It is important to cover all these topics so that you feel comfortable working with IPv6 as things are different enough from IPv4 to cause frustration if you are unfamiliar with the changes.

In addition, Microsoft has chosen to implement some IPv6 addressing behavior defaults that are different than those of some of the other OS manufacturers such as Apple's OSX, Linux, and BSD. This means that you have the potential to see different addressing behavior when all these client OS types are on the same IPv6 subnet. This is nothing to be alarmed about, but it is useful when you are trying to figure out why things are behaving differently for different OS platforms. Let's jump into the first section which covers the principal difference between IPv4 and IPv6: the available address space.

IPv6 Address Basics

The basic IPv6 address was kept relatively simple. Unlike IPv4 addresses, which come from a possible address pool of 2^{32} (approximately 4.29 billion addresses) and use a dotted decimal format like 192.0.2.1, an IPv6 address comes from a possible address pool of 2^{128} or approximately 340 *undecillion* addresses (yes, that is a real word and it is represented by 10^{36}). Honestly, it is hard to fathom a number that large. It is a number so large that even getting human scalable comparisons is difficult, so I have given up trying to explain it in those terms. There are some attempts to show you how large the IPv6 address space is, so feel free to use your favorite search engine to find them. I will instead try to put it in perspective relative to the IPv4 Internet we are familiar with today. While on the surface this does not appear to be any simpler, the reality is that the IPv6 address is simpler because it utilizes a fixed header format and uses extension headers to enhance functionality of the address. This makes IPv6 a simpler design than IPv4 even though it has a much larger address pool.

Address Format

The address formats are different for IPv4 and IPv6. Due to the large number we would have to deal with in decimals, the creators of the IPv6 RFC decided to utilize HEX to describe the addresses and chose a new delimiter to mark natural reading breaks in the address. They chose to use a colon to do that and broke the addresses apart into eight equal segments. The Internet Engineering Task Force (IETF) has still not settled on a name for these eight equal parts, but the current draft states it should be called hexadectet which can be shorted to "hextet." The IETF has an alternate informal name for these segments, a quibble which comes from a nibble being 4 bits and therefore four nibbles would make up a quad-nibble or quibble. You can review the current draft at http://tools.ietf.org/html/draft-denog-v6ops-addresspartnaming-04 to see if the IETF updates or changes it at all.

A typical IPv6 address looks something like the following: 2001:0db8:caf3:a010:bbb0:728a:4e5b:ac01 or fe80:0000:0000:0000:05ef:b5a3:2ab1:54ce.

Notice that the addresses are broken into eight equal parts (hexadectet): 128 bits total divided by 8 segments = 16 bits per segment, so each segment between the colon delimiters represents 16 bits. Such a segment contains four hexadecimal (base 16) numbers which is why you see 0-9 and also a-f. Trying to read off an IPv6 address to someone on the other end of a phone call is not easy and you can now understand why Domain Name System (DNS) is so important to IPv6 implementations. Chapter 8 covers more on IPv6 and DNS.

■ **Tip**   IPv6 has several Requests for Comments (RFCs) that cover formatting of the address. The important one to know is RFC 5952 (`http://tools.ietf.org/html/rfc5952`) which is titled "A Recommendation for IPv6 Address Text Representation."

Size of the Address Space

I like to give people who understand IPv4 a relative reference to compare IPv4 to IPv6 because that seems easier to grasp. All the available IPv4 address space is not used today (at least not currently), but for argument's sake let's say we used it all and we call that the "Internet." We would have an Internet populated with approximately 4.29 billion unique addresses.

For a variety of reasons we cover later in the chapter, IPv6 uses a default prefix length for a single subnet (virtual local area network [VLAN] or broadcast domain) of /64. This means that the first 64 bits (leftmost bits) are used for network identification and the last 64 bits (rightmost bits) are used to define the host, which results in just the host portion of an IPv6 address being 2^64. So, a single prefix in IPv6 can hold the Internet squared (2^64 = 2^32^2). You could take the entire Internet (as we have defined it previously) and square it and put it in a single prefix of /64 in IPv6. A /64 is what you would normally use for a single VLAN or a single network segment in your LAN. Imagine the whole world coming to your office and plugging in for the largest LAN party in the world.

There are practical limits. For example, your switch can't hold that many table entries. You don't actually have 4.29 billion Ethernet ports (which would only be enough for the IPv4 Internet) in a single switch (or even a lot of switches put together), and who in the world would have enough popcorn and soda to host such a big LAN party anyway (I can see Howard Wolowitz from the Big Bang Theory trying though)? But you get the idea now.

■ **Note**   IPv6 uses the idea of a prefix to represent the network address range. This practice was started in IPv4 with the adoption of Classless Inter-Domain Routing (CIDR) notation or representing the most significant bits for the network as an integer following the address. The separator or delimiter is a / and the prefix is the integer value following the / in the address. It is very common to see /64 prefixes in IPv6 as it is the default smallest prefix allocation. In practice, sometime smaller prefixes are used, but they should be avoided.

Let's scale it up from here in some reasonable increments. A typical allocation to a single "site" of IPv6 address space is a /48 which translates to 64 - 48 = 16 or 2^16 = 65,536 subnets. That seems reasonable enough. I can see practical reasons that I might need 65k subnets in a large campus or enterprise design. But remember, I have 65k subnets of the Internet squared in that /64. To make it even more interesting, many of the Regional Internet Registries (RIRs) (ARIN in this case see `https://www.arin.net/policy/nrpm.html`) are using sizing guide recommendations that say to use a /48 for every site. This means (by some people's interpretation) that a single home teleworker should get a /48 prefix delegation. Wow!

So, how many /48 prefixes do we actually have to work with out of the global IPv6 pool then? Individually that would be 2^48 (which is a huge number), but if you are a company with plans to grow then the RIRs have a different recommendation.

ARIN (https://www.arin.net/policy/nrpm.html#six582) indicates that it would like to have you request IPv6 address space based on the potential number of sites you might potentially grow to so it doesn't have to allocate you more address space later. This means if you have more than 12 sites ARIN indicates that you should request a /40, which would mean you have 48 – 40 = 8 or 2^8 = 256 /48 networks. This means you could build out 256 sites, each with 65k subnets, and each with the IPv4 Internet squared in every one of those subnets.

Even handing out /40 Internet protocol (IP) address space allocations we are still not putting a dent into the IPv6 address pool, so let's go crazy and hand out a /32 (simply to make the math easier.) If we handed out /32s to everyone who needed them we could hand out roughly 4.29 billion of them because we are back to our 2^{32}. That means everything on the Internet today could get a /32 allocation of IPv6 address space before we ran out. Remember, a /32 is 2^8 larger than the /40 so you would have 256 possible /40 networks in that prefix to work with, each with 256 sites, each with 65k subnets and each with the IPv4 Internet squared in one of those subnets. Yes, I know, it isn't easy, so Figure 3-1 is an overview diagram that might help you understand IPv6 compared to IPv4 in relative scale.

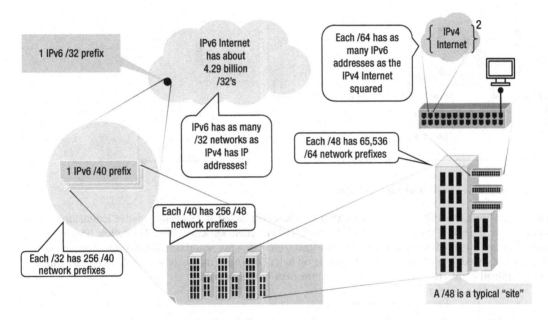

Figure 3-1. *Relative size of IPv4 to IPv6*

The practical reality is that the IPv6 address space is so large that you should not be concerned about the default /64 prefix allocation for a single VLAN/subnet. The first thing you have to do when working with IPv6 is throw away all your IPv4 thinking. I cover planning and design in the section "IPv6 Address Planning and Design," but for now just trust me, your IPv4 instincts with IPv6 are wrong.

IPv6 Address Structure

The IPv6 address structure is actually simpler than that of IPv4. Stephen Deering and Robert Hinden, the creators of the IPv6 RFC 2460 (http://tools.ietf.org/html/rfc2460), got to fix things that were wrong with the IPv4 design. There are improvements that made it into how the IPv6 protocol was designed to operate. For instance, the IPv6 header format is fixed in size to allow hardware application-specific integrated circuits (ASICs) to be optimized in dealing with IPv6. In addition, the protocol does not allow fragmentation to occur in the path of the data flow by intermediate routers (saving them from having to do all that processing) and uses ICMPv6 to make sure it can know the path MTU (maximum transmission unit) size before establishing a data flow between two end points. These are small changes, but they have a dramatic impact on network performance and efficiencies.

Packet and Header Configuration

Figure 3-2 shows the basic configuration for an IPv6 packet and the IPv6 header.

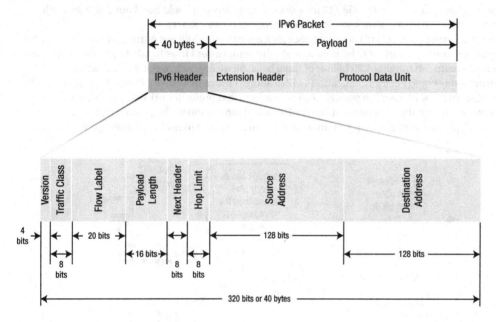

Figure 3-2. *IPv6 packet and IPv6 header configuration*

One of the bigger functional differences is that IPv6 uses something called an extension header. Extension headers effectively take the role of the Internet Header Length and Fragment Offsets in IPv4. They allow IPv6 to have predictable and well-defined extension capabilities without changing the actual IPv6 header size. Also, in IPv6 fragmentation is still allowed, it just isn't done by the router on behalf of a host; the hosts have to do that work which distributes that workload to the edge of the network, not at the distribution or core.

■ **Note**   Fragmentation policy in IPv6 is changing due to security concerns. RFC 6980 (`http://tools.ietf.org/html/rfc6980`) was recently published to address some of these concerns. The RFC outlines not allowing link-local Neighbor Discovery IPv6 packets to contain fragmentation extension headers which was part of an exploit used to circumvent first hop security solutions like RA Guard. This RFC was published in August 2013 and Windows 8.1 and Window Server 2012R2 will likely NOT have support for this RFC yet. I anticipate Microsoft will adopt the RFC recommendations and release an update.

The nice part of extension headers is that they serve a variety of roles in extending what the packet can do. These are all outlined in RFC 2460, but a short example of some are

- Hop-by-Hop Options header
- Destination Options header
- Routing header
- Fragment header
- AH (Authentication Header) and ESP (Encapsulating Security Payload) headers

There are some specific rules for the order of extension headers, but the most important is that the Hop-by-Hop extension header MUST be first. This makes sense if you think about it; a Hop-by-Hop extension header has to be processed by every node in the path so it really needs to be first. The rest have an order outlined in RFC 2460 (http://tools.ietf.org/html/rfc2460), but for the purpose of this book they do not have an impact. If you wish to read more about it, please refer to *Understanding IPv6, Third Edition* by Joseph Davies (Microsoft Press, 2012) or read the RFC.

■ **Note** Many in the IPv6 community think there should be a practical limit on the number of extension headers that can be added to an IPv6 packet. There are some reasonable calculations that indicate that about eight extension headers should suffice for most situations. Unfortunately, I am not aware of any security or network manufacturer providing a way of limiting the number of extension headers of IPv6 packets to prevent potential security risks.

IPv6 Address Representation

IPv6 addresses, as mentioned in the beginning of the chapter, look something like fe80:0000:0000:0000:05ef:b5a3:2ab1:54ce and represent 128 bits via 8 hexadectet (16 bits) separated by colons. A network in IPv6 is represented by a prefix value. A prefix is represented by a decimal value from 0-128 following a **/** and those appear after the appropriate significant bit in the IPv6 address. For example, the address 2001:0db8:caf3:a010:bbb0:728a:4e5b:ac01 in a /64 prefix would be represented as 2001:0db8:caf3:a010::**/64**.

Notice that the prefix only has the first 64 bits represented in the address (because that is what /64 defines) and then uses a shortcut in IPv6 to indicate all zeros. That shortcut is two colons in sequence. If you expanded the two colons in that address you would have four segments of 16 bits all with zeros in them as follows: 2001:0db8:caf3:a010:0000:0000:0000:0000/64.

You are also allowed to remove leading zeros from those 16-bit segments in both the address and prefix representations but only within those 16-bit hexadectets. So 2001:**0**db8:caf3:a010:bbb0:728a:4e5b:ac01 can be represented as 2001:db8:caf3:a010:bbb0:728a:4e5b:ac01 which really isn't an obvious difference. Using the fe80:**0000:0000:0000**:05ef:b5a3:2ab1:54ce you end up with fe80:**0:0:0**:05ef:b5a3:2ab1:54ce which shows clearly the advantage you gain by removing leading zeros. If you apply the zero compression rule you do even better, with fe80**::**05ef:b5a3:2ab1:54ce being the final address. The zero compression rule allows consecutive zeros in an IPv6 address to simplify reading the address. You cannot have more than one zero compression in a single address and all the compression must happen in a single quibble.

Finally, IPv6 utilizes something called Zone IDs or Scope IDs to define which address is associated with a specific interface on a host. This is important for link-local addresses which are covered in the section "Unicast." These are represented by an integer value after a % following the IPv6 address so fe80::05ef:b5a3:2ab1:54ce**%19** would indicate that the IPv6 address is associated with interface 19 on that host. For Windows the Zone ID will typically be the Interface Index value which is the unique integer that represents an interface in the OS. Zone IDs are local to the host; in other words, host A's Ethernet interface may be ZoneID 1 and connected to the same subnet as host B's Ethernet interface but its Zone ID is 9.

One of the formatting challenges you will find with IPv6 is the use of the colon (:) as the delimiter because the colon is actually used in IPv4. It is used to separate the IPv4 address from the transport (UDP or TCP) port number. So the challenge becomes how to represent the transport port number for applications. This was solved by utilizing square brackets surrounding the IPv6 address. So, in order to specify a request in a web browser to a nontraditional port, say 8080, you would use the following syntax in the browser http://[2001:db8:caf3:a010:bbb0:728a:4e5b:ac01]:8080. It is important to note this syntax is universal and not specific to web browsers so you can use it for telnet, ssh, ftp, or any other transport service.

■ **Tip** Don't try to embed your IPv4 address information into your IPv6 addresses. Often it limits what you can do with IPv6 in the long run. Remember that your eventual plan is to have an IPv6-only network, so don't tie down your design with legacy IPv4 requirements. I often see system administrators try to match IPv4 and IPv6 address designs instead of simply using DNS to manage the IP to namespace mappings to solve that problem. While there are some practical semantic things you can do, I personally have only seen successful implementations when they utilize public IPv4 addresses to IPv6 mappings. Anything with IPv4 RFC 1918 turns into a mess quickly.

Defining Common IPv6 Terminology

IPv6 does have some terminology and vocabulary that are unique to it. Luckily they aren't expansive so you should be able to start using them correctly pretty quickly. I think the most common confusion in the IPv6 lexicon is dual-stack vs. native. These two definitions are often used interchangeably and depending on the context both could be accurate or interchangeable.

Dual-stack refers to a host's network configuration in that it has both IPv4 and IPv6 running at the same time, either on the same or on different interfaces. Native refers to the fact that IPv6 is supported without a transition, proxy, or translation process. Running a native IPv6 network means your network environment is running IPv6 without those services or has a very small limited translation or proxy service in the network, typically at the edge. Additionally, it may be used in reference to having Global Unicast IPv6 addresses that are NOT part of the transition IPv6 address allocations, like 6to4 or ISATAP.

To add to the confusion, some people will use "native" to mean an IPv6-only network, specifically one that does not run IPv4. It is becoming more common to say a network is "IPv6 only" vs. "native" since the terminology of native is often shorthand to mean a dual-stack network that doesn't use transition technologies. Also, IPv6-only networks are nowhere near as common as native dual-stack deployment and it will likely remain that way for a long time. The use of the term may change as time progresses.

So don't be surprised if you hear someone say "I am running native IPv6" but when you get into the details that person is really dual-stacked. They don't have to be mutually exclusive; hence "native dual-stacked" might become the de facto when talking about IPv6 deployments. Regardless, be accommodating and ask for details so you actually know what the network configuration is before making any assumption.

Here is a short list of common IPv6 terms you will see used.

> **6rd:** Refers to IPv6 Rapid Deployment, which is designed to be utilized by Internet service providers (ISPs) for quickly deploying IPv6 services across an existing IPv4 network. 6rd uses a stateless method for mapping IPv4 to IPv6 and also uses tunneling to get those IPv6 packets out to the IPv6 Internet. It is not something normally used in enterprise, SMB, or home networks, but you might see your ISP talk about it.

> **6to4:** 6to4 is an automatic transition technology that makes use of public IPv4 addresses on a host to connect to IPv6 resources. It tunnels its IPv6 traffic to a 6to4 relay router and has its IPv4 information embedded in its IPv6 address.

> **CGN:** Carrier Grade NAT (Network Address Translation) is sometimes call LSN (Large Scale NAT) and is where an ISP will provide RFC 1918 IPv4 addresses to the CPE device and then PAT (Port Address Translation) at a central router to conserve public IPv4 address space.

> **DHCPv6 Stateful:** An IPv6 address assignment configuration that uses DHCPv6 to both assign the IPv6 address and provide all the additional information a host would require such as DNS or NTP parameters.

DHCPv6 Stateless: An IPv6 address assignment configuration that uses DHCPv6 to provide only the additional information a host would require such as DNS and NTP parameters. To obtain an IPv6 address it utilizes Stateless Address Autoconfiguration (SLAAC).

DNS64: DNS64 is commonly referenced with NAT64. It is a DNS service that will synthesize (build dynamically on the fly) an AAAA record if only an A record exists for a host. It does this with a specific IPv6 prefix that is pointed to a NAT64 device that does the translation work from IPv6 to IPv4.

DS-Lite: Dual-stack lite is a transition technology that leverages an existing IPv6 network to provide IPv4 services at the edge of the network and tunnel those IPv4 packets across the IPv6 network to a common IPv4 relay router. It is common in DS-Lite designs to run CGN at those *meet me* points with the IPv4 Internet to further conserve IPv4 addresses.

Dual-stack: As mentioned previously, dual-stack is the configuration where a host (a Windows server or client, a router, a printer, etc.) has both the IPv4 and IPv6 network stack operating.

DUID: DHCP Unique Identifier is used by a client to obtain an IP address from a DHCPv6 server. Unlike IPv4, which makes use of MAC addresses, DUIDs are not unique per prefix request on the same interface for IPv6. If you plan to reserve IPv6 addresses for specific hosts you make use of the DUID to map that reservation to the specific IPv6 address.

DAD: Duplicate Address Detection makes use of Neighbor Solicitation and Neighbor Advertisement messages via ICMPv6 to determine if an IPv6 address is already in use on the network.

EUI-64: This is a standard way of automatically generating an IPv6 address interface ID from a 48-bit MAC address.

Hexadectet: This is the 16-bit field between the : delimiter in an IPv6 address. The shortened version of the name is hextet and the slang term is quibble

ICMPv6: Internet Control Message Protocol (ICMP) version 6 is defined in RFC 4443 and is used in IPv6 for Neighbor Discovery functions as well as Path MTU Discovery and Multicast Router Discovery as well as other control functions. The most common administrative tool to use ICMPv6 is ping.

Interface Identifier: The interface ID consists of the right 64 bits of an IPv6 address. You may also see this referred to as the host ID. Privacy and EUI-64 are both used to generate the interface ID.

ISATAP: Intra-Site Automatic Tunnel Addressing Protocol is a transition technology that allows a host on an IPv4-only network to obtain an IPv6 address and connect to IPv6 resource through an ISATAP router. Depending on the prefix given by the ISATAP router it may or may not be able to connect to public IPv6 resources.

Multicast Listener Discovery: MLD is used by routers to discover hosts that are listening for multicast traffic and utilizes ICMPv6 to perform this function. It is defined in RFC 2810 and 3810 and updated in RFC 4604.

NAT64: NAT64 is used in conjunction with DNS64 and allows IPv6-only hosts to communicate with IPv4 hosts. It does this utilizing an IPv6 prefix and mapping the IPv4 host information into the IPv6 address. The IPv6-only device utilizes this NAT64 service because DNS64 tells it to via the synthetic AAAA record that was provided to the IPv6-only host.

NAT66: NAT66 is a stateful Network Address Translation method for IPv6 to IPv6 traffic. It can do both network and port translation. It operates in the same manner as NAT44. NPTv6 should be used instead of NAT66.

Native: Native refers to a network environment where the majority of devices support IPv6 and do not require transition technologies like translation, tunneling, or proxy.

Neighbor Discovery Protocol: NDP encompasses five main message types, Router Solicitation, Router Advertisements, Neighbor Solicitation, Neighbor Advertisements, and Redirect, which leverage ICMPv6 to perform all these key services.

Neighbor Advertisement: An NDP message type used to respond to Neighbor Solicitation messages.

Neighbor Solicitation: An NDP message process used for discovering the link layer address of a neighbor.

Network Prefix Translation: NPTv6 allows a router, firewall, or network proxy device to translate from one IPv6 prefix to another in a stateless manner.

Permanent Address: Any IPv6 address type that is not using the temporary address setting.

Prefix: The 64 bit leftmost value in an IPv6 address is the network prefix. A network prefix contains a routing prefix and may contain a subnet ID. The network prefix and the interface ID (64 bits) complete an IPv6 address (128 bits).

Quibble: informal term for hexadectet, comes from shortening quad nibble which would be 4 x 4 bits or 16 bits which is value of a hexadectet. See hexadectet.

Redirects: An NDP message that a router sends to a host to indicate a better first hop router for a specific destination.

Router Advertisement: An NDP message process that is used to provide hosts prefix, link MTU, routes, auto configuration, and address lifetimes.

Router Solicitation: An NDP message process used to request a Router Advertisement.

Scope ID: See Zone ID.

StateLess Address Automatic Configuration (SLAAC): A host can build an IPv6 address automatically and does not require the use of DHCPv6 on the network to do so; the only thing required for Global Unicast or ULA is a Router Advertisement with a /64 prefix. Every Windows host utilizes SLAAC for building its link-local IPv6 address. SLAAC will allow a host to dynamically build a valid IPv6 address either by a random process or by utilizing a valid 48-bit MAC address (EUI-64). It serves the same role as IPv4 Automatic Private IP Addressing (APIPA) but unlike IPv4 works for all network ranges as long as the IPv6 prefix is a /64.

Temporary Address: An IPv6 address that uses the methods described in RFC 4941 to build a limited lifetime IPv6 address for the purpose of enhancing privacy. Temporary addresses leverage the random interface ID method and are used by default in Windows clients except Windows XP.

Teredo: Teredo is a transition technology that allows a host on an IPv4 network with NAT or PAT operating to obtain an IPv6 address and connect to IPv6 resource through a Teredo relay server. Depending on the prefix given by the Teredo server it may or may not be able to connect to public IPv6 resources.

Tunnel Broker: A tunnel broker allows an IPv4 router running at a remote site via the IPv4 Internet to have a tunnel to obtain access to the IPv6 Internet. Typically a /64 prefix is allocated to the remote site and additional IPv6 prefixes can be requested if needed.

Zone ID: Also called a Scope ID, Zone IDs are an additional identifier used by the OS to uniquely identify a destination link for a specific link-local address. It is an integer value that is appended to an IPv6 link-local address using the **%** as a delimiter between the address and the Zone ID. In Windows the Zone ID is typically the interface index.

Following are some more terms that you should know. While these terms are obviously not specific to IPv6, it is important to cover them.

Anycast: An IPv6 address type used to provide a destination service to a receiver via its closest routed path. Multiple devices on the network in diverse locations can provide the service as all these destination hosts share the same IPv6 address. Anycast is often used to make services highly available. For instance, the root level name servers utilize anycast.

AfriNIC: The Internet Numbers Registry for Africa is the RIR that services the African continent. See `http://www.afrinic.net/` for details.

APNIC: Asia Pacific Network Information Centre is the RIR that services the Asian Pacific rim. See `http://www.apnic.net/` for details.

ARIN: American Registry for Internet Numbers is the RIR that services North America. See `https://www.arin.net/` for details.

EUI-64: Extended Unique Identifier 64 is defined by the IEEE in `http://standards.ieee.org/develop/regauth/tut/eui64.pdf` and is used by IPv6 but also in World Wide Names (WWNs) for storage, etc.

IANA: Internet Assigned Numbers Authority is the organization that delegates all IPv4 and IPv6 addresses. They provide these ONLY to the RIRs. See `http://www.iana.org/` for details.

LACNIC: Latin American and Caribbean Internet Address Registry is the RIR that services South America and some Caribbean locations. See `http://www.lacnic.net` for more details.

Manual Assigned: When autoconfiguration is not used to build an IPv6 address on a host. This can be done through the graphical user interface (GUI) or via scripting utilizing netsh or PowerShell.

Migration: In the context of IPv6 it is the process of moving from IPv4 to IPv6 with the end goal of having the network being IPv6 only with transition technologies for legacy IPv4 networks.

Multicast: An IPv6 address that is designed to allow a one-to-many or a one-to-a-few hosts communication. A single address multicast packet will be accepted by multiple hosts on the network. Multicast is leveraged for Neighbor Discovery.

NAT44: NAT44 is a stateful Network Address Translation method between IPv4 and IPv4. It can do both network and port translation.

Nibble: 4 bits (2^4) so in a segment or block of an IPv6 address each HEX value represents a nibble. Some people will refer to a nibble as a hexit or more rarely as a semioctet because a nibble is half of a full byte (8 bits).

Provider Assigned (PA): IP address space that is provided from a service provider for the exclusive use of its customer. When the service provider is no longer providing service for the customer the IP address space is returned to the service provider.

Provider Independent (PI): IP address space allocated from an RIR to a service provider or company for its use in its business operation. A service provider may delegate IP address space for customer use but the IP address still belongs to the service provider. See Provider Assigned for details. A business that has obtained PI IP address space is free to use the PI space as it requires and can use BGP to peer with multiple service providers to announce their PI space. This provides redundancy and allows the business to add or drop service providers as it needs over time.

RIPE NCC: Réseaux IP Européens Network Coordination Centre is the RIR that services the Europe, Middle East, and Central Asia. See `http://www.ripe.net/` for more details.

RIR: There are five Regional Internet Registries in the world covering specific geographies. Their job is to hand out IPv4 and IPv6 addresses per their governed policies.

Synthetic records: A DNS AAAA record that is provided by a DNS64 server that is generated dynamically using an IPv6 prefix and the IPv4 information from the A record DNS query. It is only generated if no AAAA record exists in DNS for the requested hostname resolution.

Transition: In the context of IPv6 it encompasses all the technologies used to get from IPv4 to IPv6 or the reverse. It would include translation, proxy, tunneling, or any other method that allows an IPv4 host to communicate with an IPv6 host.

Translation: Most often translation is used by Application Delivery Controllers (ADCs), more commonly known as load balancers. ADCs can translate from IPv4 to IPv6 and back and principally use the same technologies that were used in IPv4 to build load balancing solutions.

Unicast: An IPv6 address that is used for one-to-one host communication. Almost all regular IPv6 traffic will be unicast in nature.

UUID: Universally Unique Identifier is used in conjunction with DHCPv6 as a way of identifying a host. When used with DHCPv6 it is called the DUID or DHCPv6 Unique Identifier. UUIDs are global unique and used to identify a client or server per interface and remain constant over time; therefore they can be used as a permanent identification of a client or server. DUIDs are used in DHCPv6 for reservations instead of the 48-bit Ethernet MAC address that is used in IPv4.

Types of IPv6 Addresses

IPv6 has three types of addresses: unicast, multicast, and anycast. There are also some transitional types that are treated as part of the unicast category. This differs from IPv4 which has unicast, multicast, broadcast, and anycast. In addition to the address types, the control message types for the two protocols have changed. IPv6 has the newer ICMPv6 while IPv4 uses ICMP. Both protocols provide Transmission Control Protocol (TCP) and User Datagram Protocol (UDP) transport layers along with other transport types like Generic Routing Encapsulation (GRE).

A common question is why broadcast was left out of IPv6. The answer is simple: broadcast is simply a subset or special use case of multicast. Once this is pointed out many realize you can simply create a multicast group that all hosts listen to (ff02::1 happens to be that multicast link-local address) on a local subnet and you get the same function as broadcast. The advantage in this design of IPv6 is that the broadcast-like function via multicast is not overutilized by the OS as in IPv4 so you don't have to contend with all the bad behavior broadcasts can introduce into networks. Instead, you have to contend with multicast and its behavior requirements which are more predictable and often more modest though less understood. See the section "Multicast Addresses" for details on how IPv6 has removed the need for broadcast.

Unicast

IPv6 has several types of unicast IPv6 addresses. Every host will automatically have a link-local unicast address associated with an interface. If the host is participating in an IPv6 network it will next have either a global or a unique local address or both. Let's cover each of them here.

Global Unicast Addresses

Global Unicast IPv6 addresses are the second most common IPv6 addresses used. They are equivalent to the public IPv4 address space we are used to deploying for Internet devices. Today, Global Unicast Addresses are assigned from the 2000::/3 IPv6 prefix with each RIR assigning prefixes from that current global allocation. This Global Unicast Address space will obviously expand at some point though it will take a long time for us to consume that first allocation.

Still, application developers and security administrators should not be lazy and assume that the ONLY valid IPv6 prefixes are from that allocation for Global Unicast and should check to confirm their filters are current from time to time.

Table 3-1 shows the IPv6 prefixes that are currently allocated to each RIR.

Table 3-1. *RIR IPv6 Prefix Allocations*

RIR	IPv6 Prefix Allocation
APNIC	2400::/12
ARIN	2600::/12
LACNIC	2800::/12
RIPE NCC	2a00::/12
AfriNIC	2c00::/12

Finally, you will see two categories of Global Unicast referenced: Provider Independent (PI) and Provider Assigned (PA). The difference is pretty simple. PI space is allocated from an RIR directly to a company for its exclusive use or the use of its customers.

Typical companies that are given PI space are ISPs, large multinational companies, and Web 2.0 and Internet content companies along with corporations that have high availability requirements. It is typical for these companies to run Border Gateway Protocol (BGP) for both IPv4 and IPv6. PA space is allocated from an ISP to a customer from the ISP's PI space. It is an IPv6 prefix that does not belong to the customer (regardless of size.) If you change your ISP your PA will change too, which requires your company to renumber its network.

■ **Tip** IPv6 renumbering is a big topic on its own and there are challenges with doing IPv6 renumbering on a network. While there are some operational efficiencies put into IPv6 to make renumbering easier, it still is not a trivial project. Planning and more planning are required to make it all work. RFC 7010 (http://tools.ietf.org/html/rfc7010) goes into more details on some of the gaps in doing IPv6 renumbering. If you are just starting to deploy IPv6 it is unlikely that renumbering is on the top of your list (unless you did your IPv6 deployment wrong), but I wanted to provide some resources and perspective on what you might face later.

Unique Local Addresses

Unique local addresses are commonly called ULA (pronounced "You-LA") and are defined in RFC 4193 (`http://tools.ietf.org/html/rfc4193`). A ULA is defined by the first 7 bits (1111110) and then has a toggling eighth bit to define a Local (1) or Reserved (0) flag. The overall ULA address range is `fc00::/7` and the Local flag value is defined as 1 resulting in `fd00::/8`. The 0 flag value has not been defined yet and therefore you should not see a network make use of the ULA `fc00::/8` prefix at all.

The current common use of ULA with Microsoft products is with Microsoft DirectAccess (DA) in Windows Server 2012 and 2012 R2. DA servers will utilize a ULA address configuration for the IPv6 prefix to assign DA clients by default if the DA server is behind a border router or edge firewall that is performing NAT. While this is efficient to get a DA deployment working it is likely not the most desirable way to configure DA in the long term.

The common analogy given is that ULA is like RFC 1918 (`http://www.rfc-editor.org/rfc/rfc1918.txt`) addresses in IPv4. I don't find this analogy to be helpful because RFC 1918 addresses came about due to the shortage of public IPv4 addresses. RFC 1918 addresses with the use of NAT allow the hosts that use them to connect to the IPv4 Internet which addressed the shortage of public IPv4 addresses. There is no shortage of IPv6 addresses so the use case of ULA does not match the original use case for RFC 1918 at all. In addition, there are other IPv4 address blocks that are meant to be private but for other purposes like RFC 6598 (`http://www.rfc-editor.org/rfc/rfc6598.txt`) which defines 100.64.0.0/10 as reserved for the purpose of shared address space for ISPs deploying CGN (covered in Chapter 10).

ULA addresses should be filtered at the IPv6 Internet edge and are not allowed to be globally routable. Because NPTv6 is not widely supported today in routers or firewalls running ULA in the same way as IPv4, RFC 1918 with a NAT solution can be very difficult and I do not recommend using ULA for this reason.

ULA is appropriate for lab configurations, isolated networks that NEVER need to connect to IPv6 Internet resources, or when a secure network needs to be built that will not be accessible from the Global Unicast Address space.

One of the stated goals for ULA was to allow companies that may merge or be purchased to reduce the chances of having to readdress their network when combining them. This is a significant problem for IPv4 RFC 1918 because the chance of an address conflict is very high. Because of this, ULA uses a formula based on a timestamp to generate a random prefix to avoid these issues. I don't understand this need requirement; since Global Unicast's IPv6 addresses are unique by definition why not just simply use Global Unicast Addresses? You will never have an address conflict no matter how many mergers or breakups you go through.

A section of the IPv6 community felt it was appropriate to provide a registration service to help avoid collisions (I find this confusing but clearly IPv4 thinking prevailed), so you can request a ULA prefix from those sites or register yours at the site too. ULAs are maintained at `http://www.sixxs.net/tools/grh/ula/` and the site even states that ULAs were never intended to be registered, so what is the point? I am still trying to figure that out myself.

Finally, ULA is a bit of a religious war for those in the IPv6 community. It was brought about to replace site-local (which was deprecated) and was to appease those who thought running Global Unicast Address everywhere was somehow a concern. It is defined in RFC 4193 (`http://tools.ietf.org/search/rfc4193`) so you can read all about it and see if it is something you think you need. As a general rule of thumb I do not recommend using ULA unless you really understand its limitations or you have a valid need requirement in your design. Otherwise, use Global Unicast Addresses, either PI or PA.

Link-Local Addresses

Because link-local IPv6 addresses are assigned to every logical and physical interface in a host they are the most common IPv6 address, tied with multicast addresses. Link-local IPv6 addresses always begin with `fe80` and all link-local addresses are in the same prefix of `fe80::/64`. This means it is possible to have duplicate link-local addresses on different interfaces that are on different VLANS or subnets.

Because link-local IPv6 addresses are exactly that, link-local, having duplicate addresses is not a concern unless the duplicate addresses are on the same local link (e.g., Ethernet segment). Even with the chance of duplicate link-local addresses it rarely occurs even across multiple subnets due to the size of the IPv6 /64 prefix. The only time you might see a link-local IPv6 reused is when a network router is set up with `fe80::1`, for example, as the local default gateway or next hop link-local IPv6 address or some other standardized default gateway IPv6 convention.

If you have two different VLANS (links) connected to a single host (or router) and there are two distinct hosts with the same link-local address on each independent link how can you tell them apart from each other even though they are on different subnets? Remember that IPv6 has the concept of a Zone ID or Scope ID. In Windows these are represented after the link-local address with a **%** as a delimiter between. It turns out the Zone ID will match the Interface Index utilized by Windows to identify all the unique interfaces in use in the OS.

So, for example, you want to ping a host that has a link-local address of fe80::5ef:b5a3:2ab1:54ce but it turns out there is a matching link-local address in use on another interface on that host. These two hosts don't have a true address conflict (they are *not* on the same link), but this host that is connected to both of the networks has a dilemma to deal with. This is where the Zone ID comes in handy. In the following example, assume we have two interfaces and they have been assigned Zone ID 20 and Zone ID 21. The host I am trying to reach is off Zone ID 20; therefore, I would issue the following command: Ping fe80::5ef:b5a3:2ab1:54ce**%20**.

The output would be

```
PS C:\> ping fe80::5ef:b5a3:2ab1:54ce%20

Pinging fe80::5ef:b5a3:2ab1:54ce%20 with 32 bytes of data:
Reply from fe80::5ef:b5a3:2ab1:54ce%20: time<1ms
Reply from fe80::5ef:b5a3:2ab1:54ce%20: time<1ms
Reply from fe80::5ef:b5a3:2ab1:54ce%20: time<1ms
Reply from fe80::5ef:b5a3:2ab1:54ce%20: time<1ms

Ping statistics for fe80::5ef:b5a3:2ab1:54ce%20:
    Packets: Sent = 4, Received = 4, Lost = 0 (0% loss),
Approximate round trip times in milli-seconds:
    Minimum = 0ms, Maximum = 0ms, Average = 0ms

PS C:\>
```

Notice that my command line tools understand IPv6. Ping, tracert, nslookup, and more function just fine with IPv6 addresses. Windows has no issue with IPv6 addresses and can make use of IPv6 addresses in the same way it makes use of IPv4 addresses. If for some reason there is a service that is IPv4 specific then obviously only IPv4 addresses will be allowed. If you run across a native Windows service or function that does not work with IPv6 then there is a bug and you should open a support case with Microsoft if you need it to accept IPv6 addresses.

Special Unicast Addresses

There are some special reserved unicast addresses that should be mentioned. Specifically, they are the unspecified address and the loopback address which serve the same role as their IPv4 counterparts but have a much simpler format in IPv6.

The unspecified address in IPv6 is represented by all zeros. So the address is 0:0:0:0:0:0:0:0 or :: with zero compression applied. It is only used as a source address when an interface first comes up and does not have a unique IPv6 address on the interface yet. It is also used when representing default routes on a host with the ::/0 format.

The loopback address in IPv6 is simpler than that used in IPv4 (127.0.0.1) and is represented by all zeros except the first nibble which is 1. So the address is 0:0:0:0:0:0:0:1 or ::1 with zero compression applied. It is used when a host needs to send packets to itself. You should never see ::1 on a link or interface except for the host itself.

Unicast Transition Addresses

In addition to global, ULA, and link-local there are specific transition addresses that are used in Windows. Make no mistake, there are additional unicast addresses used for other transition methods but because they are not used in Windows I am not covering them in this book. Please refer to http://en.wikipedia.org/wiki/IPv6_transition_mechanisms to find out about other IPv6 transition technologies. It is important to note that the transition technologies covered next are all tunneling solution and have their own specific IPv6 addressing prefix and/or method for generating an IPv6 address from IPv4 information. Chapter 10 covers additional transition technology that does not have specific prefix and address types.

6to4 Transition Technology

6to4 is a native transition tunneling technology available from the Windows Vista and Window Server 2008 release on and is defined in RFC 3056, 3068, and 3964. It is designed to allow a host that has a public IPv4 address to be able to automatically assign and build itself an IPv6 address it can utilize to talk to the IPv6 Internet. 6to4 IPv6 addresses are always from the following prefix: 2002::/16.

A Windows host can autogenerate an IPv6 address by taking the IPv4 address and converting it to HEX and putting it directly after the 2002 prefix and then in the last 32 bits of the IPv6 address so it looks like 2002:<HEX conversion of IPv4 address>::<HEX conversion of IPv4 address>. It is likely easiest to see how this works with an example so let's use the RFC reserved test and documentation IPv4 address block of 192.0.2.0/24. We will pick the random IPv4 address from that block of 192.0.2.151. The autogenerated 6to4 address would be 2002:c000:0297::c000:0297.

In this example each octet in the IPv4 address is converted to HEX and entered into the corresponding location in the IPv6 address. Decimal 192 is 0xc0 in HEX, 0 is 0x0, 2 is 0x2, and 151 is 0x97. If the HEX value is below a single integer or a-f value then it is padded with a prepending 0. So 0 becomes 00 and 2 becomes 02 in this example. Just humor me now and follow along and trust that my addressing structure and math are correct.

While it is fine that Windows is able to generate its own IPv6 address how does it actually route its traffic out to the IPv6 Internet? 6to4 utilizes public 6to4 gateways (often hosted by ISPs) and these gateways have well-known public anycast IPv6 and IPv4 addresses. The IPv4 anycast address is 192.88.99.1 and uses the following IPv6 anycast address of 2002:c058:6301:: for the 6to4 router. We now have everything we need to route IPv6 traffic from the local Windows host to the IPv6 Internet via a tunnel. If the Windows OS is able to generate a 6to4 address, that ability then triggers the OS to build a default route to a public IPv6 6to4 gateway and then use a tunnel leveraging protocol 41.

Effectively, when our local Windows host is trying to connect to a public IPv6 address it generates an IPv6 packet that has a destination of the public IPv6 host it is trying to reach. Let's say that the Windows host looks in its local routing table for the default IPv6 gateway and gets 2002:c058:6301::. Then the following happens:

1. The host forwards its packet to that IPv6 gateway address.

2. Because it is a 6to4 address the payload is encapsulated (utilizing protocol 41) in IPv4 and sent it to the anycast IPv4 address of 192.88.99.1.

3. The packet is forwarded via IPv4 to the closest 6to4 gateway.

4. The 6to4 gateway decapsulates the payload and forwards the IPv6 packet (because the router is dual-stacked it can do that).

5. The IPv6 host receives the traffic and replies back.

6. The IPv6 traffic is forwarded to the closest IPv6 anycast 6to4 router (remember these routers are all dual-stacked).

7. The public IPv4 source address of the host is already embedded in the source address of the IPv6 6to4 address that the Windows host autogenerated so that is how the 6to4 gateway is able to deliver traffic back to the host via IPv4.

That is an overview of 6to4. 6to4 is also enabled by default. If you are lucky enough to have public IPv4 addresses readily available, you can test this out in a lab very quickly by simply giving your Windows client a public IPv4 address and then trying to connect to an IPv6 resource such as `http://www.cav6tf.org` or `http://test-ipv6.com/` and see if you are able to connect via IPv6. Both web sites will display if you are connecting with either IPv4 or IPv6.

If you see an IPv6 address that begins with 2002, you know it is a 6to4 address. That is what gives it away and also what allows you to filter it. You can also use the fact that it leverages protocol 41 in IPv4 to do the tunneling. It turns out you can disable 6to4 and ISATAP by filtering protocol 41 on firewalls or via your internal Layer 3 ACLs. You can also disable 6to4 via Group Policy. See the section "Microsoft Group Policy and IPv6" in Chapter 4 for disabling of 6to4 and Chapter 5 for details on PowerShell and netsh commands for 6to4. Figure 3-3 is a network overview of 6to4.

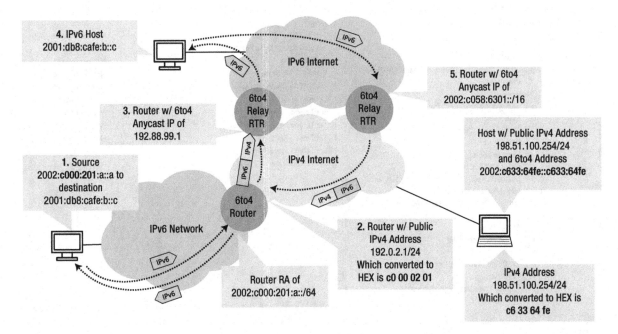

Figure 3-3. *6to4 network overview*

Additionally, you can set all the 6to4 parameters for Windows servers and clients using Group Policy. If you are using Group Policy to modify the configurations, then the following Group Policy should be set: Computer Configuration | Policies | Administrative Templates | Network | TCP/IP Settings | IPv6 Transition Technologies. Then set the 6to4 parameter to what you want. Figure 3-4 shows a screenshot of the Group Policy Management Editor and Figure 3-5 shows a screenshot of setting the 6to4 relay name parameter to corp-6to4.example.com.

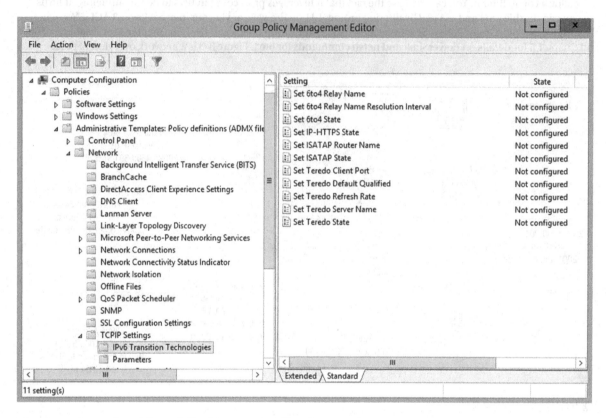

Figure 3-4. *Screenshot of Group Policy Management Editor from Windows Server 2012*

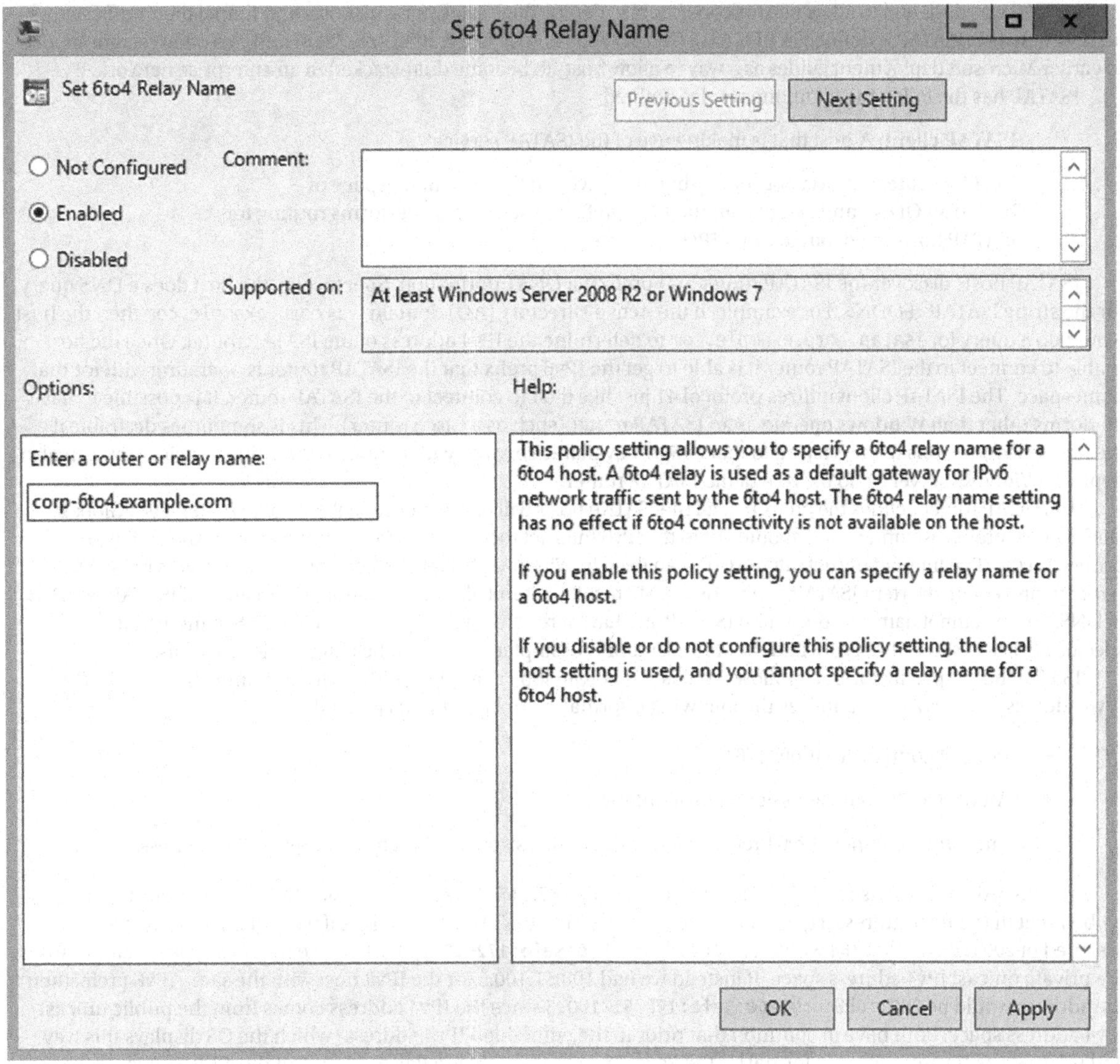

Figure 3-5. *Screenshot of 6to4 relay name parameter from Windows Server 2012*

ISATAP Transition Technology

ISATAP is a native transition tunneling technology available from the Windows Vista and Windows Server 2008 release on. It is designed to allow a host that has a public or private IPv4 address to be able to automatically assign and build itself an IPv6 address it can utilize to talk to the IPv6 intranet or IPv6 Internet. ISATAP utilizes DNS to determine what prefix it is to utilize and what gateway to use. ISATAP has the concept of global unique and private addresses depending on what the desired deployment use case requires.

ISATAP was designed to allow network operators to deploy dual-stack network hosts and tunnel their traffic across an IPv4 network. ISATAP is defined in RFC 5214 (`http://tools.ietf.org/html/rfc5214`) and was often recommended in earlier Microsoft deployment guides as a way to allow hosts to become dual-stacked in an enterprise network.

ISATAP has the following component roles defined:

ISATAP client: A host that is making use of the ISATAP service

ISATAP router: A server or router that is resolved to the DNS namespace of ISATAP.<FQDN> and assigns out the IPv6 prefix to use and also performs routing for ISATAP hosts to get out to other IPv6 resources

ISATAP hosts discover the ISATAP router and prefix via DNS information. Specifically, the host does a DNS query for the string ISATAP.<FQDN>. For example, if the Active Directory (AD) domain was `corp.example.com` then the host would do a query for `isatap.corp.example.com` to determine the IPv4 address of the ISATAP router. Once the host is able to connect to the ISATAP router it is able to get the IPv6 prefix that the ISATAP router is operating with for that namespace. The ISATAP client utilizes protocol 41 just like 6to4 to connect to the ISATAP router. It is possible to have platforms other than Windows operate as an ISATAP router (such as a Cisco router). This is sometimes desirable if the network operations team is trying to make highly available services with centralized routing policies. You can also deploy a Windows server to do the role of the ISATAP router.

An ISATAP router defines the prefix that all the ISATAP hosts will participate in. If the ISATAP router has a Global Unicast IPv6 prefix assignment and a route out to the IPv6 Internet then the ISATAP hosts would have the ability to connect to the IPv6 Internet. By default ISATAP is enabled in Windows; however, Microsoft has protections in its DNS server to prevent inadvertent ISATAP deployments. Microsoft does not allow the arbitrary publication of ISATAP.<FQDN> in DNS. So you cannot name a workstation ISATAP and have it register in DNS properly. Your DNS administrator specifically has to set up the record and the administrator is prompted to confirm he really wants to do this.

ISATAP has a specific format it follows so it is possible to look at an IPv6 address to determine if it is an ISATAP IPv6 address. An ISATAP host utilizes the following information to build out its IPv6 address:

- ISATAP Router IPv6 Prefix (/64)

- An IPv4 address it has assigned to an interface

- The format is either <IPv6 Prefix>:0:5efe:<IPv4 address> or <IPv6 Prefix>:200:5efe:<IPv4 address>

The ISATAP host will use an RFC 1918 IPv4 address like 172.17.230.211 that is assigned to a host interface and embed that in the IPv6 address it generates. The format for the ISATAP IPv6 address if we had the ISATAP prefix assigned of `2001:db8:a:b::/64` would be `2001:db8:a:b:0:5efe:172.17.230.211` since the IPv4 address comes from the private unicast IPv4 address space. If instead we had 198.51.100.5 for the IPv4 host with the same IPv6 prefix then the address would be `2001:db8:a:b:200:5efe:198.51.100.5` since the IPv4 address comes from the public unicast IPv4 address space. Both have in common that prior to the embedded IPv4 address (which the OS displays this way and is known as IPv4-compatible format) is the 5efe. Prior to the 5efe is a flag to identify if the address is a private unicast (0) or a public unicast (200) address.

So, the quickest way to tell an ISATAP address is involved in a communication is to look for the 5efe in the IPv6 address. Just be careful; if someone with an odd sense of humor manually configures an IPv6 address there is nothing to prevent him from embedding that same information into an IPv6 address he assigns to the host.

■ **Tip** If you are using something like Wireshark or Network Monitor (NetMon) to do packet captures then the displayed ISATAP address in the OS may NOT match what is displayed in the packet. The actual IPv6 packets will display in HEX so you will need to convert your ISATAP displayed IPv6 address to the actual full HEX one. For example, the `2001:db8:a:b:0:5efe:172.17.230.211` IPv6 address may look like `2001:db8:a:b:0:5efe:ac11:e6d3` in the Wireshark or NetMon output. Just know that both display formats are valid so depending on the application it may appear as either or both ways

---

In practice ISATAP is an IPv6 overlay tunnel network that runs on top of your IPv4 network. It can effectively turn your well-designed Layer 3 IPv4 network into one large single Layer 3 IPv6 subnet, so you must be careful in how you design and deploy ISATAP. Because all the hosts are joined to a common ISATAP router and participate in a common IPv6 prefix all hosts in that ISATAP domain are link-local adjacent to each other. This may not be the most desirable security configuration for your network, especially if you have worked hard in your IPv4 design to isolate hosts.

■ **Note** ISATAP *requires* a working IPv4 network. If you are having any issues with your IPv4 network ISATAP will likely have problems too depending on what the issue is.

It can also be difficult to troubleshoot and debug ISATAP problems. There are no easy client tools available to help identify when something is going wrong with the Windows client trying to connect to the ISATAP router. If your help desk is not trained on how ISATAP works and how to debug it you can end up with frustrated users and a help desk that is ill prepared to help those users. If you do plan on utilizing ISATAP you need to train your staff on how it works and how to debug it and perhaps provide some simple scripts to run to test reachability via ISATAP.

To summarize, ISATAP is enabled by default in Windows and is only utilized if an A record (in the format of ISATAP.<FQDN>) is published in DNS that the local client host is utilizing. If there is no entry then the host does not attempt to use ISATAP unless manually configured to do so via AD/GPO, PowerShell, netsh, or a registry key change. Figure 3-6 shows a typical example of an ISATAP network overview.

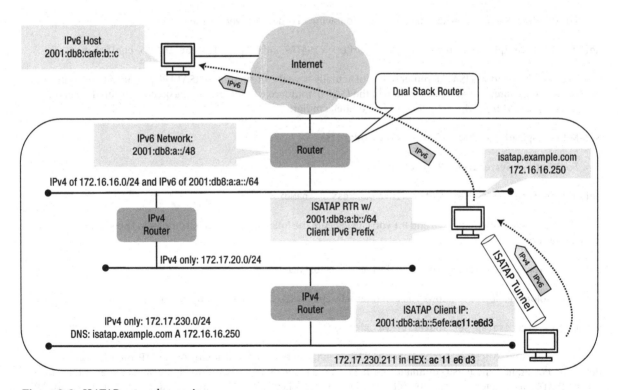

Figure 3-6. ISATAP network overview

As an administrator, if you need to build an ISATAP server the steps are straightforward. You will need an IPv6 prefix to give the ISATAP router. If your ISATAP router will forward traffic out to the IPv6 Internet or intranet it will need to be dual-stacked and have appropriate routing policies. You will need to publish the ISATAP IPv4 address via an A record in DNS and you will need to allow publication of that record. See Chapter 8 for more details on how to set up everything needed to enable ISATAP via DNS.

After the ISATAP DNS entry is built out the next thing is to configure the ISATAP router to enable both forwarding and advertising on the ISATAP tunnel interface on the server. On Windows Server 2012/R2 you can configure the ISATAP router with the following PowerShell cmdlet:

```
Set-NetIPInterface -InterfaceAlias <Name> -AddressFamily IPv6 -Forwarding Enabled -Advertising
Enabled
```

For Window Server 2008/R2 you can use the following in order to enable the forwarding and advertising:

```
netsh interface ipv6 set interface <ISATAP Interface Name or Index> forwarding=enabled
advertise=enabled
```

Next, you need to add a published route on the ISATAP tunnel interface that matches the IPv6 prefix you have reserved for ISATAP. You can do this on Windows Server 2012/R2 with the following PowerShell cmdlet:

```
New-NetRoute -DestinationPrefix <Prefix> -InterfaceAlias <Name> -AddressFamily IPv6 -Publish Yes
```

For Windows Server 2008/R2 you can use the following in order to advertise the route:

```
netsh interface ipv6 add route <Address/Prefix> <ISATAP Interface Name or Index> publish=yes
```

Because the Windows ISATAP router does not actually have the hostname of "ISATAP" you need to tell it to enable its ISATAP interface so it can function in the ISATAP router role in the IPv4 namespace. You can do that on Windows Server 2012/R2 with the following PowerShell cmdlet:

```
Set-NetIsatapConfiguration -Router <IPv4 address>
```

For Windows Server 2008/R2 you can use:

```
netsh interface isatap set router <IPv4 Address or name>
```

On Windows 7 with updates, 8 and 8.1 you can execute the following PowerShell cmdlet to specify the ISATAP router:

```
Set-NetIsatapConfiguration -Router <IPv4 address or name>
```

On an older version of Windows you can manually specify the ISATAP router by executing:

```
netsh interface isatap set router <IPv4 address>
```

See the section "Microsoft Group Policy and IPv6" in Chapter 4 for the disabling of ISATAP and Chapter 5 for details on PowerShell and netsh commands for ISATAP. See Figure 3-4 for the Group Policy Management Editor to see the ISATAP parameters you can control via GPOs (Group Policy objects). Figure 3-7 is a screenshot of the ISATAP Router Name being set to isatap.scope1.example.com.

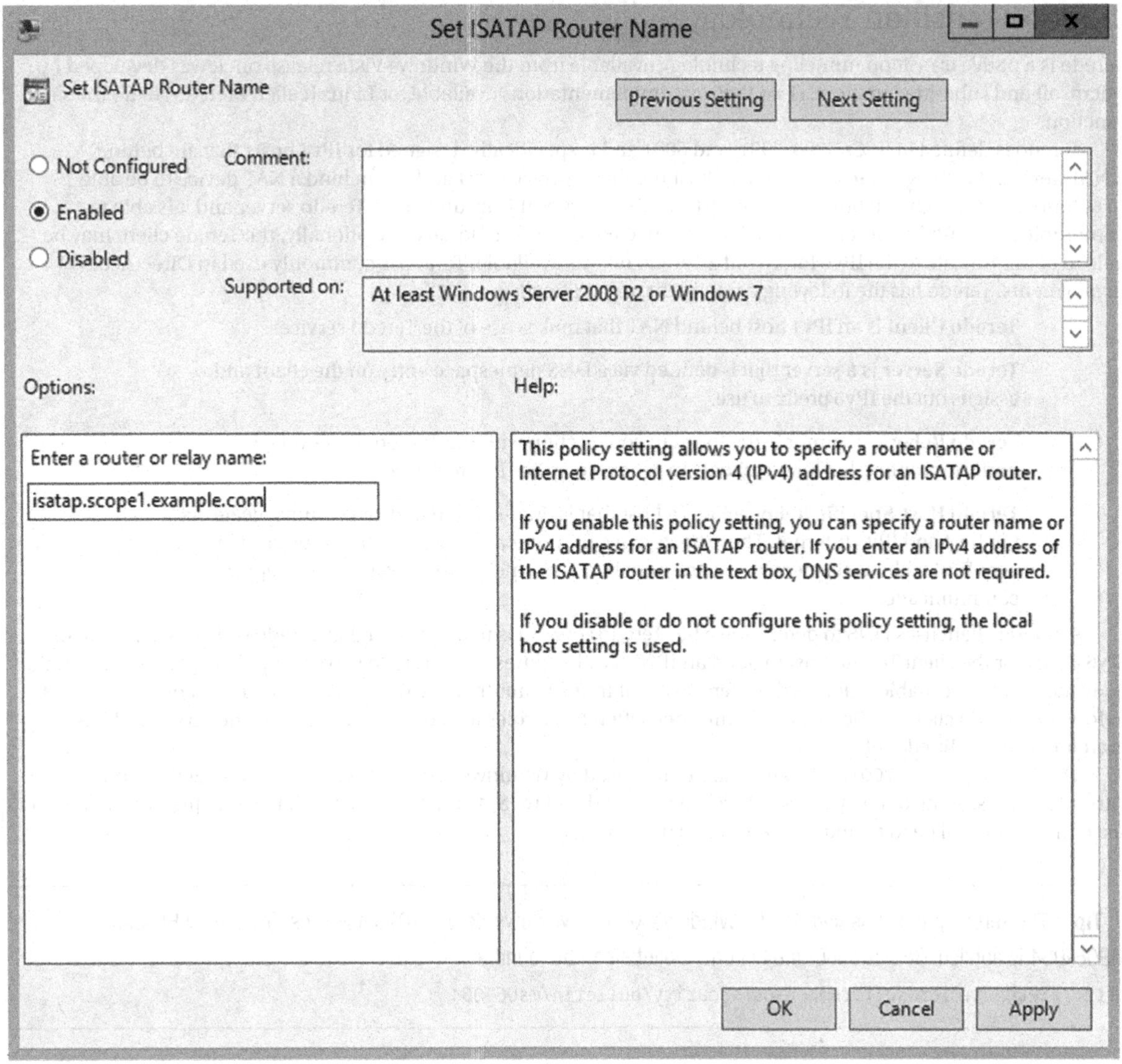

Figure 3-7. Screenshot of ISATAP router name from Windows Server 2012

A large-scale or full ISATAP deployment will involve a lot more work than what I have outlined here, but this should be enough to get you started if ISATAP is something you want to test in a lab. I do recommend that you group the Windows clients into a security group in AD and use a GPO to set the ISATAP Router Name Group Policy setting to the IPv4 ISATAP server address. Alternately, the Windows clients will use the DNS name by default to resolve the ISATAP server. Please refer to Chapter 4 for details on best practices for ISATAP and Chapter 5 for details on PowerShell.

Teredo Transition Technology

Teredo is a native transition tunneling technology available from the Windows Vista release on. It was developed by Microsoft and submitted to the IETF so there are implementations available for Linux (called Meredo) to do the same function.

Teredo is defined in RFCs 4380, 5991, and 6081 and is specifically designed for IPv4 hosts that are behind a NAT device. It is designed to allow a client host that has a private IPv4 address behind a NAT device to be able to automatically assign and build itself an IPv6 address. It does this by utilizing a Teredo server and it is able to communicate via IPv6 to other Teredo clients connected to that Teredo server. Optionally, the Teredo client may be able to communicate to the IPv6 Internet if a Teredo relay is available. Teredo is commonly used in DirectAccess deployments. Teredo has the following component roles defined:

Teredo Client is an IPv4 host behind NAT that makes use of the Teredo service.

Teredo Server is a server that is defined via a DNS namespace entry on the client and assigns out the IPv6 prefix to use.

Teredo Relay is commonly deployed in conjunction with the Teredo server role; it performs routing for Teredo clients to get out to other IPv6 resources.

Teredo Host-Specific Relay defines a host that is dual-stacked and can communicate via the IPv4 and IPv6 Internet. These hosts can communicate directly with a Teredo client over IPv4 without the need to use the Teredo relay, which saves intermediate steps in communication.

A Teredo client uses DNS to determine what Teredo server it is to utilize and that Teredo server assigns out an IPv6 prefix for the client Teredo host to build an IPv6 Teredo address. The Teredo server may also operate as a Teredo relay meaning it is capable of forwarding Teredo client traffic to another IPv6 network. This is most commonly used to forward Teredo client traffic to the IPv6 Internet. Often these roles are co-resident on the same server and it is therefore called a Teredo relay server.

The Teredo prefix is 2001::/32 and that prefix is used by Windows Vista and Windows Server 2008 through to current releases. Some older Windows OS releases used the 3ffe:831f::/32 prefix but that was deprecated and if you see it in use you will need to update the Teredo configuration.

■ **Tip** The Teredo prefix was updated for Windows XP and Windows Server 2003 if Microsoft Security Bulletin MS06-064 is applied. Details about the Security Bulletin can be found at

http://technet.microsoft.com/en-us/security/bulletin/ms06-064

Teredo NAT traversal techniques are based on STUN (Session Traversal Utilities for NAT) technology and utilize UDP. Teredo defaults to UDP port 3544 but in reality can be set to any UDP port. This makes stopping Teredo very difficult and really requires more advanced stateful packet inspection firewalls to determine if Teredo is being used on the network.

It has also been pointed out that Teredo can introduce security concerns since malware can take advantage of Teredo to do remote command and control. I don't necessarily buy the argument that Teredo is that big a concern for malware as much as it can cause difficulty understanding where your network traffic is going if enabled.

Teredo makes use of DNS to resolve the Teredo server IPv4 address. The default Teredo server in Windows is teredo.ipv6.microsoft.com which at the time of publishing resolved to 94.245.121.253. You can determine what a Windows 8 or 8.1 client is using as a Teredo server by using the following PowerShell cmdlet:

```
Get-NetTeredoConfiguration
```

Or, you can execute the following on Windows Vista or 7:

```
netsh interface teredo show state
```

Teredo is one of several options for DirectAccess (DA) clients to utilize for connectivity to the DA server. The DA server can be the Teredo server role and clients are able to get a Teredo IPv6 prefix from the DA server. The DA client is able to use the Teredo IPv6 connectivity to connect back to the corporate network via the DA server. The advantage of Teredo for DA clients is that it works for clients behind NAT devices. Because Teredo is mainly deployed as part of a DA solution it is rare to see Teredo host-specific relays in use at all. As a result, unless you do a Teredo deployment outside DA you will not have to worry about that component role.

Teredo has been available since Windows Vista and Windows Server 2008 by default. Teredo, however, is not on by default but has to be activated to be used via an application request. This can also be done via the command line or via PowerShell. Microsoft puts in a default DNS entry for a Teredo server of teredo.ipv6.microsoft.com in order to help reduce accidental misuse of Teredo services. Figure 3-8 outlines a typical Teredo configuration that has a Teredo relay server and shows the Teredo client process.

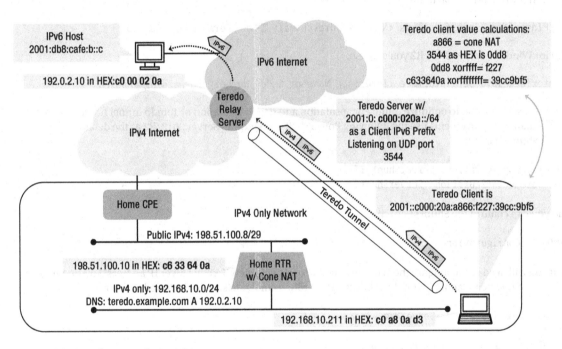

Figure 3-8. *Teredo network overview*

As an administrator, if you need to build a Teredo server and relay the steps are straightforward. Most of the time configuring Teredo is for a DA deployment and the wizard for DA will do the work, so I recommend going that route. However, if you want to do it yourself here is how.

You will need an IPv6 prefix to give the Teredo server and two consecutive public IPv4 addresses. If your Teredo router will forward traffic out to the IPv6 Internet or intranet, it will need to be dual-stacked and have appropriate routing policies. You will need to publish the first of the consecutive IPv4 public addresses as the Teredo IPv4 address via an A record in DNS. Your Teredo clients will use this IPv4 address to connect to the Teredo server. The second IPv4 address is used for detecting the type of NAT used in front of the Teredo client. The second IPv4 address MUST be consecutive at this time (it is a coding thing, not a requirement of how the detection functions) so this requirement can be challenging in certain deployment where public IPv4 addresses are hard to get.

After the Teredo server DNS entry is built out the next thing is to configure the Teredo server parameter with the first consecutive public IPv4 address.

On Windows Server 2012/R2 you can configure the Teredo server with the following PowerShell cmdlet:

```
Set-NetTeredoConfiguration -Type server -ServerName <Name or IP Address>
```

Or on Window Server 2008/R2 use:

```
netsh interface teredo set state type=server servername=<Name or IP Address>
```

Use these commands to enable the Teredo server role on the Windows server. You will need to have the existing IPv4 interfaces configured with static public IPv4 addresses prior to doing this command.

Next, you will likely want the server to have a dual purpose and use it as a Teredo relay in addition to the Teredo server role. The Teredo relay server needs to add a published route on the Teredo tunnel interface that matches the IPv6 prefix you have reserved for Teredo. You can do this on Windows Server 2012/R2 with the following PowerShell cmdlet in order to advertise that route:

```
Set-NetIPInterface -InterfaceAlias <Name> -AddressFamily IPv6 -Forwarding Enabled
```

And for Windows Server 2008/R2 you can use:

```
netsh interface ipv6 set interface <Interface Name or Index Number> forwarding=enabled
```

There is also an option to optimize traffic encapsulation and deencapsulation of Teredo tunnel traffic. To get these performance improvements use the following PowerShell on Windows Server 2012/R2 as the default behavior is to not have Shunt enabled:

```
Set-NetTeredoConfiguration -ServerShunt $True
Reset-NetTeredoConfiguration -ServerShunt
```

And you can confirm the Shunt state with:

```
Get-NetTeredoConfiguration
```

Next you will need to reconfigure the Windows clients to use your new Teredo server IP address. You do this on Windows 7 with updates, 8 and 8.1 with the following PowerShell cmdlet to specify the Teredo router:

```
Set-NetTeredoConfiguration -ServerName <name>
```

On older version of Windows you can run:

```
netsh interface teredo set state servername=<IPv4 address>
```

If you are using Group Policy to modify the Windows client configurations then the following Group Policy should be set:

```
Computer Configuration | Policies | Administrative Templates | Network | TCP/IP Settings | IPv6
Transition Technologies
```

Then set the Teredo parameter to what you want. Figure 3-9 shows a screenshot of setting the name parameter to teredo.example.com.

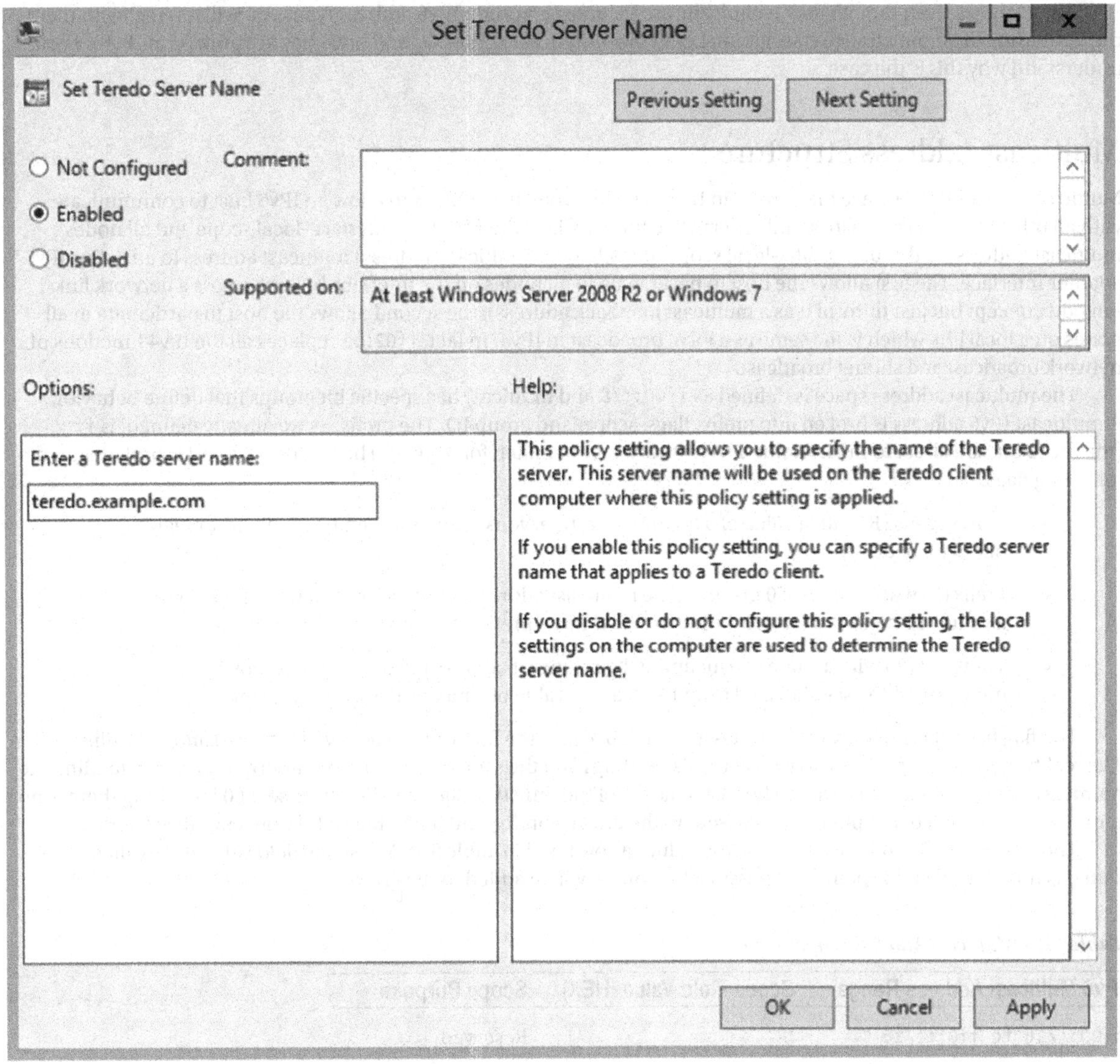

Figure 3-9. *Screenshot of Teredo name settings from Windows Server 2012*

See the section "Microsoft Group Policy and IPv6" in Chapter 4 for details on controls of Teredo along with best practices and Chapter 5 for details on PowerShell and netsh commands for Teredo. A Teredo deployment is typically done for DA and likely is something you want to test in a lab first. Again, I recommend using the DA wizard to deploy Teredo if you plan to use it as part of a DA solution.

Multicast Addresses

IPv6 makes use of multicast IPv6 addresses in a different capacity than legacy IPv4. Every host will automatically have at least one or more multicast address associated with an IPv6 interface so technically they are the most common IPv6 addresses in use. If the host has multiple IPv6 addresses it will also have multiple multicast addresses associated for each IPv6 address per interface.

The reality is, even though they technically are the most common IPv6 address types you will interact with them the least from an administrative standpoint. Let's cover multicast addresses and how they are utilized in IPv6 so you understand why this is the case.

Multicast Address Structure

Multicast IPv6 addresses have many roles in IPv6. The first role they fulfill is to allow an IPv6 host to communicate with all other IPv6 hosts on a local link. Every IPv6 hosts assigns the ff01::1 (interface-local scope and all nodes multicast address) and ff02::1 (link-local scope and all nodes multicast address) multicast address to an active IPv6 adapter interface. The first allows the host to participate in all nodes on the interface but not across a network link (an odd concept but just think of it as a multicast loopback address); the second allows the host to participate in all nodes on a local link which is the same as a local broadcast in IPv4. In fact, ff02::1 replaces all the IPv4 functions of network broadcast and subnet broadcast.

The multicast address space is defined as ff00::/8 and multicast has specific bit groups that define behavior. A multicast IPv6 address is broken into prefix, flags, scope, and group ID. The prefix, as we already defined, is ff (the first 8 bits are all set to binary value 1 so it is very easy to match for ASICS). The flag is 4 bits and is broken into the following flags:

- Rendezvous (R) with a value of 0 meaning a rendezvous point is not embedded and 1 meaning one is embedded.

- Prefix (P) with a value of 0 meaning the multicast address is not based on a unicast prefix and a value of 1 meaning that it is based on the unicast prefix.

- Transient (T) with a value of 0 meaning the multicast address is from the well-known multicast addresses allocated from IANA and a value of 1 means it is locally assigned.

The flag has 4 bits but only three values are listed because the first value is reserved (set to 0) and not utilized. The reality is you will rarely have to look at the flag settings and the scope is likely more important in understanding the multicast traffic you may encounter. The vast majority of the time the flag value in total is set at 0 indicating there is no rendezvous embedded, the prefix is not based on the unicast prefix, and it is using well-known multicast addresses.

The scope is 4 bits and is broken into the values as outlined in Table 3-2. Any scope field value not explicitly stated is unassigned at this point. It is possible that more will be added in the future.

Table 3-2. Multicast Address Scope Values

IPv6 Multicast Address Range	Scope Field Value (HEX)	Scope Purpose
ff00::/16 to ff0f::/16	0	Reserved
ffx1::/16	1	Interface-local
ffx2::/16	2	Link-local
ffx3::/16	3	Reserved
ffx4::/16	4	Admin-local
ffx5::/16	5	Site-local
ffx8::/16	8	Organization-local
ffxe::/16	E	Global
ffxf::/16	F	Reserved

Figure 3-10 shows the general multicast address format and also the flag bit values; Table 3-2 outlines the scope values.

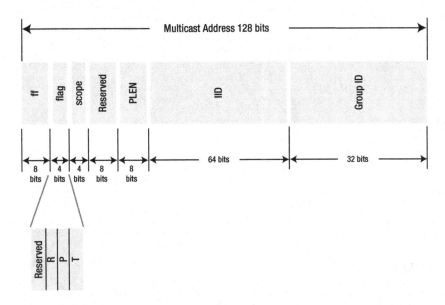

Figure 3-10. *IPv6 Multicast address structure*

Finally, the Group ID was originally 112 bits in length but has been updated into more discrete functions and the Group ID was narrowed down to 32 bits. The details of all the sections can be found in RFCs 3306, 3307, 3959, and 4489. Figure 3-10 represents the multicast address sections per RFC 4489 (`http://tools.ietf.org/html/rfc4489`).

Managing Multicast

Multicast IPv6 addresses are not as noticeable as unicast IPv6 addresses in Windows; however, every host in your IPv6 network utilizes multicast. In fact, each IPv6 address that is utilized by Windows will generate IPv6 multicast addresses automatically based on those IPv6 unicast addresses that are allocated on the host. This is the default behavior and you can see this on a host by utilizing the following netsh command:

```
netsh interface ipv6 show joins <interface id>
```

Unfortunately, there is no way to obtain the same information in PowerShell version 3. I have submitted a feature request to Microsoft to build a PowerShell cmdlet for this function so ideally it is in the works. The following example output shows the multicast addresses that are associated with Interface ID 19, which in this example is a wireless interface we used earlier.

```
PS C:\> netsh interface ipv6 show joins 19

Interface 19: Wi-Fi

Multicast Address : ff01::1
Scope            : 0
References       : 0
Last Reporter?   : Yes
```

```
Multicast Address : ff02::1
Scope             : 0
References        : 0
Last Reporter?    : Yes

Multicast Address : ff02::c
Scope             : 0
References        : 4
Last Reporter?    : Yes

Multicast Address : ff02::1:3
Scope             : 0
References        : 1
Last Reporter?    : Yes

Multicast Address : ff02::1:ff32:6ed3
Scope             : 0
References        : 1
Last Reporter?    : Yes

Multicast Address : ff02::1:ffb1:54ce
Scope             : 0
References        : 2
Last Reporter?    : Yes
```

Still, it is not common for Windows administrators to deal with or manage multicast in IPv4 or IPv6 today. Table 3-3 includes the common IPv6 multicast addresses you might see, so you have an idea what might be utilized in your environment.

Table 3-3. Common IPv6 Multicast Addresses

IPv6 Multicast Address	Description
ff01::1	Interface-local scope all-nodes
ff02::1	Link-local scope all-nodes (IPv4 broadcast)
ff02::2	Link-local scope all-routers
ff02::d	Link-local PIM routers
ff02::16	Link-local Multicast Listener Discovery v2
ff02::1:2	Link-local DHCPv6 servers or relay agents
ff02::1:3	Link-local Multicast Name Resolution (RFC 4795)
ff05::1:3	Site-local DHCPv6 servers or relay agents
ff02::c	Link-local Simple Service Discovery Protocol
ff02::fb	Link-local mDNS (Apple's Bonjour Service)
ff02::101	Link-local NTP

Neighbor Discovery—Solicited-Node

IPv6 has improved on the IPv4 link-layer address resolution process which in IPv4 is Address Resolution Protocol (ARP). The Neighbor Discovery (ND) process is really handled by ICMPv6, but in this case ICMPv6 leverages multicast to accomplish this task so I am including it in the multicast section. In IPv6 to determine the link-layer address for a given IPv6 address a special IPv6 multicast address is used called the solicited-node address. This address has a specific prefix of ff02::1:ff00:0/104. This address leaves 24 bits at the end that match the last 24 bits of the IPv6 address that the source host is trying to reach on the link-local network.

By using the special solicited-node address IPv6 reduces the number of hosts it interrupts with multicast traffic to determine the link-layer information for a specific IPv6 address. This is an advantage over using the ff02::1 link-local all-nodes multicast address, for instance, and better than what IPv4 does by utilizing broadcasts for ARP.

In the previous example output the wireless adapter had the following solicited-node IPv6 multicast addresses on the host:

```
ff02::1:ff32:6ed3
ff02::1:ffb1:54ce
```

We can see from the Get-NetIpAddress cmdlet in the example that follows that that interface has several IPv6 addresses associated with it (some output removed for clarity):

```
PS C:\> Get-NetIPAddress -InterfaceIndex 19 -AddressFamily IPv6 | ft
ifIndex IPAddress                               PrefixLength
------- ---------                               ------------
19      fe80::5ef:b5a3:2ab1:54ce%19                       64
19      2001:470:1f05:9a4:5fd:e334:6e32:6ed3             128
19      2001:470:1f05:9a4:5ef:b5a3:2ab1:54ce              64
```

The output clearly shows that the link-local address shares the last 24 bits as one of the Global Unicast Addresses which means they are the random IPv6 addresses that Windows builds for an interface instead of using EUI-64 (covered later in the section "Assigning IPv6 Addresses") and the other Global Unicast Address is the temporary address (again, covered later in the section "Assigning IPv6 Addresses") that Windows utilizes for outbound sessions.

Because both the link-local and Global Unicast random addresses share the last 24 bits only a single solicited-node address for both those addresses is built (which is very efficient) and for the temporary address another solicited-node address is built, resulting in a total of two for that particular interface ID.

Because each Windows host is listening to this solicited-node address another IPv6 host on the same link-local network can easily build a request packet with the proper IPv6 solicited-node address based on the IPv6 address it gets from DNS (or other name resolution). This also means that the requesting host only interrupts hosts that match the last 24 bits of the IPv6 address. While it is possible for two hosts on the same link-local subnet to have the same last 24 bits the likelihood is extremely rare. This results in a very efficient link-layer resolution process.

Inverse Neighbor Discovery

IPv6 also has a way to determine the link-layer address reverse resolution process which in IPv4 is Reverse Address Resolution Protocol (RARP). Inverse Neighbor Discovery (IND) uses two message types, solicitation and advertisement. Effectively the messages are used to determine the IPv6 address of a host when the host only knows a link-layer address. Again, this is a function of the ND process of ICMPv6, but it is also leveraging multicast so it is covered in this section.

There are no efficiencies gained in the IPv6 method, which uses the link-local all-nodes multicast address (effectively a broadcast) to request the IPv6 address of a specific link-layer address which is the solicitation message type. An IND advertisement message is the reply and that completes the process. IND is part of the ND process. It has some well-documented security holes (just like RARP) and it is possible to secure the ND process using SEcure Neighbor Discovery (SEND); however, SEND is not natively in Windows at this time. SEND is also only truly effective if your network is IPv6 only. If you run dual-stack you are still vulnerable to the same attack types via IPv4 so your host will potentially use IPv4 with unsecure ARP/RARP information. Until networks are IPv6 only I find it unlikely that Microsoft will add SEND support into Windows.

IPv6 Multicast and Ethernet

The final multicast process to cover is the mapping of IPv6 multicast addresses to their multicast Ethernet addresses. When IPv6 is sent on an Ethernet link the destination 48-bit MAC address is of format 33-33-xx-xx-xx-xx or 3333:xxxx:xxxx depending on manufacture standard. The last 32 bits (x values) are a direct mapping of the last 32 bits of the IPv6 address in HEX.

For IPv6 you can use the PowerShell cmdlet Get-NetNeighbor to determine the neighbor resolution that the Windows host has performed. The following example output of the wireless interface ID 19 used earlier shows the 32-bit mapping (some output removed for clarity):

```
PS C:\> Get-NetNeighbor -AddressFamily IPv6 -InterfaceIndex 19 | ft

ifIndex IPAddress                                         LinkLayerAddress
------- ---------                                         ----------------
19      ff02::1:ffb1:54ce                                 3333ffb154ce
19      ff02::1:ffa0:1e3a                                 3333ffa01e3a
19      ff02::1:ffa0:1e30                                 3333ffa01e30
19      ff02::1:ffa0:1e29                                 3333ffa01e29
19      ff02::1:ffa0:1e20                                 3333ffa01e20
19      ff02::1:ffa0:1e18                                 3333ffa01e18
19      ff02::1:ffa0:1e08                                 3333ffa01e08
19      ff02::1:ff6c:b3e0                                 3333ff6cb3e0
19      ff02::1:ff32:6ed3                                 3333ff326ed3
19      ff02::1:ff00:1012                                 3333ff001012
19      ff02::1:ff00:1009                                 3333ff001009
19      ff02::1:ff00:1003                                 3333ff001003
19      ff02::1:ff00:7d                                   3333ff00007d
19      ff02::1:3                                         333300010003
19      ff02::1:2                                         333300010002
19      ff02::16                                          333300000016
19      ff02::c                                           33330000000c
19      ff02::2                                           333300000002
19      ff02::1                                           333300000001
```

Optionally you can clear out all the entries from the ND cache for IPv6 using the following PowerShell cmdlet: Remove-NetNeighbor -AddressFamily IPv6 -Confirm:$false

There is one last important item for those who work on the network infrastructure in addition to Windows hosts. IPv6 utilizes Multicast Listener Discovery (MLD) to optimize network performance and utilization of links by reducing the number of multicast packets that are generated and forwarded. MLD is currently on version 2 and should be utilized in your network equipment if possible. You may also need to leverage Internet Group Management Protocol (IGMP) within your network depending on the support you have in your network equipment. MLD and IGMP are beyond the scope of this book but you can reference the RFCs for both protocols at

```
MLD - RFC 2710, 3810, 4604
IGMP - RFC 3376, 4604
```

■ **Note**   You can also read up on MLD in *Understanding IPv6, Third Edition* by Joseph Davies (Microsoft Press, 2012) or *IPv6 Essentials, Second Edition* by Silvia Hagen (O'Reilly Media, 2006) which both cover MLD in more depth.

As you can see from all the previous use cases, IPv6 uses multicast addresses automatically. Multicast addresses are about efficiencies in how the protocol accomplishes things and very little is left for an administrator to do. The exception would be if you are using multicast to distribute content of some kind in your network and you are either using Windows to generate the traffic for that multicast source or your Windows clients are consuming that multicast traffic. Otherwise, although it is important to know about multicast you can see it isn't something you will spend a lot of time configuring on Windows.

Anycast Addresses

The final IPv6 address type is anycast. It turns out that any unicast IPv6 address can also be an anycast IPv6 address and you can't tell the difference by looking at the address format. Anycast is actually a function of how the IPv6 address behaves more than it is its format. I consider it more a mode than a specific IPv6 address type, but regardless its function is very important when building highly available distributed resources in your network.

In its simplest form an anycast IPv6 address is an address that is assigned to multiple hosts on a network, often in different geographic network locations or peering points. An anycast IPv6 address is a destination address only so you should never see new sourced traffic from an anycast address. The goal of an anycast IPv6 address is to provide a service with a single IPv6 address or prefix and have it highly available from different locations within the network.

Figure 3-11 shows how an anycast address would function. Notice that the routers are really in control of how a source reaches an anycast destination address and the router handles the propagation of anycast IPv6 addresses. Typically a host route entry (/128) or more commonly an anycast prefix (/64) is propagated into the routing table with a limited range or weight value. Each router that has a participating anycast address will advertise the same route entry or anycast prefix. If one of the anycast IPv6 addresses fails it is withdrawn from the routing table and the next closest routing entry takes over.

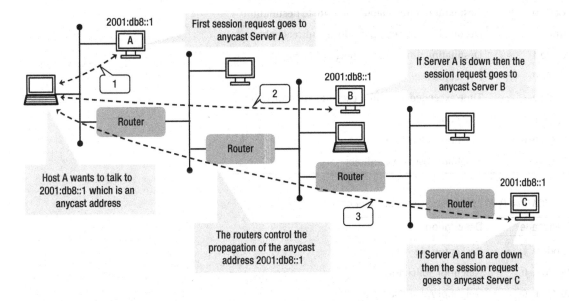

Figure 3-11. IPv6 anycast example

In summary, the function of anycast is to provide a distributed IPv6 address resource that enables high availability. Common uses of anycast are for DNS, NTP, and IPv6 transition services like 6to4 routers. In the case of 6to4 the anycast IPv4 address is 192.88.99.1 and its IPv6 address is 2002:c058:6301:: which are route injected into their appropriate protocol at their closest routing point.

ICMPv6 Protocol

One of the most significant changes from IPv4 to IPv6 is the protocol's dependence on ICMPv6 to function. In IPv4 it is not uncommon for network operators to completely block all ICMP traffic using the argument that it makes the network more secure. (This is often why you can't ping a host on some networks.) In IPv6 it is not possible to do the same as it will break the protocol.

ICMPv6 is used in ND, MLD, and Path MTU Discovery (PMTUD), which are all critical functions for IPv6. Each of these topics could take up an entire chapter in its own right but my goal is to cover the high points and cover the minimum you need to know to have an operational network for your Windows hosts.

For ICMPv6 there are two types of messages, error and informational. The type field in ICMPv6 is broken down as 0-127 for error messages and 128-255 for informational. After the type field is the code field which allows more discrete codes for the types. After the code field is a checksum and finally the message body that contains any specific message data that might be required.

Windows conforms to most IPv6 RFCs related to ICMPv6 with a few exceptions. RFC 4884 is one which is to extend ICMPv6 to support multipart messages. This should not be a significant issue for the operations of Windows as I am not aware of any other OS supporting this RFC, but this could change.

A common request I get regarding ICMPv6 is for a short list of ICMPv6 types and codes and also a list of the ICMPv6 types you have to allow for PMTUD. Table 3-4 outlines those ICMPv6 message types (the list is brief; there are many more type and code options) and Table 3-5 covers the minimum required ICMPv6 messages that are needed for PMTUD to work.

Table 3-4. *Common ICMPv6 Messages to Know*

ICMPv6 Message	Description
Type 1, Code 0	Destination unreachable, no route to destination
Type 1, Code 3	Destination unreachable, address unreachable
Type 1, Code 4	Destination unreachable, port unreachable
Type 2, Code 0	Packet too big
Type 3, Code 0	Time exceeded, hop limit exceeded in transit
Type 135, Code 0	Neighbor Solicitation
Type 136, Code 0	Neighbor Advertisement
Type 137, Code 0	Neighbor Discovery redirect

Table 3-5. *ICMPv6 Path MTU Discovery Requirements*

ICMPv6 Message	Description
Type 2, Code 0	Packet too big
Type 135, Code 0	Neighbor Solicitation
Type 136, Code 0	Neighbor Advertisement

The reality is that understanding everything that needs to happen in firewalls and routers for ICMPv6 is a huge undertaking. I recommend reviewing RFC 4890 at `http://tools.ietf.org/html/rfc4890`, which has recommendations of what ICMPv6 messages to filter on in firewall configurations.

It is likely that the one issue you will run into when using IPv6 on your network is problems with connectivity related to PMTUD. If PMTUD fails to work in IPv6 then the two hosts trying to communicate will simply fail to establish a network connection. It is a very frustrating problem to debug and may even be out of your operational control, which can add to the stress of trying to fix the problem. In short, PMTUD needs to operate end to end for a host to discover if an MTU value on some part of the link is smaller than what the host is using. If you remember, I mentioned earlier in the chapter that IPv6 no longer allows the routers to perform fragmentation. This means the hosts have to do this on their own and must have a mechanism to determine what the correct MTU size is from end to end so they know what size payload to use. This is the function of PMTUD and hence why it is so important.

■ **Note** Chapter 6 covers the Windows firewall and has the rules required for permitting PMTUD which is useful if you are required to lock down your OS much tighter than the default setting

---

Even more vexing is the reality that on standard LAN Ethernet segments everything is likely to work just fine with default MTU settings of 1500. The hosts may operate just fine even if PMTUD is blocked because the MTU matches end to end for the hosts on that network. The problem becomes apparent when using VPN, tunnels, or some other service that changes the MTU size of an intermediate link to something smaller than 1500. Suddenly your IPv6 traffic across those links will fail and you will have little idea why. My first instinct now is to use the `tracert -6 <hostname>` command to see if the network path is working and then to use the `ping -6 -l <size of payload> <hostname>` command and set the size of the payload so you can determine if you can reach the other end with a different payload size assuming ICMPv6 is not blocked everywhere. Alternately, you can use a tool like iperf to perform similar tests with different payload sizes. Iperf is not a native tool included in Windows but it is a useful tool and you can use your favorite search engine to find the most current version. One of the advantages of iperf is that it is multiplatform so you can also use it on Linux. I also recommend the Sysinternals Suite that Mark Russinovich and Bryce Cogswell created which is now owned by Microsoft. The networking utilities from Sysinternal are covered at `http://technet.microsoft.com/en-us/sysinternals/bb795532` and TCPView is particularly useful for seeing active socket sessions on a Windows host.

As a final note on ICMPv6, Microsoft introduced modifications to the ping and tracert commands in Window Vista and Windows Server 2008 to allow narrowing the protocol type. You can do this by using the switch -6 in the command. The example shows how it can be used to test only the IPv6 reachability of a DNS name.

```
PS C:\> ping -6 -l 1280 www.cav6tf.org

Pinging cav6tf.org [2001:470:0:11a::403e:a5c5] with 1280 bytes of data:
Reply from 2001:470:0:11a::403e:a5c5: time=40ms
Reply from 2001:470:0:11a::403e:a5c5: time=24ms
Reply from 2001:470:0:11a::403e:a5c5: time=29ms
Reply from 2001:470:0:11a::403e:a5c5: time=32ms

Ping statistics for 2001:470:0:11a::403e:a5c5:
    Packets: Sent = 4, Received = 4, Lost = 0 (0% loss),
Approximate round trip times in milli-seconds:
    Minimum = 24ms, Maximum = 40ms, Average = 31ms
```

As the output shows, even though `www.cav6tf.org` has both an IPv4 A record in DNS and an IPv6 AAAA record, it only used ICMPv6 to test the connection.

Assigning IPv6 Addresses

IPv6 uses similar tools and services to assign IP addresses to hosts as IPv4. However, there are differences because the IPv6 protocol was designed for some different use cases that IPv4 never considered. Understanding how to assign IPv6 addresses is critical for many Windows administrators as they likely do that function for IPv4 today. This section covers the different ways to assign IPv6 addresses and, I hope, why you will use one method vs. another.

Autoassigning Addresses

While IPv4 has the ability to autoassign addresses (commonly known as Automatic Private IP Addressing or APIPA) as outlined in RFC 3927 (http://tools.ietf.org/html/rfc3927), IPv6 has extended capabilities past what IPv4 is able to do. IPv4's autoassigned address range is 169.254.0.0/16 and is effectively a link-local scope and very limited in function. APIPA is unable to autoassign IPv4 addresses from a range that would allow it to communicate with the public Internet. It is designed for small peer-to-peer or ad hoc networks where a host might want to reach a printer or a file share. So how is IPv6 unique? It can utilize an autoassigning method that allows it to get a valid IPv6 address on any network that advertises the right information.

First I will cover how it performs the same function as IPv4 autoassigning which is for link-local addresses. Then I will cover how Windows obtains a Global Unicast or ULA from the RA process. There are two methods to do this: SLAAC and DHCPv6.

Before we get into all the details around autoassigning addresses we need to cover the topic of interface IDs and how they are generated.

Interface IDs

An interface identifier is defined as the rightmost 64 bits of an IPv6 address. This differs from the prefix that consists of the leftmost 64 bits. This means that functionally all IPv6 addresses have a natural split in their address at the midway point. This isn't always true as you can make prefixes as specific as you like; however, it is not a normal practice and breaks the ability of a host to autoassign addresses.

Interface IDs in Windows have two options, the random and EUI-64 methods to generate the interface ID. These interface IDs behaviors can be controlled and the default settings differ for Windows versions and for a Windows client vs. a server. Let's cover EUI-64 first.

EUI-64 Interface ID

EUI-64 makes use of the 48-bit MAC address (IEEE 802 address) of the Windows host interface. It can also make use of the newer IEEE EUI-64 addresses, but those are not in use commonly today (except in Firewire). We will cover the IEEE 802 48-bit MAC address types that are commonly used with Ethernet to build the EUI-64 interface IDs for IPv6 addresses.

A 48-bit MAC address is split in half and fffe is stuffed into the middle of the MAC address. This means we are adding 16 bits to the existing 48 bits of the MAC address which results in 64 bits.The seventh and eighth bits of the address (from the left) may also be modified. The seventh bit is the universal/local role and the eighth bit is the individual/group role. Usually only the seventh bit is modified. When these modifications are made in IPv6 the technical term for the interface ID is "Modified EUI-64" though it is often just shortened to EUI-64. Almost all other OS IPv6 implementations do the Modified EUI-64 standard. Figure 3-12 has an example of building out an EUI-64 address.

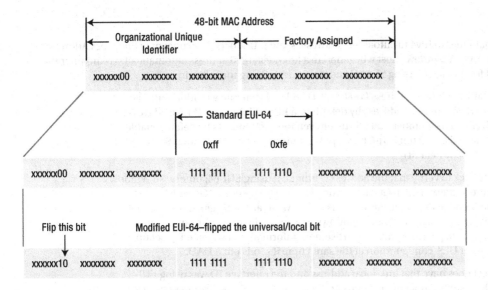

Figure 3-12. *EUI-64 from a 48-bit MAC address*

Autoconfiguration (in other words the IPv6 address wasn't manually configured) for Windows XP and Windows Server 2003 both utilized EUI-64 by default to generate the interface ID portion of an IPv6 address. Windows Vista, Windows 7, Windows 8, Windows 8.1, Windows Server 2008, Windows Server 2008R2, Windows Server 2012, and Windows Server 2012R2 all use the randomly generated method.

Random IDs (Non-EUI-64)

The great news is that random interface IDs on Windows hosts are actually really simple. Windows randomly generates an interface ID when using this method. Windows (except Windows XP and Windows Server 2003) does this by default so you have to turn off this privacy setting if you want to use EUI-64. This is done with the following netsh:

```
#- shutting off random extension (force EUI-64)
netsh interface ipv6 set global randomizeidentifiers=disabled store=active
netsh interface ipv6 set global randomizeidentifiers=disabled store=persistent
```

And with Powershell cmdlets:

```
# - turn off random addressing (make it do EUI-64)
Set-NetIPv6Protocol -RandomizeIdentifiers Disabled
# - turn back on random addressing
Set-NetIPv6Protocol -RandomizeIdentifiers Enabled
```

Both the EUI-64 and random ID methods generate permanent IPv6 addresses. This is to distinguish from a temporary address which is yet another privacy method used by Windows (more on that later). Now that we know how interface IDs are made let's dive in and tackle SLAAC.

SLAAC

IPv6 expands on the capabilities of IPv4 to autoassign addresses and introduced the concept of StateLess Address AutoConfiguration or SLAAC. A Windows host will generate a link-local IPv6 address automatically (remember the `fe80::/64` range is used for link-local) using SLAAC and it does it by doing the following:

1. Builds a tentative link-local address (`fe80::/64`) and will generate a random interface ID to build an IPv6 link-local address by default or a EUI-64 interface ID IPv6 address if random is disabled (remember that all current versions of Windows by default enable random interface IDs and not EUI-64, except for Windows XP and Windows Server 2003 which use EUI-64 by default)

2. Does a DAD check to verify that the address is unique if using EUI-64; otherwise Windows starts using the address right away, not waiting for the DAD process (Optimistic DAD) since the likelihood of duplicate addresses is so low with randomly generated interface IDs. When using Optimistic DAD the Windows host immediately sends out a Router Solicitation trying to get the Router Advertisement information it will need to set up a Global Unicast or ULA configuration at the same time it sends out a DAD.

3. If another host does have that link-local address and the interface ID was using EUI-64 then the host stops autoconfigurations and removes the link-local address from the interface and the host must be manually configured. If the interface ID is using the default random method then the Windows host will attempt another nine times to build random interface IDs. If all ten random interface IDs fail DAD then the Windows host will remove the last link-local address from the interface and the host must be manually configured.

4. If there are no conflicts then the tentative address is valid (becomes permanent) and the Windows host will use that link-local address on the interface.

SLAAC for link-local serves the same function as APIPA, but things get much more interesting when SLAAC is used for automatically generating a valid IPv6 address based on the Router Advertisement (RA) messages that are being advertised on the network. A router with the appropriate flag options and sending out multicast RAs will allow hosts on that subnet (VLAN) to automatically build an IPv6 address from the prefix(es) it advertises.

When the multicast RA is received by the Windows host it will use the prefix information in the RA to automatically generate an IPv6 address in that prefix. In the section "Size of the Address Space" I have noted that the smallest IPv6 prefix should be a /64 and here is the explanation why: it is the only way to allow a host to automatically generate an interface ID via the random or EUI-64 method. A standard prefix advertised in an RA must be a /64 for SLAAC to function properly and RFC 4862 (`http://tools.ietf.org/html/rfc4862`) defines the process. In summary, SLAAC does the following:

1. The hosts send out a Router Solicitation (RS) message to speed up the RA process to determine what prefix the RA is advertising if it hasn't already received an RA. Windows with the random method set for the interface ID will use Optimistic DAD and send out the RS at the same time it is doing DAD.

2. If no RA is received or the RA does not have the A flag set then some other address configuration protocol has to be used (currently this would be DHCPv6). On Windows Vista and Windows Server 2008 if no RA is present then those hosts do not attempt to use DHCPv6. For Windows 7 and Windows Server 2008 R2 and greater if no RA is present the hosts still attempt to utilize DHCPv6.

3. If an RA is received then the Windows host will generate an IPv6 address for each prefix included in the RA with the following conditions:

- If the Autonomous flag (A flag) is set in the RA the prefix and interface ID (random or EUI-64 methods) are used to generate a tentative address.

- The Windows host runs DAD to verify it is unique for EUI-64; otherwise it does Optimistic DAD and starts using the IPv6 address immediately.

- If the address is in use and was using the EUI-64 method the Windows hosts halts the process and must be manually configured. If the random method was used for the interface ID then Windows will generate another random Interface ID and do DAD again. It will do this ten times before it halts the process and the host must be manually configured.

- If there are no conflicts then the Windows host will use the address and initialize the interface.

4. If the Managed Address Configuration flag (M flag) is set in the RA then DHCPv6 is used.

5. If the Other Stateful Configuration flag (O flag) is set in the RA then the Windows host uses SLAAC to build an IPv6 address (with either the EUI-64 or random method for building the interface ID) but uses DHCPv6 to obtain other configuration information (like DNS server IP addresses).

Windows Vista and Window Server 2008 up to the most current versions will configure many if not all of its IPv6 interfaces automatically. It will configure link-local addresses for each interface using the random method to make the interface ID. If there is a Global Unicast and/or a unique local prefix advertised in the RA and the A flag is set then it will also generate an IPv6 address for the global and ULA prefixes.

■ **Note**   An interesting behavior for Windows 7 and Windows Server 2008R2 and greater is that the host will reuse the random interface ID that was generated in the link-local IPv6 address in the Global Unicast and/or ULA. This gives the side benefit that the ND solicited-node multicast address matches for the link-local and Global Unicast and/or ULA addresses.

Before we jump into DHCPv6 I need to quickly explain temporary IPv6 addresses and how they are used in Windows.

Temporary IPv6 Addresses

Windows Vista, Windows 7, Windows 8, and Windows 8.1 have an additional behavior that is not enabled by default in Windows Server 2008, Windows Server 2008R2, Windows Server 2012, or Windows Server 2012R2, which is that they will also generate a temporary IPv6 address in addition to their permanent EUI-64 or random interface ID generated IPv6 addresses. Section 3.3 of RFC 4941 (`http://tools.ietf.org/html/rfc4941`), which is the RFC that outlines privacy extensions for SLAAC, covers the generation of temporary IPv6 addresses.

Windows clients generate a temporary IPv6 address for every Global Unicast and ULA permanent IPv6 address they have on every interface that is active and has IPv6 enabled. A temporary address is used for outbound sessions from the Windows client. Temporary addresses rotate over time depending on the timers set in the local RA or set using the `Set-NetIPv6Protocol` PowerShell cmdlet. If the timers on the Windows client are lower than those provided in the RA message then those will be used; otherwise the RA timer settings are used. The valid lifetime value is the one that determines when a new random interface ID is generated and used to create a new temporary address for the Windows client.

■ **Tip**   A permanent IPv6 address is a Global Unicast or ULA that is assigned to the interface either via autoconfiguration (SLAAC or DHCPv6) or manually that doesn't change for as long as the interface is active (enabled). A temporary IPv6 address is a Global Unicast or ULA that uses a random interface ID in order to build an IPv6 address that will have a limited lifetime and is designed to provide more privacy for a client

---

Temporary addresses afford end users better privacy than the standard permanent addresses that Windows autoconfigures on an interface. Temporary addresses are not registered in DNS dynamically by the Windows client. Only the permanent Global Unicast or ULA addresses are registered in Dynamic DNS (DDNS) for AD purposes.

Because the permanent addresses do not change if the host does not move subnets or have a reset on their interface it logically makes sense that these are the addresses that are used to register with AD. The permanent address is the one that other AD hosts will want to use to connect to the Windows client.

For instance, if the help desk needs to connect to a remote Windows 8 client it will want to name resolve to the permanent Global Unicast IPv6 address the host has entered into AD DNS. A temporary address may have expired and is no longer actively accepting sessions on the Windows 8 client. Thus, the permanent IPv6 address makes the most sense to register in DDNS. Link-local IPv6 addresses are not registered in DDNS at all.

You can turn off temporary address behavior with the follow PowerShell cmdlet:

```
# - turn off temporary addressing
Set-NetIPv6Protocol -UseTemporaryAddresses Disabled
# - turn back on temporary addressing
Set-NetIPv6Protocol -UseTemporaryAddresses Enabled
```

And you can use netsh to do the same.

```
# - shutting off temporary addresses
netsh interface ipv6 set privacy state=disabled store=active
netsh interface ipv6 set privacy state=disabled store=persistent
```

You will have to disable and reenable the adapter to purge the old temporary IPv6 addresses that were in use on the Windows client. If you do not do this then you will have to wait for the temporary address to expire. It is possible to use temporary addresses on Windows servers; simply use the netsh or PowerShell cmdlets to enable them. However, I do not recommend using temporary addresses on servers.

I am sure you may have noticed the unfortunate naming used in the netsh command for controlling temporary addresses. It can be confusing and looks like you are setting the interface ID parameters, which control if you are doing EUI-64 or random, but you are actually setting the behavior of Windows to generate an additional temporary address to use for privacy purposes.

A random interface ID is really all about randomly generating an interface ID 64 bit value. Temporary IPv6 addresses are all about end user privacy by generating temporal addresses for outbound sessions (and it happens to leverage the random interface ID process to make those temporary addresses). Clear as mud, right? Let's move on to DHCPv6 before it gets any more confusing.

DHCPv6

The next autoassigning method for IPv6 is Dynamic Host Configuration Protocol version 6 (DHCPv6) and it is defined in RFC 3315 (http://tools.ietf.org/html/rfc3315). Chapter 9 covers DHCPv6 in depth so I recommend jumping to that chapter if you are looking for detailed configuration; this section is just an overview.

DHCPv6 has many operational similarities to DHCP (used for IPv4), but it is critical to know how DHCPv6 differs. The key difference between the two is that in DHCPv6, the DHCPv6 server does *not* provide default gateway information. This causes a lot of confusion so let's quickly discuss how hosts determine their default gateway.

If you recall, routers use RA to communicate information to hosts on the local subnet. RAs contain a variety of information, but the creators of IPv6 made the assumption that any router that is providing RAs must also be capable of being the default gateway on the network. There are ways to set different values in the RA (effectively preferences) for the default gateway so the DHCPv6 server does not need to provide this information. It was a functional separation of duty. It was thought it would help avoid errors in DHCP server settings. If a DHCP server administrator misconfigures the default gateway value it breaks network functionality. If instead the router that is already on the local subnet provides that information there is no room for error since it is physically attached to that subnet. Just as with RFC 6106 (IPv6 Router Advertisement Options for DNS Configuration) this design choice is still being debated to some extent in IPv6 working groups. There are many administrators (operators in the working group parlance) who wish to have feature parity between DHCPv6 and DHCP, and I would not be surprised to see this potential change at a later date.

The other interesting part of IPv6 is that your next hop values are (by default) link-local IPv6 addresses. This means that the default gateway next hop entry in your OS will have a link-local IPv6 entry it will use to forward traffic. This can be very confusing because in IPv4 your next hop entry for a default gateway will be an IPv4 address in the same network as the configuration on the interface. The reality is that IPv4 does not assign multiple IPv4 addresses to an interface at once, so there is no relative comparison unfortunately. For example, in IPv4 we expect to see (some output modified for clarity and formatting) the following:

```
PS C:\> Get-NetIPAddress -InterfaceIndex 19 -AddressFamily IPv4 | ft
ifIndex IPAddress            PrefixLength PrefixOrigin SuffixOrigin AddressState PolicyStore
------- ---------            ------------ ------------ ------------ ------------ -----------
19      192.168.10.160            24 Dhcp         Dhcp         Preferred    ActiveStore
PS C:\> Get-NetRoute -AddressFamily IPv4 -DestinationPrefix 0.0.0.0/0
ifIndex DestinationPrefix    NextHop                                   RouteMetric PolicyStore
------- -----------------    -------                                   ----------- -----------19
0.0.0.0/0            192.168.10.1                                        0 ActiveStore
```

For IPv6, the following sample output shows a link-local next hop for the host's default gateway even though the Windows client clearly has an IPv6 Global Unicast Address:

```
PS C:\> Get-NetIPAddress -InterfaceIndex 19 -AddressFamily IPv6 | ft
ifIndex IPAddress                          PrefixLength PrefixOrigin
------- ---------                          ------------ ------------
19      fe80::5ef:b5a3:2ab1:54ce%19             64 WellKnown
19      2001:470:1f05:9a4:d9dd:874f:2926:bc3a  128 RouterAdv...
19      2001:470:1f05:9a4:88bb:391c:d39f:d7a3  128 RouterAdv...
19      2001:470:1f05:9a4:5ef:b5a3:2ab1:54ce    64 RouterAdv...
PS C:\> Get-NetRoute -AddressFamily IPv6 -DestinationPrefix ::/
ifIndex DestinationPrefix    NextHop                                   RouteMetric PolicyStore
------- -----------------    -------                                   ----------- -----------19
::/0            fe80::3285:a9ff:fe6c:b3e0                                256 ActiveStore
```

Comparing the two you can clearly see the next hop value being link-local in IPv6, which is not the case in IPv4 because it does not have multiple IP addresses to choose from. Now that you understand one of the bigger operational differences between IPv4 and IPv6 let's quickly cover DHCPv6.

DHCPv6 makes use of several flags that are advertised in RAs to control the behavior that clients utilize (see Chapter 9 for details). You will see three settings:

- A flag or Autonomous flag, often mistakenly called the autoconfiguration or auto flag

- M flag or Managed Address Configuration flag

- O flag or Other Stateful Configuration flag

You can determine how a Windows client or server will build out an IPv6 address based on these flag combinations. In summary, for the standard configurations

- If the A flag is set (value is set to 1) then the host will utilize SLAAC to build an IPv6 address based on the prefix information in the RA and if turned off the hosts will not attempt to utilize SLAAC

- If the M flag is set (value is set to 1) then the host will utilize DHCPv6 to obtain everything except the default gateway

- If the O flag is set (value is set to 1) then the host will utilize DHCPv6 to obtain other configuration settings (like DNS or NTP parameters)

Let's cover two special uses cases that happen if these flags are in specific combinations.

DHCPv6 Stateful

When an RA has the M flag on (value is set to 1) and the O flag on (value is set to 1) it is referred to as DHCPv6 Stateful. This combination is telling you to obtain an IPv6 address from the DHCPv6 server and to also obtain all your other configuration settings from the DHCPv6 server—like DNS or NTP parameters via DHCPv6 option code.

DHCPv6 Stateless

When an RA has the O flag on (value is set to 1), the M flag off (value is set to 0), and the A flag on (value is set to 1) it is referred to as DHCPv6 Stateless. This combination is saying to the host, generate an IPv6 address via SLAAC but request your other configuration settings from the DHCPv6 server like DNS or NTP parameters via DHCPv6 option code. This provides a method for clients to obtain critical services like DNS name servers even though they generated an IPv6 address via SLAAC. Remember, an RA does not contain any additional information besides the IPv6 prefixes available on that subnet and, by inference, the default gateway.

Assigning Both SLAAC and DHCPv6

It should be noted that you can still have the A flag on (value set to 1) along with the M and O flags being on (both values set to 1). In this configuration, Windows hosts will obtain an IPv6 address via DHCPv6 and also generate a SLAAC address. If the DHCPv6 server is providing a prefix that is the same as what the RA is advertising (they don't have to be the same) then your host will have two IPv6 addresses from the same prefix—one assigned from DHCPv6 and one from SLAAC. If the DHCPv6 prefix provided is different from the prefix advertised in the RA then the host will obtain one from the DHCPv6 prefix and generate a SLAAC address from the RA prefix. This is why typically you will set the A flag off in the RAs if you plan on utilizing only DHCPv6 for your clients.

One of the common reasons you may see this combination is the lack of a DHCPv6 client for Android. Because Android is unable to use DHCPv6 due to not having a DHCPv6 client, SLAAC must be enabled for devices that run Android to obtain an IPv6 address. Unfortunately, because Android does not have a DHCPv6 client it is unable to leverage the O flag to obtain any optional parameter, the most important being a name server IP address. This means that you will need to supply a name server to the handset in some other way, most likely by manually setting it up. Alternately, you can dual-stack the network and provide that information via IPv4 as Android does have DHCP working for IPv4. This is really only an issue for wireless networks at this time since Android is principally used in cellular and tablet devices that do not have wired Ethernet ports.

> ■ **Note** I hope that Android will add DHCPv6 support soon to help resolve this last standing issue of having a clean DHCPv6 vs. SLAAC design. At this point, it is difficult to give clear guidance about which approach is better. If you run an enterprise network with Windows I recommend using DHCPv6. If you need to support Android devices be aware you will need to have SLAAC enabled.

The good news is that Windows has had a robust DHCPv6 client since Windows Vista and Windows Server 2008. In addition, Windows Server 2008 and beyond have supported proper DHCPv6 operations as a service along with integration into DNS. Chapter 9 covers in more detail how to configure Windows Server for DHCPv6 and how to manage Windows clients.

Manually Assigning IPv6 Addresses

Finally, you can always manually set the IPv6 address of a Windows client or server. You can use netsh, PowerShell, or the GUI to perform this task. The following PowerShell shows an example of how to manually set IPv6 address parameters for a host. Chapter 5 has more details on using PowerShell to set all sorts of IPv6 parameters.

```
# Set the IP address on the interface for the first time using
New-NetIPAddress -InterfaceIndex 12 -IPAddress 2001:0db8:cafe:0010::1 -PrefixLength 64
-DefaultGateway 2001:0db8:cafe:0010::254
# If you are modifying an existing server IP stack you will need to use
Set-NetIPAddress -InterfaceIndex 12 -IPAddress 2001:0db8:cafe:0010::2 -PrefixLength 64
```

Alternately, you can simply set the IPv6 parameters for an interface by navigating to change adapter settings (Control Panel\Network and Internet\Network Connections) to select adapter properties via the GUI. Figure 3-13 shows the adapter properties; in the screenshot it shows settings for a Wi-Fi adapter. Figure 3-14 shows the actual IPv6 properties for that Wi-Fi adapter and has sample manual IPv6 address configuration information in the fields.

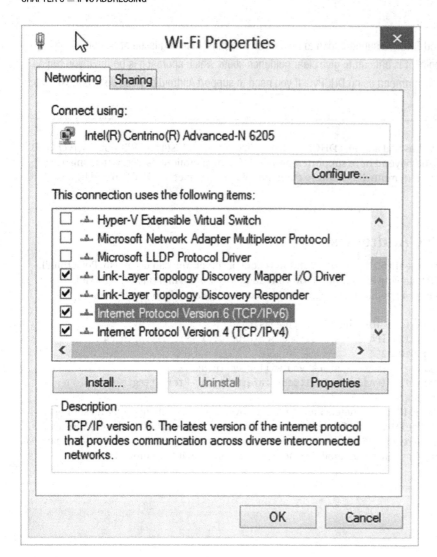

Figure 3-13. *Screenshot of adapter properties on Windows 8*

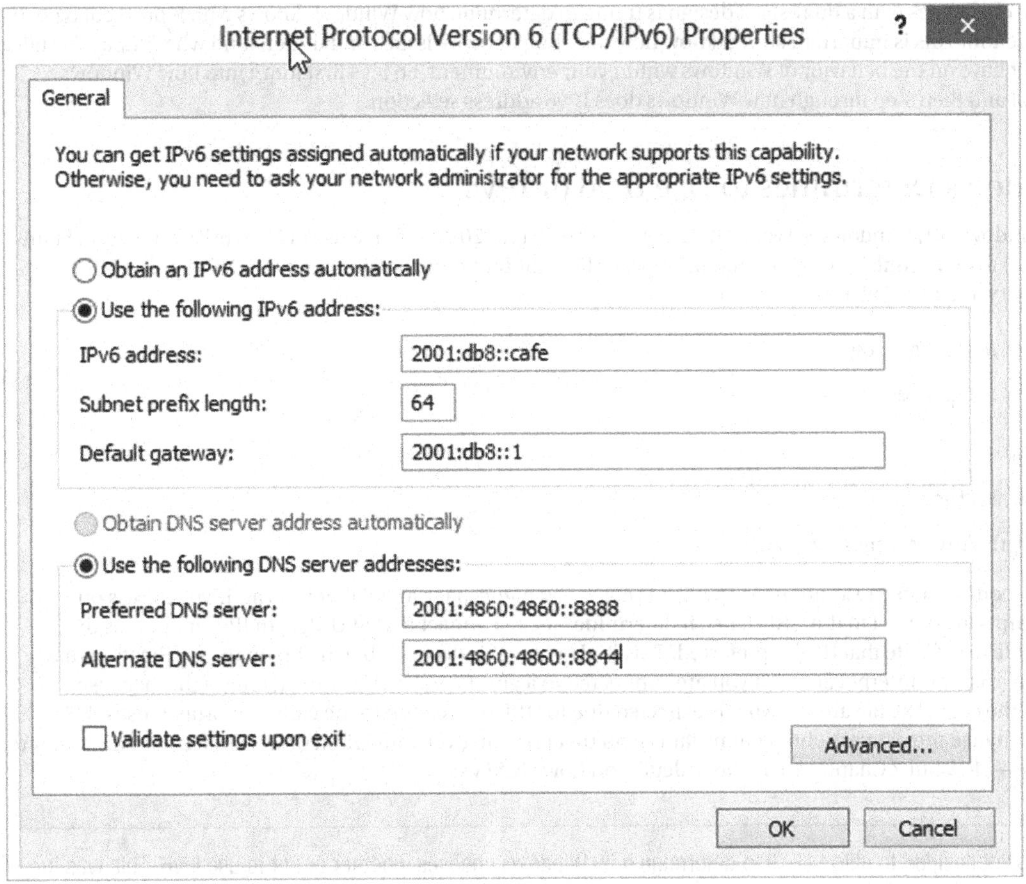

Figure 3-14. *Screenshot of IPv6 properties on Windows 8*

Manual configuration of IPv6 addresses should be limited to Windows servers and I recommend utilizing PowerShell to set all parameters on a Windows host. There are technically only a handful of Windows servers that have roles that require a manually assigned IP address (IPv4 or IPv6). It will be required for the DHCPv6 server and it is useful on the DNS and AD servers. For all other server roles you should consult with the appropriate deployment guides to determine if the server requires manual IP address configuration. The alternative is to use reservations in DHCPv6 to set the IPv6 address of the server. As long as that DHCPv6 service is available your servers will obtain their proper address. I realize that many administrators chose to manually configure all their servers to avoid this dependency. Consider using an IP Address Management (IPAM) solution so you don't accidentally duplicate addresses. The advantage of DHCP is that manual address assignment mistakes don't happen.

Windows OS Address Behavior

Windows has arguably the best IPv6 implementation of all OSs available in the market today. It is robust, has many of the RFC and industry standards implemented, and has many methods for managing its behavior. It has been updated regularly as standards have changed and is a demonstration of Microsoft's commitment to IPv6 as the next-generation protocol for the Internet. As outlined in Chapter 2, the new networking stack developed for Windows Vista and Windows Server 2008 is capable of providing native IPv4 or IPv6 services plus transition services.

One of the challenges with a dual-stack design is trying to determine how Windows knows which protocol type to use for a connection. This is important so you know how to debug network issues and understand what impact certain decisions might have on the behavior of Windows within your environment. So let's first jump into how Windows picks a protocol and then step through how Windows does IPv6 address selection.

How Windows Determines to Use IPv6 or IPv4

Windows 8, Windows 8.1, Windows Server 2012, and Windows Server 2012R2 make use of Network Connection Status Indicator (NCSI) to determine if the OS should use IPv6 or IPv4 for outbound session requests. NCSI performs a simple DNS query and http call. For IPv6 it uses

- `ipv6.msftncsi.com`

- `http://ipv6.msftncsi.com/ncsi.txt`

For IPv4 it uses

- `www.msftncsi.com`

- `http://www.msftncsi.com/ncsi.txt`

NCSI first requests name resolution for `ipv6.msftncsi.com` namespace and if it detects an IPv6 address on the host it attempts to connect to the URL. Once it determines it can connect to that URL with IPv6 it updates the prefix policy table to indicate that IPv6 is preferred. This is also how Windows is able to pop up the notification that a capture portal exists for Internet access if you are connected to a guest wireless network. It knows this because the contents of the `ncsi.txt` file are not what is expected due to URL redirection to the capture portal. It uses this information to change the network connection status icon that pops up over your wired or wireless icon in the system tray of Windows—slick huh? Chapter 10 includes details on how NCSI works.

■ **Note** Microsoft decided to utilize NCSI to determine how Windows chooses whether or not to use IPv6. This was in contrast to the RFC 6555 method commonly called Happy Eyeballs. I consider Microsoft's NCSI solution to be a partial Happy Eyeballs implementation and there are advantages to Microsoft's decision. See Chapter 10 for more details on the pros and cons of Microsoft's NCSI.

Default Address Selection Behavior of IPv6

One of the hardest things to understand when working with IPv6 is how Windows is selecting IPv6 addresses to use. At first it might seem like black magic or a cruel Jedi mind trick, but the reality is all OSs that support IPv6 have to conform to a common address selection process.

Windows is not unique in this respect so once you have walked through this process for Windows the rules should apply for other OSs too. Review the address selection process summarized next so you are familiar with it, but don't memorize it. First, it has changed over time and second you can reference the RFCs when you really need to dig into the details. I would not be surprised if some additional updates occur so keep an eye on the RFCs and the Windows Network Blog on TechNet to know if things are changing. The Windows Network Blog can be found at `http://blogs.technet.com/b/networking/` and the current RFC 6724 (`http://tools.ietf.org/html/rfc6724`) is what you should track.

Default Address Selection Process

RFC 6724 defines the default address selection process a host should utilize for IPv6 (and is an update to RFC 3484). Unlike standard IPv4 behavior, IPv6 allows a host to have multiple IPv6 addresses assigned per interface. This introduces the implicit problem of choosing an IPv6 address for either listening (for a service) or sourcing traffic (when trying to connect to a remote service).

Working through it all gets rather complex, and here I am attempting to *simplify* it greatly. With simplification comes loss of technical detail; you can't have them both. The goal is to provide a framework to quickly map out what is happening for most situations. You might run into situations that require reading the full RFC 6724 plus running Network Monitor or Wireshark to really figure out what is happening. Ideally your IPv6 deployment is not so complex that you will not be able to use the summary provided.

Windows Vista, Windows 7 (without the IPv6 Readiness Update—available at http://support.microsoft.com/kb/2750841), Windows Server 2008, and Windows Server 2008R2 (without the IPv6 Readiness Update) use the older RFC 3484 (http://tools.ietf.org/html/rfc3484) address selection process. Please refer to that earlier RFC for slight differences in behavior. Windows 8, Windows 8.1, Windows Server 2012, and Windows Server 2012R2 utilize RFC 6724 along with Windows 7 and Windows Server 2008R2 when they have the IPv6 Readiness Update applied.

RFC 6724 Summary

Based on RFC 6724 (review the RFC for specific behavior) this is a summary of how both the source and destination address selection process will work. I am going to focus more on the source process because that is more challenging. The RFC has an excellent summary from section 2 of the RFC:

> The algorithms use several criteria in making their decisions. The combined effect is to prefer destination/source address pairs for which the two addresses are of equal scope or type, prefer smaller scopes over larger scopes for the destination address, prefer non-deprecated source addresses, avoid the use of transitional addresses when native addresses are available, and all else being equal, prefer address pairs having the longest possible common prefix. For source address selection, temporary addresses [RFC4941] are preferred over public addresses. In mobile situations [RFC6275], home addresses are preferred over care-of addresses. If an address is simultaneously a home address and a care-of address (indicating the mobile node is "at home" for that address), then the home/care-of address is preferred over addresses that are solely a home address or solely a care-of address.

The RFC then goes into a complex set of rules. Basically, the goal of RFC 6724 is to provide a standard algorithm for source address selection and destination address selection. For source you want to choose the best sourcing address on a host to communicate with a specific destination address. For destination address selection you need to sort the list of possible destinations addresses (that you obtained through a name resolution process, likely DNS) in some preferential order.

So first, we should go over how RFC 6724 defines the conditions for comparing addresses. In the rules it compares two possible source addresses (SA and SB) vs. a destination address (D). For Windows some of the rules are not needed so I will leave the numbering but simply note not needed instead of details. In addition to the list, I have provided a source address selection flowchart in Figure 3-15. As a quick reminder, a scope in IPv6 was defined in the section "Multicast Addresses." Following is the rules list. The ones in bold are especially useful to think about when troubleshooting.

1. Prefer a source address if it equals the destination address (this seems really obvious but the RFC authors are making standard rules for everyone to conform to)

    a. If SA = D then prefer SA

    b. If SB = D then prefer SB

2. Prefer an appropriate scope for the source address

   a. If the scope of SA is smaller than the scope of SB and if the scope of SA is smaller than the scope of D then prefer SB; otherwise prefer SA

   b. If the scope of SB is smaller than the scope of SA and if the scope of SB is smaller than the scope of D then prefer SA; otherwise prefer SB

3. If one source address is preferred and the other deprecated, use the preferred address

4. Rules for Mobile IPv6—not in Windows—skip it

5. Prefer an outgoing interface that matches the destination

   a. If SA is assigned to an outgoing interface and that will be used to send traffic to D, prefer SA

   b. If SB is assigned to an outgoing interface and that will be used to send traffic to D, prefer SB

   c. If neither is assigned or both are assigned they are the same level of preference

6. Prefer a matching label

   a. If Label of SA = Label of D and Label of SB <> Label of D, prefer SA

   b. If Label of SB = Label of D and Label of SA <> Label of D, prefer SB

7. **Prefer temporary IPv6 addresses**

   a. If SA is a temporary address and SB is a permanent global or ULA then prefer SA

   b. If SB is a temporary address and SA is a permanent global or ULA then prefer SB

8. **Prefer longest prefix match**

   a. If the common prefix length of SA and D is greater than SB and D, prefer SA

   b. If the common prefix length of SB and D is greater than SA and D, prefer SB

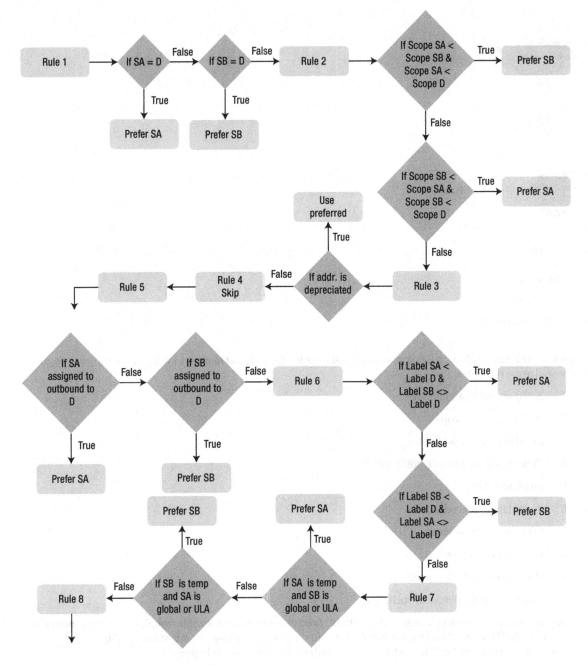

Figure 3-15. RFC 6724 source address selection rules (summary)

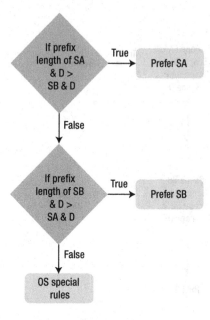

Figure 3-15. *(continued)*

Destination address selection has similar rules and instead of the logic statements I will just use the titles because they summarize the rules well.

1. Avoid unusable destinations

2. Prefer matching scopes

3. Avoid deprecated addresses

4. Prefer home addresses (Mobile IPv6) skip

5. Prefer matching label

6. Prefer higher precedence

7. **Prefer native transport**

8. Prefer smaller scope

9. **Use longest matching prefix**

10. Otherwise, leave the order unchanged

I have bolded the rules that you might have to think about in some situations while troubleshooting. Remember, most of the time the Windows OS is just going to do the right thing. Occasionally you might have to dig into the process and if so, I recommend pulling up RFC 6724 to really understand what is happening.

IPv6 Address Planning and Design

The chance to build a new network from the ground up is a rare opportunity. I have spoken to many administrators who wish they could change something about the network they are supporting today, but they must live within the confines of what their predecessor designed and deployed.

One of the unique aspects of adopting IPv6 is that you can build a new network topology and overcome some of the legacy limitations that may have had an impact on your decisions in the past. This isn't to say that IPv6 is a full ground-up chance to rebuild your network. It is unlikely you will redesign your WAN circuit configurations or change the LAN switchport configurations you have today. After all, MPLS labels and VLAN tags don't really care if the payload is IPv4 or IPv6. However, you can redesign around address limitations that may have been artificially imposed with the selection of too small a subnet mask in IPv4. There are other advantages you can gain too, but first you need a basic understanding of how IPv6 utilizes prefixes and how to subnet those prefixes without introducing a lot of extra math. I really try to stick to the "keep it simple" motto with IPv6.

Size of Prefix and Subnetting

The default prefix size for an IPv6 address is a /64. This prefix is used for a single subnet or VLAN and provides an effectively unlimited number of IPv6 addresses on that subnet. The reason I can say that is because you will exhaust all the physical resources in your network before you ever reach even a fraction of the number of IPv6 addresses that can be derived from a prefix of that size. Recall that the lower 64 bits were the interface ID and those bits are set manually, by DHCPv6 or via SLAAC or a combination of both.

A /64 prefix is only a portion of a larger prefix that the company or ISP will maintain. Often a single-site location (see the section "Size of the Address Space") will have a /48 prefix. This /48 prefix can be subnetted into smaller networks of varying size depending on the needs of the site. It is common in IPv4 to break up address space to fit the need requirements of the hosts in that network. For IPv6 you no longer do this. Why? Because you no longer have to worry about how many hosts are in a subnet or VLAN; we are using a /64 prefix so we will never run out of IPv6 addresses for any number of hosts in that subnet.

So how do we determine how to break up our network prefixes? Should we simply break up the /48 into 65,536 /64 networks and have that many individual prefixes in our routing table for that site location? Or, is there a more efficient way to go about this. It turns out that we can do routing summarization in IPv6 just like we do in IPv4 and that we can reduce the impact of IPv6 on our routing and switching equipment by doing some basic summarization.

One of the easiest ways to subnet a prefix is to break the network on nibble boundaries. As a reminder, a nibble is a 4-bit value (2^4 or 16 possible values) and in this case that represents a single HEX character in an IPv6 address. By following this simple rule we will be able to subnet a prefix to more reasonable allocations but still be able to read the IPv6 address quickly to know what network it belongs in. Using the nibble boundary trick I call "counting by 4 rule" and you will see why shortly.

Nibble Boundaries

Nibble boundaries are an efficient way to subnet a larger prefix into smaller more discrete network segments that can be summarized easily and also to match functional requirements if necessary. When subnetting use natural nibble boundaries (count in increments of 4 for the prefix when selecting subnets, i.e., /60 /56 /52) which is where my counting by 4 rule comes from. The following outlines subdividing a single /48 network into more usable networks:

- /48 = 65,536 networks of /64

- /52 = 4,096 networks of /64 and 16 subnets

- /56 = 256 networks of /64 and 256 subnets

- /60 = 16 networks of /64 and 4,096 subnets

To quickly review the math let's look at the /60 prefix. A /60 has 16 /64 subnets or $2^{64}-2^{60} = 2^4 = 16$ or 16 subnets. Each subnet has 16 /64 networks and there are 4,096 /60 prefixes in a /48. The math for that is $2^{60}-2^{48} = 2^{12} = 4,096$ total subnets of /60 in that /48 prefix. It is likely that most organizations can conform to this standard rule of 4 as you can find one of the network subnet and prefix combinations listed that would work for your site.

Remember, you are not necessarily limited to a /48. If your organization is large enough you could qualify for a /44 or a /40 (see that, still incrementing by 4) and you need to look at what your requirements will be over the next 10 to 20 years to be able to really determine the high end of what you should ask for. The general rule of thumb with IPv6 is to ask for more than you need so you don't have to go back and ask for more.

A more complex design and plan for addressing are outside the scope of this book. Just remember at a minimum to use prefixes that are broken on nibble boundaries and count by 4!

Routing

The Internet routing architecture is a complex subject and this section does not address running IPv6 in a public peering or a multihomed BGP configuration. Rather, the goal is to show how routers behave for hosts to interact with them. IPv6 routing is an important topic and if you require knowledge on routing I suggest picking up *IPv6 for Enterprise Networks* by Shannon McFarland, Muninder Sambi, Nikhil Sharma, and Sanjay Hooda (Cisco Press, 2011) or *Day One: Exploring IPv6* by Chris Grundemann (Juniper Networks Books, 2011) or the more advanced *Day One: Advanced IPv6 Configuration* by Chris Grundemann (Juniper Networks Books, 2011).

With the goal of how a router interacts with a Windows host we should look at what the router provides the subnet it is attached to that has client or server hosts connected. First are RAs. Second will be Router Solicitations (RSs).

Router Advertisements

A router will provide RAs on every VLAN or subnet it is connected to and configured to do so. RAs are one of the standard ND message types and likely the only ND message type that you might configure parameters for proper operation. All other ND message types are pretty much automatic and require no administrative settings.

RAs leverage ICMPv6 (type 134) and have a hop limit set to 255 as they are only designed to be used on a local link. RA messages provide hosts prefix, link MTU, routes, autoconfiguration, and address lifetimes. The common RA flags that would actually be set by an administrator are the A, M, and O flag options. Windows Server 2008 and greater will automatically start sending RAs on their connected interfaces if the Routing and Remote Access service is installed on the server in order to operate the server as an IPv6 router. Windows 7, Windows 8, and Windows 8.1 will also start periodically sending out RAs if Internet Connection Sharing (ICS) is enabled. Details on ICS can be found

- For Window Vista at http://windows.microsoft.com/en-US/windows-vista/Using-ICS-Internet-Connection-Sharing

- For Windows 7 at http://windows.microsoft.com/en-us/windows7/set-up-a-shared-internet-connection-using-ics-internet-connection-sharing

- For Windows 8 at http://windows.microsoft.com/en-us/windows-8/using-ics-internet-connection-sharing

An RA is sent out periodically on a local link by the router or in response to an RS.

Router Solicitations

A router will respond to a host that sends out an RS message when it is attempting to do a Router Discovery process. A host will send an RS which leverages ICMPv6 (type 133) in order to quickly obtain prefix, link MTU, routes, and autoconfiguration information from all routers on all the hosts' connected interfaces. This will likely occur during the OS boot process so it can quickly bring up its adapter interfaces. It will also do this when an adapter is disabled and reenabled or if a link is dropped and reconnected. RSs happen automatically; there is nothing to configure. They are simply part of the ND process in Windows.

Additional IPv6 Addressing Resources

There are many RFCs written that cover IPv6 addressing. They are the standards that are used to define how IPv6 addresses are built and used—for example, `http://tools.ietf.org/html/rfc4291` is the current RFC outlining IPv6 addressing architecture written by Robert Hinden and Stephen Deering; you don't get much better than that. That being said, not everyone is a fan of reading RFCs and sometimes they are not as helpful for practical issues related to a specific OS.

In the case of Windows, the best collection of practical resources can be found at the Microsoft TechNet web site, `http://technet.microsoft.com/en-us/network/bb530961.aspx`. The site has current and timely information on networking and access technologies for Windows and the web site is a wonderful place to start if you need help on any of those topics.

CHAPTER 4

■ ■ ■

IPv6 Best Practices for Windows

Often when planning and designing dual-stack and/or IPv6 networks it is useful to have a best practice guide to reference when practical experience in deploying a technology is not forthcoming to those working on the project. For IPv6 this can be challenging.

While IPv6 as a protocol has been around for a long time (the first RFC [Request for Comments] on IPv6 was published in 1995), the amount of community knowledge about IPv6 for Microsoft Windows is rather limited. There are some excellent books available about the IPv6 protocol, IPv6 security, IPv6 networking, and even IPv6 planning. However, there is not a collection of IPv6 best practices for Microsoft Windows. This chapter hopes to address that gap.

Microsoft Best Practice Resources

Microsoft provides guidance to its customers in several ways. First, Microsoft published the *Infrastructure Planning and Design (IPD) Guides*, which can be found at `http://technet.microsoft.com/library/cc196387.aspx`. These guides cover a variety of Microsoft product technologies. Microsoft also has the Solution Accelerators program that provides tools around planning, deploying, and managing Microsoft technologies and these can be found at `http://technet.microsoft.com/en-us/solutionaccelerators/default`.

Unfortunately, while all of these resources are good, they do not specifically address IPv6 planning and design or operating a dual-stack environment. In addition, almost none of the resources call out specific dual-stack or IPv6 use cases, and often they do not even mention IPv6.

It is not an uncommon assumption that if a design and deployment works with IPv4, it will logically work with IPv6. Unfortunately, this is not always the case. It is interesting to note that Microsoft no longer tests its own software in IPv4-only configurations. This effectively means that those that intentionally turn off IPv6 are running a configuration that is not validated and tested by Microsoft. Microsoft has been doing this since 2008, so it is not a recent development.

Finally, the best resource for Microsoft content is TechNet. A simple search on Microsoft TechNet will get you a tremendous amount of information regarding IPv6. More important, Microsoft has a specific URL (uniform resource locator) for IPv6 which directs you to all the TechNet information: `http://www.microsoft.com/ipv6`.

That URL at the time of publishing redirects to `http://technet.microsoft.com/en-us/network/bb530961.aspx`.

Also, there is a specific URL for current IPv6 support in Microsoft products (and it is actively updated) at `http://technet.microsoft.com/en-us/network/hh994905`.

You will want to keep tabs on this page to understand which Microsoft product technologies are supporting IPv6 but also what web and cloud services (such as `bing.com` or Azure) have support for IPv6 (`bing.com` does and Azure does not). Note that Office 365 has numerous services associated with it and currently only a partial selection of those services support IPv6.

IPv6 Best Practices for Windows

IPv6 best practices for Windows can cover a wide variety of topics and there needs to be a strategy to tackle the order. For the purposes of this book it makes some sense to start from the Internet and move back to a company's internal infrastructure. Why? This guarantees that you will be able to get IPv6 working at each critical point in your environment.

It is undesirable to get IPv6 working at your client access layer if it is not possible to use IPv6 end to end to the public IPv6 Internet. While many people find this statement odd, let me propose to you the following: would you ever build out your corporate IPv4 network and NOT connect it to the Internet today? Aside from some lab situations, most people would simply say you are crazy if you did not give people Internet access. Some may argue that remote access solutions like DirectAccess (DA) would not require public IPv6 Internet access. I would argue to reach the full potential of DA as a remote access solution, having IPv6 Internet access is critical so that you can content filter and perhaps have better routing control of the host and how it accesses Internet resources.

This argument holds just as true for IPv6. There is a good reason I recommend having IPv6 Internet access available too. IPv6 was implemented within Windows to be on by default and to be preferred. The same happens to be true with Apple's OSX and iOS operating systems and with all major *nix distributions such as Linux and BSD.

■ **Note**   It cannot be emphasized enough that Microsoft Windows from Vista and Server 2008 up to all current releases has IPv6 *ON* by default and *PREFERRED*. See Chapter 3 for details about this point as well as some of the caveats that have been released recently.

So the impact of your networking or infrastructure team turning on IPv6 can be immediate and alarmingly disruptive if not done correctly. The moment most Windows administrators hear this their first instinct is to run to their servers and clients and turn IPv6 off. This would be a huge mistake. The reality is that IPv6 is likely already running happily on your network. It just happens to be limited to a local virtual local area network (VLAN) or existing subnet range within your network. It turns out that IPv6 makes use of that link-local technology mentioned in Chapter 3 along with name resolution to establish connections with each other. It is common practice to put your servers in a common VLAN or unique subnet with IPv4 today (and this practice will continue with IPv6). Therefore, it is not unusual that your servers are already exchanging network traffic with each other via IPv6—you just didn't know they were doing that.

In fact, the unsuspecting use of IPv6 is so common that Microsoft has had many support cases opened due to administrators turning off IPv6 (Why are they turning off IPv6? I am not sure) and breaking their functional Windows network. Often after Microsoft support people figure out what the administrator has done, they simply ask the administrator to turn IPv6 back on and everything starts working again. That this solution works isn't a mystery; remember what was mentioned earlier. It is on by default and preferred. If we had a running IPv4 network and turned off IPv4 would you expect your server to run well?

While it isn't all that simple, do realize that turning OFF IPv6 can have just as adverse an impact on your network as not correctly deploying IPv6. This is why you need to read the best practices and get a plan together to deploy IPv6 correctly the first time! To quote Benjamin Franklin, "An ounce of prevention is worth a pound of cure."

IPv6 Best Practices Overview

Using the principle mentioned earlier of moving from the Internet back to a company's internal resources, the following order was developed. It is designed to allow us to have a logical order to discuss all the relevant Microsoft technologies. Don't get hung up on the order of items, if you don't need something in the list, skip it. The next sections will cover.

1. IPv6 Transition Technologies
   - 6to4
   - ISATAP
   - Teredo

2. Internet (IPv6 and IPv4)
   - Internet Edge
   - Firewalls
   - DirectAccess

3. DMZ Services
   - Email
   - DNS
   - High Availability
   - Remote Access

4. Microsoft Exchange

5. Microsoft Lync

6. Microsoft IIS and SharePoint

7. Microsoft SQL

8. Microsoft Active Directory and Group Policy

9. Microsoft File and Print

10. Microsoft Windows Server

11. Microsoft Windows Client

12. Remote Offices

IPv6 Transition Technologies

When Microsoft rebuilt the networking stack in Windows and built in IPv6 it made some specific decisions around transition technologies. What are transition technologies? They are technology solutions designed to ease the transition from IPv4 to IPv6. The goal was to make the transition to the IPv6 Internet seamless for end users. Remember, Microsoft produces a Windows operating system (OS) that is used by home consumers all the way up to large-scale enterprise class servers. These OS versions share a remarkable amount of underlying code and the networking stack happens to be a significant part of that shared functionality.

Microsoft decided to include three main transition technologies in the OS to help IPv4 Internet hosts reach IPv6 Internet resources. These technologies are 6to4, ISATAP, and Teredo.

For the majority of Windows environments I recommend turning OFF all the transition technologies but leaving IPv6 enabled. There are a variety of reasons for this recommendation, but in its simplest form it comes down to this: for most deployments of Windows in enterprise settings, and in small- to medium-sized business settings, you want predictable behavior from your client and server hosts. Transition technologies can introduce unexpected behavior in the OS. However, due to the need for almost all IPv4 networks to migrate to dual-stack and eventually IPv6 only, I recommend leaving IPv6 enabled.

■ **Note** Best practices are to leave IPv6 *ON* but to disable all transition technologies. Specifically, turn *OFF* 6to4, ISATAP, and Teredo on both Windows Server and Client hosts. If you are deploying DirectAccess then depending on your design you may use one of the transition technologies. This is fine as the design is accounting for the specific use of the transition technology.

6to4

The first transition technology is 6to4 and it is defined in RFC 3056, 3068, and 3964. 6to4 has some very specific requirements of the IPv4 network. It needs the host to have a public IPv4 address. In other words, it cannot have an RFC 1918 or private reserved IPv4 address. RFC 1918 addresses come from the ranges 10.0.0.0/8, 172.16.0.0/12, and 192.168.0.0/16. It is unusual in today's IPv4 Internet where IPv4 addresses are becoming scarce to see workstations or servers that have public IPv4 addresses. There are some larger and older organizations that still use public IPv4 everywhere, but this is not the norm. However, it is important to know the impact that 6to4 will have on hosts that do have public IPv4 addresses.

6to4 utilizes the public IPv4 address to dynamically build a legitimate Global Unicast IPv6 address and is able to use tunneling (using protocol 41) to connect to public 6to4 routers utilizing IPv4 as a transit. This allow the 6to4 host to connect to the IPv6 Internet via the 6to4 relay router (which uses the anycast IPv4 address of 192.88.99.1). Because the host has a globally unique IPv6 address derived from its globally unique IPv4 address, the remote IPv6 host that is returning traffic simply sends its traffic back to its closest 6to4 relay router. That 6to4 relay router is able to forward the traffic to the 6to4 host via its IPv4 address and the connection is complete. Because a host can switch dynamically between 6to4 and IPv4 transmissions it can be difficult to figure out how a host is receiving or sending traffic. For these reasons it is not recommended to run 6to4 unless you have specifically designed a solution around it. Chapter 3 provides more details and the specifics of how 6to4 does this. Figure 4-1 shows an example overview of how 6to4 is able to allow an isolated IPv6 network can use 6to4 to connect to the IPv6 Internet via an IPv4 Internet connection.

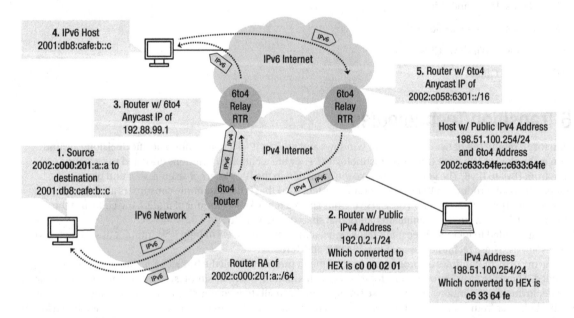

Figure 4-1. 6to4 overview

ISATAP

The next technology is Intra-Site Automatic Tunnel Addressing Protocol (ISATAP), which was designed to allow network operators to deploy dual-stack network hosts and tunnel their traffic across an IPv4 network. ISATAP is defined in RFC 5214 and was often recommended in earlier Microsoft deployment guides as a way to allow hosts to become dual-stacked in an enterprise network.

Often you would choose to use ISATAP so that specific technology solutions that required IPv6 like DirectAccess were able to talk to all the hosts in an existing enterprise network without having to run IPv6 on the routers, switches or firewalls within an enterprise. Today, DirectAccess has NAT64/DNS64 built into the product so the requirement that all the hosts in an enterprise network be dual-stack is no longer as important. IPv6 is still needed to make DA work but it is hidden by the use of NAT64/DNS64. Even though most deployments of DirectAccess will leverage NAT64/DNS64 it is still possible and in some cases appropriate to do a deployment leveraging ISATAP. More detail on DA is covered later in the section "Direct Access."

ISATAP utilizes IPv4 DNS to learn the location of an ISATAP router. An ISATAP router defines the prefix that all the ISATAP hosts will participate in, allowing the ISATAP router to provide IPv6 access to hosts that participate in ISATAP. By default ISATAP is enabled in Windows; however, Microsoft has protections in its DNS (Domain Name System) server to prevent unwanted ISATAP networks. Microsoft does not allow the simple publication of ISATAP.<FQDN> in DNS. So you cannot name a workstation ISATAP and have it register in the DNS properly. Your DNS administrator has to specifically set up the record and she is prompted to confirm she really wants to do this. Your DNS administrator will then have to specifically configure the DNS server block list to allow ISATAP. Details on the global query block list can be found at http://technet.microsoft.com/en-us/library/cc794902(v=WS.10).aspx.

There are three major issues when attempting to deploy ISATAP. First, it depends on IPv4 DNS to work properly and for the host to properly resolve the DNS query for the ISATAP router from ISATAP.<FQDN>, so, for example, ISATAP.EXAMPLE.COM.

Second, ISATAP in Windows Client has no agent or other notification software to tell you it is working. Thus, if there are any problems with the ISATAP router, there is no obvious way to know whether or not your host has IPv6 access. There is no status indicator in Windows Client to alert users and often help desk staff are flooded with complaints of "network problems" with no clue as to what is going on. Worse, these problems can be intermediate and difficult to troubleshoot. There is an ISATAP monitor in the DirectAccess console in Windows Server 2012 and Windows Server 2012R2.

Finally, ISATAP functionally makes your IPv4 network one large flat layer 2 network from an IPv6 perspective. If you utilize VLANs to segment users and devices into functional roles and you have firewall or access control list (ACL) rules on your network devices to control what they can access, then you have a problem. Because all the hosts are joined to a common ISATAP router and participate in a common IPv6 prefix, all hosts in that ISATAP domain are link-local adjacent to each other. This may not be the most desirable security configuration for your network. For these reasons it is not recommended to run ISATAP unless you have specifically designed a solution around it.

Chapter 3 covers more details on how ISATAP functions. Figure 4-2 shows an example overview of how an ISATAP client can connect to an IPv6 Internet host from an IPv4-only network.

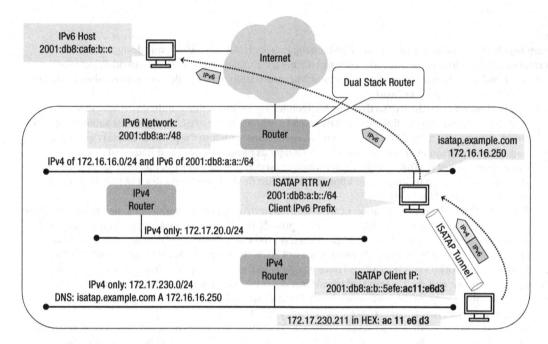

Figure 4-2. *ISATAP overview*

Teredo

The last transition technology is Teredo. Teredo was developed by Microsoft, though there are implementations available for Linux (Meredo) to do the same function. Teredo is defined in RFC 4380, 5991, and 6081 and is specifically designed for IPv4 hosts that are behind Network Address Translation (NAT) devices.

Teredo makes use of NAT traversal methods to allow the host to connect to a Teredo server. If the Teredo client wishes to connect to the IPv6 Internet, then the Teredo server needs also to have the Teredo relay function built into it and to assign Global Unicast IPv6 prefixes to the Teredo clients. Teredo NAT traversal techniques are based on Session Traversal Utilities for NAT (STUN) technology. You can find more information about STUN at http://en.wikipedia.org/wiki/STUN.

Teredo is an interesting technology for solving some difficult IPv4 NAT deployment issues for client machines. It has also been pointed out that it can introduce security concerns since malware can take advantage of Teredo to do remote command and control. I don't necessarily buy the argument that Teredo is that big of a concern for malware as much as it can cause difficulty understanding where your network traffic is going. Teredo makes use of DNS to determine a legitimate Teredo server. The default Teredo server in Windows is teredo.ipv6.microsoft.com which at the time of publishing resolved to 94.245.121.253.

Teredo is one of several options for DirectAccess clients to utilize for connectivity to the DA server. The DA server is the Teredo server role and clients are able to get an IPv6 prefix via the DA server. The DA client is able to use the IPv6 connectivity to connect back to the corporate network. The advantage of Teredo for DA clients is that it works behind NAT devices; however, it does require that the DA server have two public IPv4 addresses on its external interface.

Because Teredo works behind NAT and because more enterprise and SMB networks utilize NAT, it is not recommended to run Teredo unless you have specifically designed a solution around it. You can find more details about how Teredo works in Chapter 3. Figure 4-3 shows an example overview of how a Teredo client can connect to an IPv6 Internet host from behind an IPv4 NAT device by utilizing a Teredo Relay Server.

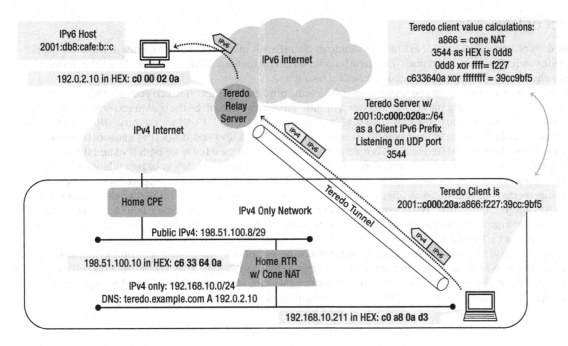

Figure 4-3. *Teredo overview*

IPv6 Transition Technologies Key Takeaways

As with all best practice recommendations you need to consider what you are trying to accomplish. As a general practice, and as I've already stated, I recommend turning OFF the IPv6 transition technologies in Windows. Specifically, turn off 6to4, ISATAP, and Teredo. You have options on how to do this.

For stand-alone (non–domain joined) clients and servers you will need to use PowerShell, netsh, and registry key settings to control the various transition technologies. You will need administrator rights on the host also. If you have a domain you can utilize Group Policy to set these configuration options, or you can also leverage PowerShell, netsh, or the registry. Remember, you are turning off only the transition technologies, not IPv6. In fact, you will likely want to check to make sure IPv6 is not turned off so that you know it will function properly when you do turn on IPv6 within your infrastructure.

Internet

The Internet today is primarily an IPv4 network. In fact, the vast majority of enterprise and small- to medium-size business networks built and deployed today are IPv4-**only** networks. They were never designed or built to run IPv6.

With the recent depletion events of the global IPv4 address pool it has become necessary to deploy IPv6 for the Internet to continue to grow and function. Internet service providers (ISPs) have been deploying IPv6 on their backbones over the last several years and recently have been providing IPv6 access to their customers natively through broadband services such as DSL, Metro Ethernet, and Cable but also through 4G LTE services from mobile operators. This means today that it is possible to request IPv6 address space from your ISP and have some reasonable expectation the ISP will be able to deliver it. Some service providers have not waited for customers to request IPv6 and are simply providing IPv6 with new orders.

Impact of IPv6

But what does ordering IPv6 on your existing IPv4 Internet circuit really mean? There are a couple of ways that the ISP can provide you IPv6 service. It can drop you a new broadband circuit that runs IPv6. This is unlikely to be the method most ISPs choose due to the costs of additional physical resources.

The other option is to provide you IPv6 access via the same physical medium on which your IPv4 is provided. This is effectively dual-stacking your current service. For most customers this will be the option you will utilize to get IPv6 Internet access in addition to continuing to get IPv4 Internet access. Your ISP will assign you an IPv6 address block from its global address assignment similar to how it provides you an IPv4 address or IPv4 network block today. This is called provider assigned (PA) and still is the most common method used today for both IPv4 and IPv6.

If you are an enterprise that runs Border Gateway Protocol (BGP) with several ISPs to be redundant and you have your own Autonomous System Number (ASN) and IPv4 provider independent (PI) address space then you need to make arrangements with your Regional Internet Registrar (RIR) address provider (for North America this is ARIN) to get an IPv6 PI address assignment. For many customers this makes the most sense to reduce how many global unicast IPv6 addresses you run on your network. It also reduces the amount of network renumbering you will have to do later if you decide to change ISPs for any reason.

Best practices will vary a bit for how you connect to the Internet, but for enterprises it is recommended they obtain PI IPv6 address space and run multihomed BGP to ensure high availability. They should obtain a sufficiently large enough IPv6 address prefix to allow them to grow for several years, accounting for the RIR address provider's policies. Figure 4-4 is a typical enterprise IPv6 peering configuration.

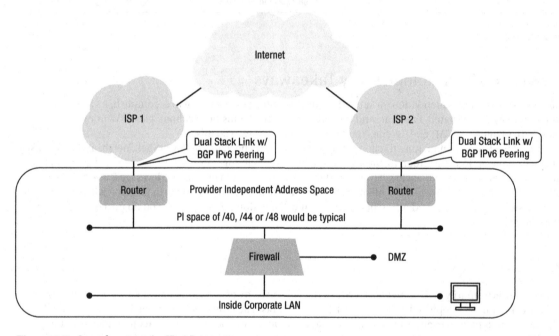

Figure 4-4. *Sample enterprise IPv6 Internet access*

Smaller enterprises and SMBs might leverage PA IPv6 address space just as they do for IPv4. The principal difference is that IPv6 addresses will be used internally as well as externally. There is no NAT or PAT with IPv6 as there is no need to do address translation to conserve address space. Remember that a single subnet in IPv6 is a /64 which is the same amount of addresses as the entire IPv4 Internet squared. The challenge with PA IPv6 addresses is the fact that if you switch ISPs you will have to renumber your IPv6 network. Fortunately, IPv6 has better methods for renumbering networks, but it is still a laborious process. Additionally, if you wish to be highly vailable with IPv6 and you decide to use multiple ISPs (multihoming) but do not use BGP, then you are left deploying both PA IPv6 prefixes (ISP 1 and ISP 2) throughout your network. Additional challenges come with that sort of design such as source address selection (RFC 6724), Network Prefix Translation (NPTv6), and other issues. At this time, either use BGP for multihoming or stay with a single ISP so that you have a single IPv6 prefix to manage and deploy. Figure 4-5 is a typical small enterprise or SMB IPv6 peering configuration.

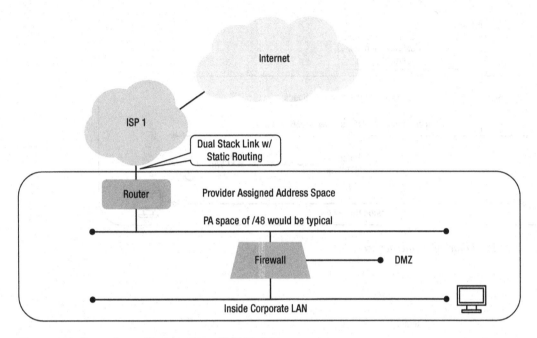

Figure 4-5. *Example small enterprise or SMB IPv6 Internet access*

If you are a home business, mobile subscriber, or a small branch office then you will likely only have the option to leverage PA IPv6 address space. It will likely be dual-stacked with IPv4 and have a smaller prefix allocation than the former solutions. It is not unusual to see /60 or /64 prefix allocations in these cases. In some unusual situations you will see /128 IPv6 address allocations, but these should be the exception and not the rule. If your ISP is providing /128 IPv6 addressing then it makes sense to look for a new ISP as there is NO reason it should be allocating you a single IPv6 address. Figure 4-6 is a typical home office IPv6 configuration and Figure 4-7 is a typical mobile subscriber IPv6 configuration. Please refer to Chapter 3 for more details on address planning and design.

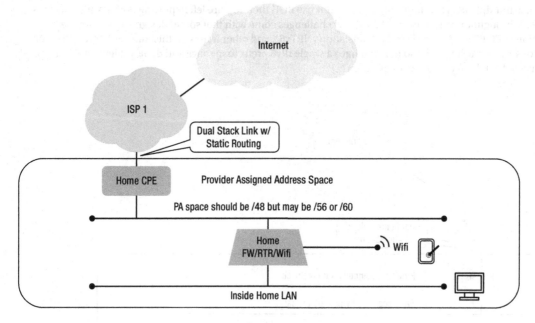

Figure 4-6. *Sample IPv6 home office Internet access*

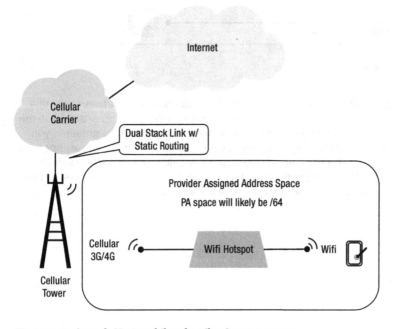

Figure 4-7. *Sample IPv6 mobile subscriber Internet access*

IPv6 Internet Key Takeaways

The reality is there are two Internets in operation today. The largest and most widely used is the IPv4 Internet; however, the limitations that IPv4 has with address depletion and NAT/PAT protocol problems really hamper the capabilities of what the IPv4 Internet is able to provide. The smaller but growing Internet is based on IPv6.

What many people do not realize is that if you do not have IPv6 today you do not have full access to the full "Internet." There is the potential that some services and web sites will only be available via IPv6, and if you still only have IPv4 you are unable (currently) to access that content or service. This is why this chapter repeats the advice to dual-stack your network. In fact, the IPv6 community has a rule of thumb for the preferred methods of obtaining IPv6 access in ascending order of preference.

- Prefer Dual-Stack/Native IPv6

- Tunnel when you must

- Translate when you are desperate

So, what does this mean? The rule of thumb tells you that dual-stack is the first and best step in moving to Native IPv6. What is the difference between dual-stack and native IPv6? Technically native IPv6 means you are only running IPv6, no IPv4. Dual-stack means you are running both IPv4 and IPv6 at the same time on the same host. Tunneling is a solution when you have to span across areas of your network that are IPv4 only and cannot support IPv6. Translation occurs when you have to provide a method for IPv4 to talk to IPv6 and IPv6 to IPv4. A better description is that you need a protocol converter. C-3PO from Star Wars was a protocol converter; the only reason Uncle Owen bought him was because he could speak Bocce. If Uncle Owen knew how to speak the binary language of moisture evaporators he wouldn't have needed C-3PO.

Internet Edge

The first actual piece of equipment that a company will have to configure and initially run IPv6 on will likely be its Internet Edge router. If the company is running a highly available and redundant Internet connection configuration, then it is likely making use of BGP. If it is only getting Internet service from a single ISP, then it likely is not using BGP and is doing a static routing solution.

The Internet Edge design goal should be full dual-stack support, and upgrading equipment to be able to perform this function is important. Remember, the goal is to provide full IPv6 functionality at the Internet Edge. While there are transition solutions available to enable web, mail, and DNS content to be translated, the most efficient process is to get your Internet routers, switches, and firewalls working with IPv6 in addition to IPv4.

Basic IPv6 Internet Edge Requirements

Most enterprise networks rely on a network team whose members are responsible for Internet Edge access for IPv4; however, for commercial and SMB it is very common for system administrators to also design, deploy, and operationally maintain this area. There are some key items for the Internet Edge when enabling IPv6.

Enterprises that are multihomed prefer native IPv6 BGP peering and do not rely on IPv4 BGP peering for IPv6 BGP. You should run separate BGP IPv4 and IPv6 neighbor configurations for each protocol per service provider link. The rationale is that if there are problems with your IPv4 or IPv6 peering they do NOT impact the other protocol. So problems in your IPv4 peering would not impact your ability to peer for IPv6.

Remember with Windows (and for practical purposes all other modern OSs today) IPv6 is enabled by default and preferred. This makes it critical to have the same service-level agreement (SLA) for IPv6 as you have for IPv4. If you decide to not have the same availability and SLA support from your providers then interruption of IPv6 services can have an undesirable effect on your end users. While most modern OSs have some form of Happy Eyeballs (RFC 6555) in place, it does not mean that IPv6 outages are any more acceptable than IPv4 outages. Reduce your help desk and trouble ticket load and make them the same.

Just as with IPv4, you should apply appropriate ingress and egress filters for IPv6 prefixes. For instance, you should only take inbound traffic destined for your prefix and only allow your specific IPv6 prefix outbound. Also, you should provide global ICMPv6 protections that are appropriate. Chapter 6 covers those.

If you have to maintain and support the routers and switches at their Internet Edge you want to ensure you have enough CPU (central processing unit) and memory to handle IPv6 routing table growth and also to accommodate your existing IPv4 routing tables. This means that you may opt for simpler Edge deployments and utilize static routing where you can. IPv6 addresses use more space in memory than do their IPv4 counterparts. The addition of IPv6 can have a severe impact on both the memory and the CPU. The CPU can be impacted by hardware that still requires the CPU to forward IPv6 traffic versus those that have been upgraded to do IPv6 forwarding in hardware.

It is standard practice today to statically assign an IPv4 address for devices like firewalls, routers, and loopbacks plus management interfaces of other devices. There is no reason that you would not continue this practice with IPv6. You can do some simple things to make your network more secure at the same time while not overly complicating the network configuration. For instance, have DNS entries (forward and reverse) set up for your Edge devices. Do not embed your IPv4 information in your IPv6 address. Remember that IPv6 is represented in HEX so switch to using some of the HEX values that exceed the standard IPv4 address range possibility of 0-255. Standard IPv4 default gateways are often .1 or .254 so consider setting your IPv6 default router RA to utilize FFFF in the last 16 bits or something meaningful to your network. Also, remember that network devices will typically utilize their link-local address to advertise to other hosts on that link-local subnet. This means you need to be able to modify both the link-local address and the global unicast address (GUA) on the devices. It makes sense to make the last 64 bits match between the link-local and global unicast address.

While the next best practice is optional it still is recommended to set up support for `ipv6-literal.net` DNS names for Edge devices in case DNS is not available. This enables those devices to utilize local name resolution to still find each other. There are not a lot of cases in which you will need IPv6 literals, but it is nice to know it is there and properly configured in case something does go wrong. Chapter 8 provides more details on IPv6 literals.

Finally, it is best practice to turn on RA-Guard and where appropriate MAC filters on Edge ports to reduce default gateway errors and rogue DHCPv6 services. This also prevents spoofing, prevents abuses of how the IPv6 protocol operates, and also helps to reduce errors that might occur.

IPv6 Internet Edge Key Takeaways

Sometimes it is not possible to get native IPv6 service from your ISP. If it is not possible to have native IPv6 service then a tunnel solution across IPv4 may be your only option until your ISP makes native IPv6 service available. If that is the case consider using the following methods to work around this limitation:

- *Switch ISPs.* It isn't a popular recommendation but if you cannot utilize a tunnel service, look at other service providers to obtain IPv6 native peering. Most of the major ISP players in the United States have IPv6 available, but you may have to push your account manager to get the right information including whether there are additional costs associated with it. Typically there are no additional costs or fees associated with running IPv6. If there are, consider switching providers. There is no logical reason for there to be additional costs associated with IPv6.

- *Utilize Hurricane Electric's tunnel broker services.* They will even do BGP peering through the tunnel and allow you to advertise your PI IPv6 prefix through them. More details can be found at http://www.tunnelbroker.net/.

If you cannot use a tunnel and you cannot get native IPv6 services from your ISP then it is best to wait on your IPv6 deployment. Yes, I said it, wait.

■ **Note**   Best practices are to have native or dual-stack IPv6 Internet access. As a partial solution use a tunnel broker as a backup IPv6 Internet connection. Otherwise, if you cannot get native IPv6 service then **WAIT** until you can!

You really need to have a reliable IPv6 connection, and native IPv6 service is the best practice. If you want to test a lab or just have some greater availability via a second BGP peer, then a tunneled solution is fine. You should still plan on getting a second native IPv6 connection, but a tunneled solution can hold you over while you work that out. Figure 4-8 shows an example of IPv6 BGP Peering and Figure 4-9 of IPv6 BGP Peering using a tunnel broker service.

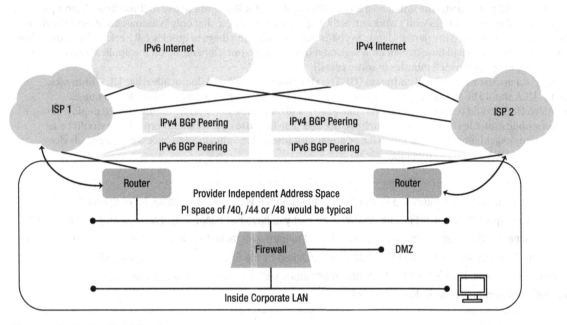

Figure 4-8. *IPv6 w/ BGP Peering*

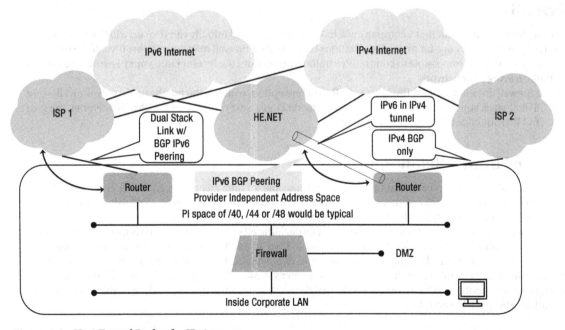

Figure 4-9. *IPv6 Tunnel Broker for IPv6 access*

It is important that you do NOT deploy 6to4 at your Internet Edge and run public IPv6 services with those 6to4 addresses. 6to4 will eventually be deprecated and, due to its asymmetrical routing behavior, is not predictable in performance, latency, and path.

If you are unable to turn up a proper IPv6 Internet Edge solution do NOT turn on your internal access (client) ports with an IPv6 prefix as you will potentially break your IPv4 Internet access. Remember, Windows from Vista and Server 2008 on will prefer IPv6, and if that host has an IPv6 address it will attempt to use it. If you don't have a path out to the public IPv6 Internet, things won't work correctly. It is important to note that only Windows 8.1, 8, and Windows 7 with the correct update have the partial Happy Eyeballs support, allowing them to quickly fall back to IPv4. Any other Windows Client machine will have to wait for a session request to time out. Depending on the applications or OS this could be a very long time (over 2 minutes in some cases!).

Finally, do not use unique local addresses (ULA) on the Internet Edge and do not advertise ULA addresses externally. ULA should be filtered at your Internet Edge to prevent sending or receiving that address range. Additionally, ULA should be limited in use. It is designed for testing, labs, and perhaps some limited deployments where nonpublic routable IPv6 addresses might be needed. The only use case for the Internet Edge would be an out-of-band management network or loopback addresses for internal monitoring and access of Internet devices. Otherwise, keep ULA off the Internet Edge.

■ **Note**　If your Internet Edge hardware is unable to support IPv6 it will need to be replaced or upgraded. It is important to have good IPv6 support in your hardware so that you have like capabilities between IPv4 and IPv6. Often with older equipment IPv6 was a second-class citizen and the hardware lacked application specific integrated circuit (ASIC) optimization. This meant that any IPv6 traffic was handled by the CPU, which can have a significant impact on network performance. Now is the time to invest smart; make sure your Internet Edge hardware can perform in a comparable fashion with IPv6 as it does with IPv4.

Firewalls

The second piece of equipment that a company will have to configure and initially run IPv6 on will likely be its firewall. This can be a challenge for many organizations because their firewall may not support IPv6. If the firewall does not support IPv6 it is impossible to control IPv6 traffic coming from the Internet into your network, nor can you control traffic leaving your network.

If your firewall does not support IPv6 you are left with one option, which is the purchase of a new firewall—one that has full dual-stack support and is able to properly provide Edge security functions for IPv6. Remember, the goal is to provide full IPv6 functionality at the Internet Edge.

Basic IPv6 Firewall Requirements

For enterprise deployments, typically a security team is responsible for firewall policies and an operations team to handle enforcement. However, for commercial, SMB, and home it is common for system administrators or end users to also design, deploy, and operationally maintain these devices.

Some best practices for firewall policies include not duplicating all your IPv4 rules. IPv6 is a unique networking protocol and IPv4 rules do not necessarily map one for one to IPv6. In addition, you will often run only a subset of IPv6 services compared to IPv4 when starting with your IPv6 deployment. There is no reason to put every IPv4 rule into the IPv6 policy as it is unlikely you have all the same services in place. When developing firewall policies for IPv6, do not migrate IPv4 specific port configurations to IPv6 if the services which are being made available to connect to are only going to be available on IPv4.

ICMP rules for IPv4 traditionally have been very restrictive. Because IPv6 uses ICMPv6 extensively for many functions you will have to apply new policies to make sure you are not fundamentally breaking the protocol. IPv6 does not work properly if things like path MTU (maximum transmission unit) discovery are not operational. Path MTU discovery relies on ICMPv6.

One of the advantages you will continue to have in IPv6 is the ability to group rules on prefix boundaries. This becomes a more unique advantage with IPv6 because the firewall functions as a router. With a dual-stack solution it is possible for a firewall to do correlation and event analysis for both IPv4 and IPv6. It is also possible to run a separate firewall for IPv4 versus IPv6 depending on the need requirements of the company. It makes sense that if you have dual-stacked everywhere in your network, you should block all tunneling and transition technologies for IPv6. There is no reason to run them as you are providing native IPv6 for all hosts.

Most major firewall manufacturers today have some sort of Intrusion Prevention System (IPS) and/or Intrusion Detection System (IDS) in their product. You should make sure these solutions are IPv6 enabled and are aware of IPv6 and can perform inspection and matching for both IPv6 and tunneled traffic in either IPv4 or IPv6.

Finally, I recommend that you leverage the local client and server host-based firewalls to help protect those devices in addition to your network firewall. IPv6 is designed to return the Internet to what was originally the desire for network protocols: no translation with device-to-device communications. This means that having a good host-based firewall reduces the chances of something malicious happening to that device. All Microsoft Windows Clients have a robust firewall that is enabled by default. Windows Server also has a robust firewall and is enabled by default; however, depending on the services running on the server, the firewall will be modified by Server Manager or other tools to enable appropriate access.

IPv6 Firewall Key Takeaways

Firewall functions will differ between IPv4 and IPv6 due to differences in how the protocols behave and are defined. Firewalls will provide IP and port ingress and egress access controls for both protocols. IPv4 firewalls also provide both NAT and PAT functions along with Stateful Packet Inspection (SPI). IPv6 does not have equivalent NAT and PAT functions (only prefix translation—see RFC 6296), so it is reasonable that the firewall will not do these functions. It becomes difficult then to map IPv4 to IPv6 for these functions.

Almost all major firewall manufacturers are supporting IPv6 natively today. Microsoft's commercial firewall product is Forefront Threat Management Gateway (TMG) and unfortunately at this time TMG does not support native IPv6 and is now at end of life. If you are utilizing Forefront TMG then you will need to install a separate IPv6 firewall. You also have the alternative to migrate to a firewall product that can support both IPv4 and IPv6. Current common industry standard firewalls that do support IPv6 are the Cisco ASA, Juniper SRX & ISG, Sonicwall, Fortinet, Palo Alto Networks, and Checkpoint (this is not a complete list by any means but these are some of the common manufacturers).

Windows Vista, Windows 7, Windows 8, and Windows 8.1 client platforms have the Windows firewall on by default and will perform firewall functions for both IPv4 and IPv6. Rules for the firewall can be configured via Group Policy, GUI, or PowerShell. In addition, a host firewall for Windows Server 2008/ R2 and Windows Server 2012/R2 can be enabled and similar Group Policy, GUI, or PowerShell functions can be employed to manage those platforms as well. The Windows Firewall with Advanced Security (WFAS) on both client and server also manage the IPsec VPN configuration for both IPv4 and IPv6. More details on the WFAS can be found at http://technet.microsoft.com/en-us/library/hh831365.aspx.

DirectAccess

DirectAccess is unique to Microsoft; it is a technology included originally in Windows Server 2008 and later enhanced in Windows Server 2012 and Window Server 2012R2. It is targeted at SMB and enterprise customers who wish to have a robust remote access solution that allows client devices to always be connected to the company network. It has some nice features such as manage out, which allows a help desk team to remotely manage a DA client (as long as it has some sort of Internet access) with all the same tools they use on the corporate network. It leverages all the same authentication, authorization, and control policies that corporate information technology (IT) teams use to manage their internal corporate resources. These DA clients just happen to not be on the corporate network.

DirectAccess and IPv6

For many, the IPv6 requirements for DA are confusing at best and bewildering at worst. First let's define what DA is and how it is designed and used in a Windows network and then tackle the discussion of how it leverages IPv6.

DA is a remote access solution from Microsoft that allows Windows 7, Windows 8, and Windows 8.1 domain-joined clients to be always on and connected to their enterprise network in a secure and seamless way via the Internet. It does this by utilizing a secure connection over IPv4 using 6to4, Teredo, or IP-HTTPS as connection options. It can do this from any IPv4 Internet connection and can establish a connection back to the corporate Windows domain even before users log into their computers. It truly is an always-on persistent and bidirectional remote access solution. Figure 4-10 shows a sample DA client connecting to a DA server. It lists a DA prefix of 2001:db8:cafe:1::/64 which is the IPv6 prefix allocated to the DA server to hand out IPv6 addresses to the DA clients so they can connect back to the corporate network.

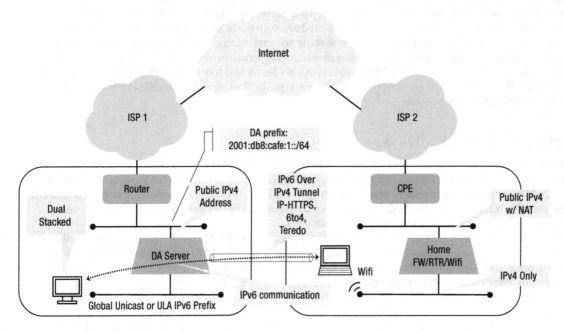

Figure 4-10. *Overview of DirectAccess*

The IPv6 protocol for internal Windows resources that DA clients are trying to reach is a requirement for a DA deployment for Windows Server 2008 and 2008 R2. IPv6 is still used and required for Windows Server 2012 and 2012 R2; however, you are given a built-in transition that allows you to limit your IPv6 deployment. You can leverage NAT64/DNS64 to avoid having to dual-stack all your internal Windows resources that DA clients would need to connect to for services. Figure 4-11 shows the IPv6 end-to-end requirement with Windows Server 2008 and 2008R2.

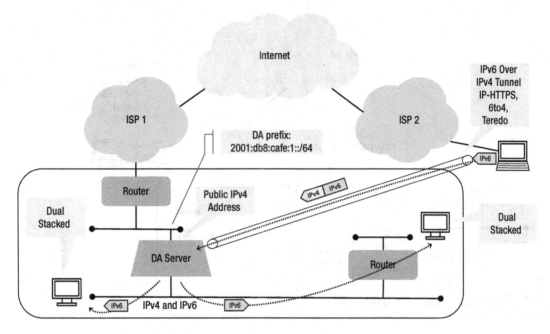

Figure 4-11. *DirectAccess solution with Windows Server 2008 and 2008R2*

The new enhancements in Windows Server 2012 and 2012R2–based DirectAccess is that the DA server uses NAT64/DNS64 to allow DA clients (IPv6-only hosts) access to intranet servers and resources that are only available over IPv4. This capability was available in Window Server 2008 and 2008R2 if Forefront Unified Access Gateway (UAG) was utilized. This reduces the overall footprint requirement of IPv6 support on the internal network; however, do realize that the clients are still IPv6-only nodes on the network and will NOT have an IPv4 internal address. The DA server does translation between IPv6 and IPv4 for every DA client. There is a moderate performance hit, but it is still an excellent solution for customers who cannot immediately dual-stack their enterprise network. Also, NAT64/DNS64 limits the ability of an enterprise to perform the manage-out function that is typically one of the attractive features of DA. Manage out is the ability of the corporate IT team to reach out to a DA client and remotely push policy (like Group Policy) or connect to the client to perform any sort of function (like remote desktop assistance). The NAT64/DNS64 solution only allows the DA client that is running IPv6 to reach an internal resource that is available only on IPv4. It doesn't work the other way around, so an IPv4 resource can't reach out to an IPv6 resource.

Windows Server 2008 and 2008R2 running DirectAccess natively have no NAT64/DNS64 solution available. The solution is to deploy NAT64/DNS64 by utilizing Forefront UAG. If you do not utilize Forefront UAG then the standard DA solutions with Windows Server 2008 and 2008R2 *require* IPv6 support on the internal network. Figure 4-12 shows what you can do with Windows Server 2008 or 2008R2 with Forefront UAG or alternatively with Windows Server 2012 and 2012R2 with the built-in NAT64/DNS64 capabilities.

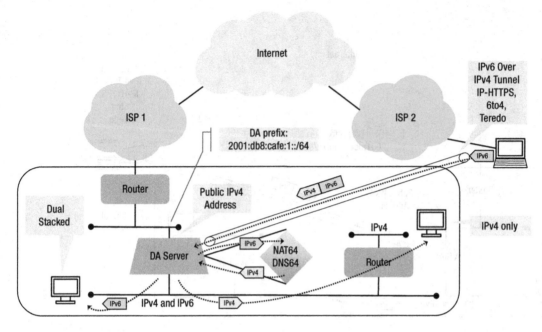

Figure 4-12. *DirectAccess solution with Windows Server 2012 and 2012R2 or alternately Windows 2008 or 2008R2 with Forefront UAG deployed*

There are multiple ways to implement IPv6, but the recommended best practice is to dual-stack to allow all clients and servers to reach all IPv6-enabled servers and clients on the internal network or access the network via a DA solution. This means that DA clients would have access to all resources on the network and solutions such as manage out would work without issue.

A formerly common design option for DA deployment was ISATAP to allow full functionality for manage out. DA clients can then be remotely managed by servers that participate in ISATAP assuming the ISATAP router and DA server have IPv6 routing available between them. If they do not, then this solution will not work.

The additional benefit of ISATAP is that it can be a limited deployment for only those devices that need to be reached by the DA clients. Not all Windows servers would be required to participate in the ISATAP configuration. Typically a domain controller, DNS server, Exchange Server CAS and UM role and/or a Lync Server plus file and print servers, and a SharePoint server would be considered. By having those servers participate in the ISATAP deployment, they are reachable from the DA clients. While previous versions of Lync had issues interoperating with DA, Lync 2013 has IPv6 support and can operate in a DA environment. I still do not consider running voice and video services over DA to be best practice. If you do plan on providing Lync 2013 over DA make sure to evaluate split tunnel options so that Lync services happen directly across the Internet connection, which will reduce latency and tunnel overhead issues.

Finally, a Server Load Balancer that does IPv6 to IPv4 (SLB64) as a translation solution can be deployed if only web and DNS are required, but this is very limiting and not recommended unless it meets a specific use case for the DA clients. Often SLB64 is one of many solutions provided by application delivery controllers (ADCs). Chapter 10 provides more information on SLB64.

DirectAccess IPv6 Key Takeaways

So while all DA clients utilize IPv6 to access resources back on their corporate network via the DA server, those resources do NOT necessarily have to run IPv6. It depends on whether a translation solution such as Forefront UAG with NAT64/DNS64 is present or if the newer Windows Server 2012 or 2012R2 has been deployed with NAT64/DNS64 enabled. It is worth noting that DA clients can only be Windows 7 Enterprise or Ultimate and Windows 8 Enterprise and must be domain-joined, so no Windows Vista, XP, or non–domain joined clients will work.

In earlier deployment guides for DA it is often recommended to use ISATAP, but for a production deployment best practice is NOT to utilize ISATAP but to properly dual-stack your network. If your design must include ISATAP (for some reason you cannot convince your network team to get IPv6 working) then utilize a service block ISATAP IPv6 solution to terminate all the ISATAP tunnels in a common area; it will reduce errors and ease troubleshooting. A service block is a highly available group of network resources designed to provide a single network service in an enterprise network. It is typically modular (block like) in design and limited in scope for a specific service. Network designs typically have several modular service blocks that operate in their environment and ISATAP would simply be one of those service blocks.

■ **Note**   See Microsoft TechNet at `http://technet.microsoft.com/library/hh831416` for more and detailed information on DirectAccess deployment.

DMZ Services

Networks of all sizes end up needing to provide service to the Internet at large. For home users it is more common to run a simple virtual private network (VPN) service to allow you to connect back to your home office. SMB and enterprise networks might run a variety of services like e-mail, DNS, web sites behind load balancers, and VPN solutions. All of these external facing services are grouped in this section.

E-mail

One of the most commonly deployed Microsoft products is Microsoft Exchange, which is principally used for e-mail. Exchange 2007 and 2010 have a specific role in their recommended deployment topology that needs to be addressed when utilizing IPv6.

This section covers the specific Exchange 2007 and 2010 role of serving as an Edge Transport service, and that service's deployment in an enterprise demilitarized zone (DMZ) or Internet Edge environment. This role does not exist in Exchange 2013. Details about migrating these Exchange roles can be found at `http://technet.microsoft.com/en-us/library/jj150569%28v=exchg.150%29.aspx`.

In Microsoft Exchange 2013, the Front-End Transport service fulfills a similar role to the older Edge Transport service.

Microsoft Exchange in the DMZ and IPv6

Any Microsoft Windows server relies on IPv6 for connectivity between hosts if the servers are able to communicate with IPv6 link-local addresses or GUAs and resolve host names with AAAA records. It is important for Exchange administrators to realize that this is true for Microsoft Exchange solutions. If the Microsoft Exchange servers are within the same VLAN or subnet then the Exchange servers will prefer to use IPv6 to do all host-to-host communications and will prefer to do so utilizing link-local addresses.

If ULAs or GUAs are used and AAAA host records are available for the servers then IPv6 will also be the preferred method for host-to-host communication across a routed network. For this to work IPv6 routing and end-to-end reachability have to be working for IPv6.

If an Exchange server in the Edge role performs an external DNS lookup and resolves an MX record to an IPv6 or AAAA record and it has a native IPv6 address it will attempt to communicate using IPv6. If the server is non–domain joined (and typically an Exchange server in Edge Transport role is not domain joined) then the server will also attempt to use transition technology IPv6 addresses to communicate.

What impact the transition service has on Exchange depends on the service role Exchange is providing. In an Edge role in the DMZ where communications are simple mail transfer protocol (SMTP), Exchange will exhibit slightly more sophisticated default behavior due to how Exchange deals with MX record types. Exchange will attempt to connect with IPv6 if an MX record has an IPv6 MX entry available. A key difference is that if the Exchange server is in a DMZ with public IPv4 addresses prior to attempting to deliver via IPv4 it will attempt to utilize a 6to4 transition technology to see if it can deliver SMTP mail via that 6to4 connection if it is non–domain joined. Remember, the OS prefers IPv6 when possible. If ISATAP is enabled in the DMZ (not recommended), the Exchange server will then attempt to use the ISATAP tunnel prior to 6to4. If Exchange is unable to connect to the host via IPv6 it will immediately attempt to connect to the IPv4 MX address returned in the MX zone records. If that fails then the Exchange server will queue the mail for delivery at whatever default timers are set by the Exchange administrator because by this point it has exhausted all its MX record options for both IPv6 and IPv4.

Microsoft Exchange in the DMZ IPv6 Key Takeaways

The best practice for Exchange administrators is to turn off all the IPv6 transitions technology solutions on the Exchange server regardless of whether IPv6 is enabled or not. Unfortunately, this recommendation is not in the Exchange IPD, but make sure it is done. It avoids the following issues:

- If the non–domain joined Exchange host has a public IPv4 address it will prevent it from using 6to4 and ISATAP.

- You may introduce unnecessary latency in your SMTP delivery if 6to4 is attempted, but your firewall is blocking 6to4 causing the IPv6 attempt to time out. This means your server fails back to IPv4, but it may repeat this for every message it attempts to deliver.

The IPD recommends that the either the Edge role servers be stand-alone workgroup mode or a separate domain be put in place specifically for those servers. Most enterprise deployments elect to do a workgroup solution; hence the transition technologies are on by default. The IPD has not been updated at all with IPv6-specific recommendations at this time. I recommend turning off all the transition technologies on all Exchange server roles and to audit your platforms before doing the change to determine if your servers were already using IPv6 to deliver any services. If your platform was doing IPv6 via a transition technology, make sure you will not break the service by disabling the transition technologies.

There are legitimate reasons to leave the transition services enabled; just document and define your use case for having it on. Otherwise use the best practice and turn them off.

DNS

Depending on the environment, DNS may or may not be deployed in the DMZ. DNS is a very common service to leverage SaaS (software as a service) from Internet players like UltraDNS or Dyn. It is also not unusual to use web hosting providers to provide external DNS services. Finally, smaller SMB or home offices may utilize their ISP to provide DNS, especially in the case of resolvers.

Microsoft since Window Server 2003 has a DNS service that operated on Windows Server that can function as a public IPv4 and IPv6 DNS resolver. Microsoft's implementation of DNS can provide both record types over either network protocol. This means, for example, that the DNS server could be IPv4 only but able to provide AAAA IPv6 resource record responses back to a host via IPv4. Most enterprise solutions will either leverage SaaS or a commercial appliance like Infoblox's DNS, DHCP, and IP Address Management (DDI) product to provide public DNS services in the DMZ. SMB and home offices rarely run DNS services publicly, but if they do here are some best practices. Refer to Chapter 8 for details on IPv6 and DNS.

Microsoft DNS and IPv6

Microsoft first released a DNS server in Windows NT 3.51. DNS is a critical component of running Active Directory (AD) and for basic name-to-IP-address resolution. Since the release of Windows Server 2008 IPv6 has been on equal footing in Windows DNS and has all the same capabilities as IPv4. Dynamic DNS is utilized by both clients and servers and works for both IPv4 and IPv6. It should be noted that a Windows host will only register via dynamic DNS its global unicast address or unique local address. It will not register any multicast or link-local addresses in dynamic DNS.

It is possible for hosts on the same VLAN or subnet to resolve host names utilizing something other than a Microsoft DNS server. Zero-configuration (zeroconf) networking technologies are also present in Windows hosts and are implemented in Link-Local Multicast Name Resolution (LLMNR). LLMNR works over both IPv4 and IPv6, with the Windows host preferring IPv6 as expected.

Depending on the transition technology utilized, a Microsoft client or server may or may not do a dynamic DNS entry using that transition IPv6 address. This becomes an important consideration when deploying technologies such as DirectAccess. If you wish to use the manage-out option with DA, then having proper dynamic DNS entries is critically important. See Chapter 8 for more detail on IPv6 and DNS.

Microsoft DNS IPv6 Key Takeaways

Best practices for a robust and stable Active Directory infrastructure is to run AD-integrated DNS. Microsoft's DNS service can be highly available due to its dynamic and distributed nature which leverages automatic replication. Replication can happen over IPv4 or IPv6.

DNS servers should be dual-stacked so that they are able to respond to DNS queries over either IPv4 or IPv6. If DNS is the only role on that server, consider implementing a tighter advanced firewall configuration on that server to protect it from other requests for services that will interrupt its primary function. Also, make sure that the DNS server has an appropriate ICMPv6 policy so that it has no issue with larger MTU sizes or path MTU discovery (PMTUD).

High Availability

One of the principal locations where high availability comes into play for enterprise and SMB is around DMZ services. Services like e-mail, DNS, and VPN are all critical infrastructure components and having them highly available has become common practice. This can be achieved in different ways. One solution is to leverage server load balancers (SLB) to accomplish this. These can be deployed for local load balancing (same data center typically) or distributed for a global load balancing solution (diverse data centers).

Traditionally load balancers did not provide more complex application inspection and proxy functions; thus, as these became commonplace in the industry the load balancer was rebranded an Application Delivery Controller (ADC). ADCs are the most common enterprise solution for applications to make them highly available. Other solutions can include the use of third-party cloud or hosting providers, building applications on distributed platforms, and finally leveraging Anycast. Details on Anycast can be found in Chapter 3.

While ADCs are likely the most common way enterprise and SMBs will deploy highly available services, Microsoft does include in Windows Server the capability to utilize network load balancing (NLB) and failover clustering. Older versions of Windows included component load balancing, but that has been removed from the OS. Microsoft Cluster Service (MSCS) is designed to address failure of a server and so in Windows 2008 and 2008R2 the service was renamed to Windows Server Failover Cluster. NLB is Microsoft's solution to cluster Windows Server hosts together and provide stateless load balancing. It is an appropriate solution for things like web services on Microsoft Internet Information Server. Because it is stateless by design, it limits the capabilities and where it can be used.

HA–Application Delivery Controllers and IPv6

A unique capability of ADCs is that they can be utilized to translate between IPv4 and IPv6. Because of this capability they can be used as a strategic tool in solving IPv6 transition. They can be used at the IPv6 Internet Edge for enterprise DMZ applications such as web, DNS, or mail services that are not dual-stacked yet. Alternatively, they can be used to allow IPv6 clients to access IPv4 resources for an intranet application that is not yet IPv6 enabled. They can also allow IPv6 clients to connect to IPv4 Internet resources via the proxy function in the same way.

Because the ADC has both an IPv6 and IPv4 address it is able to translate and proxy services in either direction depending on the need requirements. ADCs in their traditional role allow public virtual IP addresses (VIP) to be load balanced and/or policy routed to real server IP addresses on the intranet or DMZ. It is also not uncommon in IPv4 configurations to have a NAT pool. For IPv6, ADCs can either have a routed configuration which routes a specific IPv6 prefix through the device or it can have an IPv6 prefix allocation to source traffic from the ADC for load balancing. The following list shows the possible load balancing protocol options available with most ADC manufacturers that support IPv6.

- IPv6 VIP addresses to IPv6 real server address pools

- IPv6 VIP addresses to IPv4 real server address pools

- IPv4 VIP addresses to IPv6 real server address pools

- IPv4 VIP addresses to IPv4 real server address pools

Many also have the additional capability to work with a device that can perform DNS64 (DNS64 builds synthetic IPv6 AAAA records if there are no native IPv6 records for a resource) for IPv6-only clients and then map that to the NAT64 function in the ADC device. This allows the ADC to proxy the IPv6 to IPv4 session. Figure 4-13 shows a typical use case of IPv6 VIP to an IPv4 real server.

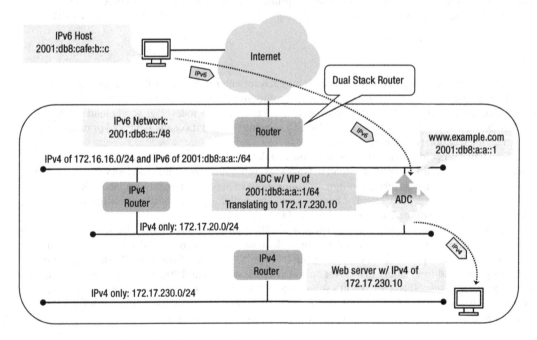

Figure 4-13. *Example ADC load balancing IPv6 to IPv4*

HA–ADC IPv6 Key Takeaways

Best practices for high availability can dovetail with the need to provide IPv6 access to DMZ resources. ADCs can provide both functions at a cost-effective price point. While they do not replace the robustness of a dual-stack or native IPv6 solution offering, they can be leveraged during the transition period that many companies, big and small, will have to go through to enable IPv6 on their network.

There are some concerns for Windows deployments that administrators should be aware of in the use of ADCs. ADCs only provide specific application functions such as web, DNS, and some other basic TCP services. If you have a complex custom application suite the ADC may not be able to properly provide a transition technology solution so make sure to test before you buy. Also remember that you are introducing more devices into the transaction and therefore complicating troubleshooting. You may need to build flow diagrams to understand where your applications are sending traffic to determine what the problem is if one comes up. Because your applications MUST use the ADC to provide the translation, it is possible for the ADC to become a bottleneck and a source of traffic congestion.

Finally, most ADCs do not have prefix translation as an option or have limited functionality in that area. Prefix translation is a functional equivalent of NAT (it seems we can't escape some derivation of NAT), so do not do design or look for solutions around prefix translation unless you have validated it is working in a functional manner for your needs on the platform you have selected.

■ **Note** For more detailed information about ADCs' performance and functions around IPv6, see Scott Hogg's article titled "How to Shop for Application Delivery Controllers" in **Network World** (February 2012), at
`http://www.networkworld.com/reviews/2012/021312-ipv6-application-delivery-controllers-side-255478.html`.

Microsoft NLB and IPv6

Microsoft NLB is capable of providing both IPv4 and IPv6 NLB. The optimal configuration for Microsoft NLB will reduce the amount of flooding that must happen at layer 2 within the network. Your options to reduce the impact on your network equipment are to select unicast mode or if you select multicast mode to use the Internet Group Management Protocol (IGMP) multicast option. This allows your network team to turn on IGMP snooping, which reduces the flooding issue present with multicast only.

A key difference between IPv4 and IPv6 behavior will depend on the hardware and software support you have in your switches. While IPv4 can leverage IGMP for multicast management and most switch platforms have that available today, IPv6 requires Multicast Listener Discovery (MLD). MLD is not as commonly available and may require a software or hardware upgrade. If you are unable to provision MLD, then unicast mode is the most desirable as it will reduce the amount of flooding that will happen in your switching environment.

Multiple Microsoft Windows servers can belong to an NLB cluster; however, if all servers are removed or are down in a cluster your switch will default to flooding for discovery purposes for any payload destined for the shared NLB IPv4 or IPv6 address. One of the challenges for IPv6 is that you will need to maintain a list of IPv6 addresses that are shared in the NLB configuration. The NLB setup screen does not accept FQDN entries, which means typing mistakes can be costly, so avoid typing them and use cut and paste to reduce errors. Luckily you should only have to build out the cluster IPv6 configuration once.

Best practices are to utilize ADCs for load balancing of traffic for both IPv4 and IPv6. In addition, utilizing ADCs to perform IPv4/IPv6 translation services is preferred. However, companies that cannot afford ADCs but already have Microsoft Windows Server deployed in their environment can leverage Microsoft NLB for both IPv4 and IPv6 capabilities.

It is important to limit the VLAN or layer 2 subnet that the Microsoft NLB servers are in. It reduces the impact of flooding other server resources and also allows you to control which switches in your network have that VLAN. This reduces the packet forwarding that happens and reduces the traffic seen on switches that do not have any hosts connected to that VLAN. Microsoft recommends utilizing unicast mode for NLB. It reduces the configuration work in the network and also reduces the broadcast traffic on the switches.

Remote Access

Microsoft's principal Remote Access solution in Server 2012 and 2012R2 is DirectAccess; however, you can also leverage the Routing and Remote Access (RRAS) Unified Server role now. This means you can also run a Remote Access VPN client solution on the DA server to handle non–domain joined clients (it will work with domain-joined clients, too) which was not possible in Server 2008 or 2008R2. Before Server 2012 and 2012R2, DA and RRAS could not be co-resident on the same server unless you utilized Forefront UAG, which is a separate product purchase and license.

Microsoft's RRAS solution can handle both client VPN and site-to-site VPN and in Server 2012 and 2012R2 it can now leverage Microsoft NLB to be highly available. Microsoft NLB can have up to eight nodes in this configuration to share load, but sessions cannot dynamically move across nodes in case of a failure of a server. In addition, Microsoft NLB does not provide session-state failover. Any clients that are connected to a failed server when a failure occurs will have to reestablish their connection to a new server in the cluster.

Microsoft also added a new Remote Access service role in Server 2012R2 called Web Application Proxy (WAP). WAP allows remote computers to securely access internal corporate applications from outside the network. It provides a reverse proxy role with strong authentication and allows companies to publish applications externally. This new role was put into the product to address the Bring Your Own Device (BYOD) trend that is happening in the market. Details about WAP can be found on TechNet at `http://technet.microsoft.com/en-us/library/dn280944.aspx`.

Client VPN and IPv6

RRAS is capable of supporting both IPv4 and IPv6 in full tunnel or split tunnel configuration. There are limitations to the supported platforms and deployment models, but Microsoft's solution is really a Microsoft on Microsoft story. The principal reason for deploying RRAS will be to support Windows 7 and Windows 8 clients. While RRAS is capable of supporting standard PPTP and L2TP/IPSec, the feature and functions that RRAS provides are enhanced with Windows Client as the VPN endpoint.

The RRAS server should be dual-stacked in order to function as a DA server but also with the RRAS role. You can do specific VPN configurations on the server utilizing PowerShell. In prior deployment options positioning the DA server behind a firewall and utilizing NAT was not possible. This is no longer the case with Windows Server 2012 and 2012R2. The RRAS service never had this restriction and depending on the deployment scenario it may be appropriate to utilize a firewall or NAT with an RRAS solution.

The RRAS and DA functions are one of the few times it may make sense to have a dedicated virtualization platform. The server can still run Hyper-V and be managed by System Center Virtual Machine Manager (SCVMM), but you want to isolate specific network interfaces to the particular Hyper-V server instance running for DA or RRAS. If you will be running a combined DA and RRAS behind a NAT and firewall then the VM can run on your normal SCVMM configuration.

Figure 4-14 shows a standard single-site RRAS deployment.

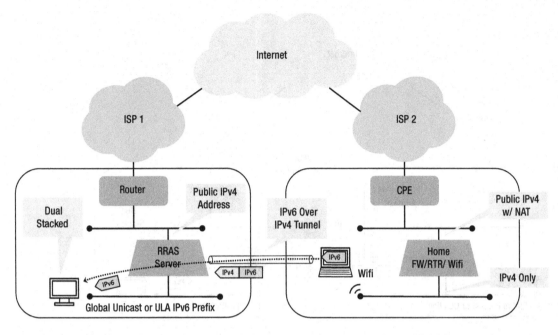

Figure 4-14. *Windows Client VPN*

Client VPN IPv6 Key Takeaways

Best practices for an RRAS Server is to run dual-stack on Windows Server 2012 or 2012R2. Depending on the deployment, you may have dual interfaces too. If the design is to be co-resident with DA (only possible on Windows 2012 or greater) then you will have to select appropriate IPv6 routing and tunneling methods. There are also restrictions on the combinations of services on a server that may run in an NLB configuration.

Review the Microsoft Remote Access web site for details on all the configuration requirements that should be performed to ensure a proper solution. The URL is `http://technet.microsoft.com/en-us/network/dd420463.aspx`.

Site-to-Site VPN and IPv6

Windows RRAS is capable of supporting both IPv4 and IPv6 for site-to-site VPN tunnel configurations. The site-to-site solution is best leveraged as a Windows-to-Windows configuration, although it is possible to build configurations to work with third-party VPN products like Cisco's ASA or Juniper's SRX or Netscreen.

There are specific VPN solutions for leveraging Windows Azure: Windows Azure Connect handles secure machine-to-machine VPN, and Windows Azure Virtual Network connects site to site. Unfortunately at this time the Windows Azure Virtual Network only supports IPv4. This may change, so keep an eye on the Windows Azure Virtual Network documentation overview page which should reflect when IPv6 support comes out. The URL for this site is `http://www.windowsazure.com/en-us/documentation/services/virtual-network/`.

The Windows Azure Virtual Network content on MSDN is located at the following URL: `http://msdn.microsoft.com/en-us/library/windowsazure/jj156007.aspx`.

Figure 4-15 shows a typical RRAS site-to-site VPN over an IPv4 public Internet but with a dual-stack internal network.

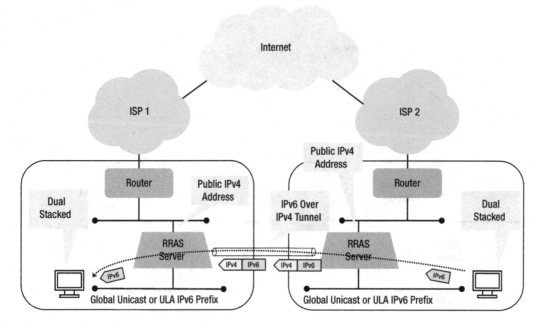

Figure 4-15. *Windows site-to-site VPN*

Best practices for an RRAS Server performing site-to-site VPN is identical to one running for Client VPN. The only caveat that is different is when integrating with Windows Azure Virtual Network you will only be able to configure IPv4 VPNs.

Microsoft Exchange

In the section "Microsoft Exchange" we covered Microsoft Exchange with its role in the DMZ. This section is targeted at the rest of the network and what additional impact IPv6 might have on Exchange and how you deploy it.

Microsoft Exchange and IPv6

This section covers the specific Exchange 2010 roles of Client Access Server (CAS), Hub Transport, Unified Messaging (UM), and its deployment in an enterprise environment. These roles may be affected by IPv6 in hybrid cloud hosting solutions depending on whether you select a PaaS (platform as a service) or an IaaS (infrastructure as a service) environment. Also, there is specific guidance for hybrid solutions for Exchange with Office 365 and those guidelines should be followed for proper support.

In Microsoft Exchange 2013 the Front-End Transport service fulfills a similar role to the older Edge Transport service which was covered earlier. Microsoft Exchange 2013 was completely rearchitected due to Microsoft's own needs in Office 365 and therefore it principally only has two building blocks. The first is CAS to make up the CAS Array and the second is Mailbox Servers, which make up the Database Availability Group (DAG). More details on the changes can be found in this excellent blog post on the Exchange Team blog site at the following URL:
http://blogs.technet.com/b/exchange/archive/2013/01/23/exchange-2013-server-role-architecture.aspx.

General Exchange design and deployment guidance can be found at
http://technet.microsoft.com/en-us/library/bb124558%28v=exchg.150%29.aspx.

Microsoft Exchange will rely on IPv6 for network connectivity between hosts if the servers are able to communicate with IPv6 link local addresses or Global Unicast Addresses by resolving host names with DNS AAAA records.

This is true for all the Exchange server roles for 2010, specifically UM, Hub Transport, and Client Access. It is also true for Exchange 2013 for the CASs and Mailbox Servers. The exception for both is if link-local addresses are the only IPv6 addresses available, and all the roles are on separate VLANS. Then all network traffic will utilize IPv4 if all the transition technologies are turned off for the servers.

All the same IPv6 requirements of the Edge Transport role apply to the other roles; however, they are typically not deployed in environments that could potentially utilize public IPv4 addresses. Please refer to the previous section for Microsoft Exchange IPv6 requirements. The specific features that have IPv6 support are outlined at `http://technet.microsoft.com/en-us/library/gg144561.aspx`.

The feature descriptions at this URL are updated as the features gain IPv6 support.

Because Microsoft still recommends utilizing ADCs for high availability and load distribution, having a dual-stack capable ADC is important.

Microsoft Exchange IPv6 Key Takeaways

Best practices for Exchange 2010 and 2013 roles is to turn off all the IPv6 transition technology solutions on the server. The Exchange servers should still run as dual-stack so they are ready for IPv6 when it is enabled. This recommendation is not in the Exchange IPD but it should be done to address the following:

- If a DNS query returns an AAAA and an A record, the IPv6 AAAA record will be utilized first for the session attempt; this includes all IPv6 transition and tunneling technology solutions except Teredo.

- Allow dual-stack capable ADCs to distribute traffic to each appropriate Exchange role as required on either IPv4 or IPv6.

Turning off the transition solutions on these Exchange servers can be handled via Group Policy in AD or by PowerShell. Additionally, transition solutions are not recommended unless you have specifically designed a solution to utilize them. By doing this it will ease the troubleshooting process for IPv6 connectivity and help determine when things are really broken.

You can find the relevant Group Policy Objects via Group Policy Management Editor snap-in at `Computer Configuration|Policies|Administrative Templates|Network|TCP/IP Settings|IPv6 Transition`. See Chapter 3 for more information about how to use Group Policy to set 6to4, ISATAP, Teredo, and IP-HTTPS. Finally, unfortunately there is not full parity of features for IPv6 in Exchange. Specifically, there is no support for IP Allow List providers and IP Block List providers in the Connection Filtering agent; nor is there support for Sender reputation in the Protocol Analysis agent.

Microsoft Lync

Microsoft Lync (formerly Office Communications Server or OCS) is the unified communications solution that encompasses instant messaging (IM), presence, voice, video, and remote meetings. The most current release of Microsoft Lync 2013 has IPv6 support; however, Lync 2010 has no IPv6 support. The previous version of OCS 2007 was also IPv4 only.

Microsoft Lync and IPv6

One of the principal challenges to gaining IPv6 support in Lync 2013 was the fact that the Session Initiation Protocol (SIP) that Lync utilizes to perform basic call setup and control functions was not IPv6-enabled until April 2011. The RFC for IPv6 SIP is `IPv6 Transition in the Session Initiation Protocol (SIP)`. You can find the RFC at `http://tools.ietf.org/html/rfc6157`.

This RFC explains why Lync 2010 does not have IPv6 support, as Microsoft felt it was more important to work on other features rather than worry about IPv6 due to the lack of protocol support in SIP.

The deployment model for Lync 2013 and all its associated roles can function on a dual-stack Windows server; however, this does not mean all the communications from the Lync server to external services (such as a SIP provider) will happen over IPv6. In fact, it is unlikely that many SIP providers are supporting IPv6 at this time. This means that Lync 2013 will still utilize IPv4 to do external SIP communications. However, Lync 2013 will communicate with the internal Exchange server, AD, and file and print servers if Global Unicast IPv6 addressing is utilized in the network. See http://technet.microsoft.com/en-us/library/jj204624.aspx for planning and configuration guidance for Lync.

If you are deploying Lync clients over DA they will utilize IPv6 to communicate with the Lync server, but you may run into issues with specific functions not operating as expected. It is not uncommon for enterprises to run all their own infrastructure and have a comprehensive Exchange and Lync deployment. In that configuration everything should run fine in a dual-stack configuration. Depending on the DA design it is possible to provide traffic separation (split tunnel) and allow the Lync client to connect to Lync Edge servers directly and bypass the DA process. For some secure network environments this may not be an option. While Lync 2013 will function for all services over DA, the Lync team has not validated this deployment model—so caveat emptor.

For SMB or home office configurations, often Office 365 is used and may be run in a hybrid configuration with Lync or Exchange as the hosted service. In these situations it may be difficult to determine what service is utilizing IPv6 versus IPv4 due to the fact that Office 365 is not running all available services on both IPv4 and IPv6.

Office 365 2013 has full IPv6 support; however, you should check the specific IPv6 Office 365 site for status at http://community.office365.com/en-us/wikis/manage/office-365-ipv6.aspx. Chapter 10 provides more details on Microsoft cloud offering.

■ **Note**   There is also a generic *IPv6 Support in Microsoft Products and Services* web site which is excellent resource. It can be found at http://technet.microsoft.com/en-us/network/hh994905.aspx.

Microsoft Lync IPv6 Key Takeaways

Best practices for Lync are identical to those for Exchange, which is to turn off all transition technologies on the Windows Server and to dual-stack. If you anticipate using DirectAccess and Lync on premises make sure to dual-stack and have appropriate IPv6 routing in place on the DA server so that DA clients can connect to Lync.

It is still recommended to utilize ADCs with Lync 2013 and by having dual-stack servers it allows the greatest flexibility in the ADC configuration to support end client and server requests.

Microsoft IIS and SharePoint

Microsoft Internet Information Server (IIS) is the web server platform for Windows. The current version on Windows Server 2012R2 is IIS 8.5 and can be installed by adding the Web Server Role via Server Manager or PowerShell. SharePoint leverages IIS and therefore the recommendations for IIS are appropriate for SharePoint. SharePoint does, however, have some unique aspects about it that deserve special consideration when dealing with IPv6.

Microsoft SharePoint and IPv6

Microsoft SharePoint utilizes IIS to run its web services' front end. Because IIS has full IPv6 capabilities, SharePoint by extension also has IPv6 capabilities. SharePoint and IIS are able to run web services simultaneously on both IPv4 and IPv6 and therefore it is recommended that the IIS server be dual-stacked.

SharePoint also relies on Microsoft SQL Server and if SQL is installed on a remote host it will use IPv6 as its primary transport if Global Unicast or ULA IPv6 is available. Because SharePoint may make use of UNC path information it is critical that proper DNS be in place so that IPv6 literals do not have to be used. The use of IPv6 literals will potentially cause problems with the URL tools used in SharePoint, so a working DNS solution is critical.

SharePoint also relies on AD DS for user authentication, and that too can leverage IPv6 if Global Unicast Addressing or ULA is available. There may be cases where web parts or externally embedded context is available over IPv4 only. It is important for the SharePoint server to be dual-stacked to be able to support pulling that content. Also, clients that are connecting to the dual-stack server should be dual-stacked themselves if external content is provided through both IPv4 and IPv6, otherwise content may not render correctly.

This situation can easily be tested by setting up IPv4-only and IPv6-only clients and connecting to the SharePoint site. If content is missing on the page then likely a content part is only available over one protocol or the other.

Microsoft IIS and IPv6

Microsoft IIS is a versatile web server and can provide functions besides the front-end web role for SharePoint. It is also used by Microsoft Exchange and Lync for various roles, AD for the Certificate Server role, and other Microsoft products whenever a web server is required. In all these cases it is appropriate to gain the greatest flexibility from the platform by dual-stacking the Windows Server. This means that IIS will have the ability to provide content over either or both protocols.

For Certificate Services, IIS is able to appropriately issue certificates with IPv6 address information and provide Certificate Authority (CA) and Certificate Revocation List (CRL) services via IPv6 too.

IIS when used with Microsoft Exchange for the CAS role is able to provide front-end web, SSL, and active sync services via IPv6 in addition to IPv4. Because Microsoft is now recommending ADCs instead of Microsoft's native NLB for the CAS role, IPv6 to IPv6 ADC functions are critical for IPv6 or dual-stack deployments.

Microsoft SharePoint, IIS, and IPv6 Key Takeaways

Best practices for IIS and SharePoint are identical (in case you haven't caught on to the recurring theme) to those for Exchange and Lync, which is to turn off all transition technologies on Windows Server and to dual-stack. Because an ADC will likely be utilized at some point to make your web services highly available you can leverage the ADC to handle the transition to IPv6 until you can get the server dual-stacked. Remember that it is a tool in a migration strategy; don't leave it that way! You want IIS and SharePoint to be able to communicate with IPv6 natively.

Microsoft SQL Server

Microsoft SQL Server is the premier database platform for Windows. The current version on Windows Server 2012R2 is SQL Server 2012 and is available in three versions: Enterprise, Business Intelligence, and Standard. SQL Server leverages Windows Server, and therefore the recommendations for IPv6 on Windows Server mentioned later are appropriate. SQL Server does, however, have some unique aspects about it that deserve special consideration when dealing with IPv6.

Microsoft SQL Server and IPv6

Microsoft SQL Server is often used to store unique web or custom attributes from web transactions. Often some of the information stored in a SQL Server database consists of things like IPv4 addresses. These are used to address things like fraud prevention, or to help with uniqueness of a session transaction.

Some of the biggest challenges around IPv6 for SQL Server have nothing to do with running SQL Server over IPv6 for the transaction. The challenges have to do with how database fields are defined within SQL Server. Because IPv4 has been the principal networking protocol for the Internet since its inception, there are many applications and backend systems that assume the values they are storing relating to networking information are IPv4 only. Because IPv6 values are now being passed to these systems, one of the challenges can be determining if the SQL Server fields are properly set up. Is SQL Server properly storing the IPv6 values, or are they simply erroring out?

Storing an IPv6 address value can be a challenge. Normalizing data is an important aspect of data analysis. Some standards have to be agreed upon in terms of how an IPv6 addresses are stored. Chapter 3 covers some rules for displaying IPv6 addresses, rules like removing leading zeros and using double colons (::) to do zero compression. These rules cause all sorts of problems when trying to do searches on IPv6 addresses. For instance, which of the following expressions should I invoke if I am looking for the IPv6 address of 2001:db8::1 in my database?

```
2001:0db8:0000:0000:0000:0000:0000:0001
2001:db8:0:0:0:0:0:1
2001:db8::1
```

As you can clearly see, the only safe method is to fully expand the address for searching and matching. This means there needs to be logic put in place to capture a search for 2001:db8::1 and turn it into a search for 2001:0db8:0000:0000:0000:0000:0000:0001. But what about the case where some third party is providing the data? What if they do not normalize it in the same way? Then perhaps the match will still happen only for 2001:db8::1.

While clearly the problem I've is not unique to IPv6, the issue is a larger one in IPv6. There are simple issues like the fact that IPv6 addresses are in HEX and not decimal values. These mean that doing simple processing on an address requires more complex logic if the database is being used for something like automation or inventory control of IPv6 addresses.

Because Windows Server has full IPv6 capabilities, SQL Server by extension also has IPv6 capabilities. SQL Server is able to run services simultaneously on both IPv4 and IPv6, and therefore should be run on a dual-stacked Windows Server.

Microsoft SQL Server on Windows Server will use IPv6 as its primary transport if Global Unicast or Unique Local Address (ULA) IPv6 is available. Because SQL Server may make use of UNC path information, it is critical that proper DNS be in place so that IPv6 literals do not have to be used. A working DNS solution is critical for Windows, and by extension for SQL Server.

SQL Server can also leverage AD DS for user authentication, and that too can leverage IPv6 if Global Unicast Addressing or ULA is available. Dual-stacking will allow the most transparent functional use of SQL Server. However there are times you will want to explicitly call out which protocol to use for a session connection when building out your SQL Server configuration. The database connection request from the remote server determines that behavior. Simply run the service on both IPv4 and IPv6, and let the remote host determine which protocol to use.

Microsoft SQL Server and IPv6 Key Takeaways

Best practices for SQL Server are identical to those for Exchange, Lync, IIS, and SharePoint. Turn off all transition technologies on Windows Server, and run in a dual-stack configuration. Because an ADC will likely be utilized at some point to handle load balancing for SQL Server, you can leverage the ADC to handle the transition to IPv6 until you can get the server dual-stacked. Remember that ADC is a tool in a migration strategy; don't leave ADC in place permenantly. You want SQL Server to be able to communicate via IPv6 natively. Finally, you will have to work with your application and database teams to address how IPv6 values are kept in SQL Server tables. If SQL Server is being used to store things like web server log files, then normalizing the IPv6 addresses will be an important part of the work you do with your application and database teams.

Microsoft Active Directory and Group Policy

Microsoft has had IPv6 enabled and preferred since Windows Server 2008 and Windows Vista. Because of this, it is enabled for the entire OS, and all of its core functions were rewritten to fully support IPv6. The impact of this cannot be understated. It means that basic things like all IP address fields had to accept both IPv4 and IPv6 formats plus a wide variety of changes within the core OS to accommodate IPv6. Simple things like logging outputs and database fields all had to account for the new address format for IPv6.

The support and capabilities of IPv6 in AD and Group Policy have matured over time and with Windows Server 2012R2 there have been additional improvements in managing and controlling IPv6 protocol behavior via AD and Group Policy.

Microsoft Active Directory and IPv6

Because the Windows OS utilizes Winsock and other standardized application programming interfaces (APIs) and drivers developed by Microsoft, it was logical that one of the key services that Windows provides, Active Directory Domain Services, would fully utilize IPv6.

If servers running AD have Global Unicast or ULA IPv6 available between them, they will perform functions like replication, authentications, and authorization over that IPv6 connection. Specifically, these behaviors are still controlled via Sites and Services/Sites/Subnets so you will need to document where your new IPv6 prefixes are deployed relative to your IPv4. Table 4-1 shows an example site to IPv4 subnet and IPv6 prefix correlation table.

Table 4-1. *Example IPv4 to IPv6 Address Correlation Table*

Sites	IPv4 Subnets	IPv6 Prefix
A	10.1.0.0/16	2001:db8:cafe::/48
B	10.2.0.0/16	2001:db8:ca11::/48
C	10.3.0.0/16	2001:db8:caab::/48

Building a correlation table like the one shown in Table 4-1 will allow you to match the replication and authentication behavior between IPv4 and IPv6. If you do not do this you will get different behavior for these services running on IPv6 versus IPv4. Depending on how your replication and authentication schema is built out for remote sites this could be a significant issue. Figure 4-16 shows how the site topology and IPv4 and IPv6 configurations match up. Figure 4-17 is a screenshot of what the configuration looks like in AD Sites and Services.

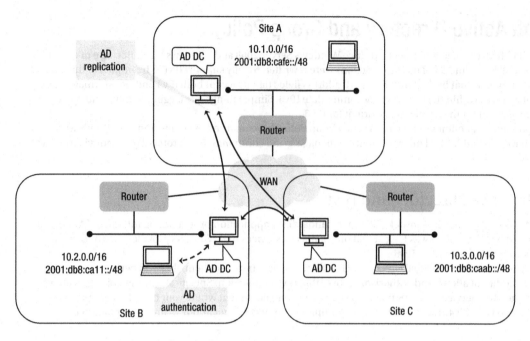

Figure 4-16. *Example AD site diagram for replication and authentication*

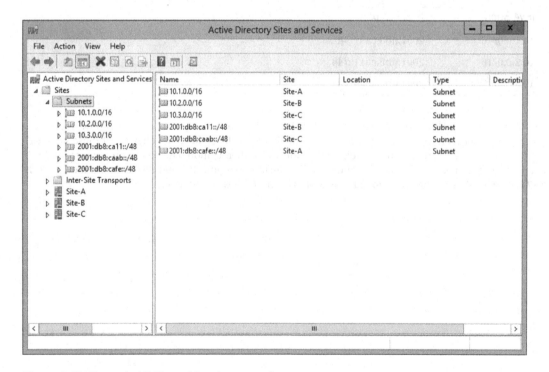

Figure 4-17. *Example AD Site and Services screenshot*

Microsoft Group Policy and IPv6

One of the challenges for Group Policy is that Group Policy Objects (GPOs) can only be pushed to hosts that are able to connect to their appropriate AD domain controllers. Remember that Group Policy relies on AD and therefore leverages the replication process that AD uses for the push of policy configurations throughout the network. AD domain controllers should therefore be dual-stacked so that GPOs can be pushed to both IPv4 and IPv6 hosts.

If your environment still has Windows XP or Server 2003 then you must have IPv4 on the server as you should not run IPv6 on XP or Server 2003. Also, for specific use cases where clients are IPv6 only (such as DA clients), the server must be able to provide the GPOs over IPv6. An exception would be if the DA Server has NAT64/DNS64 enabled for the DA clients. Then the DA client would then be able to connect to the server via a proxied IPv4 session.

■ **Note**   End of support for Windows XP is April 8, 2014—more details are at `http://www.microsoft.com/en-us/windows/endofsupport.aspx`. Most important, do NOT run IPv6 on Windows XP or Windows Server 2003 as these products are not current in their IPv6 support!

Microsoft has added additional GPO capabilities in Windows Server 2012R2 and Windows 8.1 which provides the ability to do IPv6 item-level targeting. This means that you can now specify a range of IPv6 addresses (a prefix) and these policies for the IP address ranges can do both IPv4 and IPv6 simultaneously. In addition, Microsoft has added Group Policy Preferences for Printers and for VPN Properties.

IPv6-specific GPOs are available to control host behavior also. Unfortunately, many of the public sites outside Microsoft that document them are for the purpose of disabling IPv6. Microsoft has publicly stated to NOT disable IPv6 and that doing so will often break some application functionality. For reference, `http://support.microsoft.com/kb/929852` has the information on the IPv6 registry keys and GPOs for controlling IPv6.

In summary, you need to create and configure a new registry key value (it doesn't exist by default). The value location is `HKEY_LOCAL_MACHINE\SYSTEM\CurrentControlSet\Services\tcpip6\Parameters\DisableComponents` and you will notice that "DisabledComponents" doesn't exist so you have to create it as a DWORD type. Once you do that you can use the following diagram and table to disable specific parameters for ALL interfaces on a host. These are global parameters so if you need more specific controls, then the prefix policy table and netsh and/or PowerShell may be better options. Figure 4-18 shows all the Group Policy IPv6 registry bit values and what they mean. Table 4-2 shows some common bit value combinations that might be used for the "DisabledComponents" registry key.

Registry Value (type DWORD) for "DisabledComponents"	Bit 7	Default value is 0 or off. If set to 1 then it disables all IP-HTTPS interfaces.
	Bit 6	Default value is 0 or off. It is reserved.
	Bit 5	Default value is 0 or off. If set to 1 then it sets the default prefix policy table to prefer IPv4 over IPv6.
	Bit 4	Default value is 0 or off. If set to 1 then it disables all LAN and PPP interfaces but NOT tunnel based interfaces like 6to4, ISATAP, Teredo and IP-HTTPS.
	Bit 3	Default value is 0 or off. If set to 1 then it disables all Teredo interfaces.
	Bit 2	Default value is 0 or off. If set to 1 then it disables all ISATAP interfaces.
	Bit 1	Default value is 0 or off. If set to 1 then it disable all 6to4 interfaces.
	Bit 0	Default value is 0 or off. If set to 1 then it disables all the tunnel interfaces which include 6to4, ISATAP, Teredo and IP-HTTPS.

Figure 4-18. *Group Policy IPv6 registry bit values*

Table 4-2. *Group Policy IPv6 Registry Value Combinations Table*

TCP/IP IPv6 Functionality	"DisabledComponents" Registry Value in HEX
Disable all tunnel interfaces	0x1
Disable 6to4	0x2
Disable ISATAP	0x4
Disable Teredo	0x8
Disable Teredo and 6to4	0xA (0x2 + 0x8 = 0xA)
Disable all LAN and PPP interfaces	0x10
Disable all LAN, PPP and tunnel interfaces	0x11 (0x1 + 0x10 = 0x11)
Prefer IPv4 over IPv6	0x20
Disable IP-HTTPS	0x80
Disable IPv6 over all interface and prefer IPv4	0xFF (set all bits to true)

Microsoft Active Directory, Group Policy, and IPv6 Key Takeaways

Requirements for Active Directory and Group Policy with IPv6 really come down to upkeep. It is making sure you are doing all the day-to-day maintenance stuff for both IPv4 and IPv6—for instance, adding the appropriate IPv6 prefixes (/48 down to /64s) to Sites and Services/Sites/Subnets so that replication and authentication flow matches what you originally designed for IPv4. Making sure that you are applying your GPO Policy Preferences against both the IPv4 and IPv6 networks if you use IP addresses as a target.

More information about Sites and Services/Sites/Subnets can be found at http://technet.microsoft.com/en-us/library/cc740187%28v=ws.10%29.aspx.

The good news is that Windows Server will leverage the information you put into AD's Sites and Services to do many things correctly within your AD domain. While Microsoft Exchange has its own defined mail forward and mail routing policies the Exchange servers still utilize AD (and therefore the Sites and Services properties) to forward authentication requests to the correct domain controller. The same is true for almost all other services that Microsoft provides.

Microsoft File and Print

Microsoft Windows Server is often used for file and print services. Employees, contractors, and now even virtual machine instances need to access files on central shares and to print information required to perform their job. For this reason it is important that these servers have IPv6 available to allow native IPv6 client device access.

IPv6 with Microsoft File and Print

Microsoft Windows Server 2008, 2008R2, 2012, and 2012R2 are all capable of supporting IPv6 natively. If they are dual-stacked they are also able to provide some proxy-like functions for file and print. For example, if a request to print something from a client that is IPv6 only can be put in the print server queue, even though a printer may only support IPv4, it is possible for the print server to still provide print jobs to that printer via IPv4.

This works in the same manner for file storage. You can now see why dual-stacking is so important. If the two clients are attempting to directly communicate but do NOT have a common protocol (IPv4 or IPv6) they will be unable to access any files from the other device. This is more common in workgroup or peer-to-peer configurations, but a single file server that is not dual-stacked is effectively invisible or unavailable to one protocol or the other.

Microsoft's BranchCache is a bandwidth optimization solution for providing file access performance improvements. It is fully IPv4 and IPv6 capable and can optimize file usage across branch office locations. More details about BranchCache can be found at http://technet.microsoft.com/en-us/network/dd425028.

File and Print IPv6 Key Takeaways

Microsoft Windows Server 2008, 2008R2, 2012, and 2012R2 are able to act as file and print servers and communicate with IPv6 to clients and printers. However, many older printers do not support IPv6. This is why it is critical that the server be dual-stacked and have IPv4 access so it can communicate with older printers or other third-party devices whose life cycle has not yet been reached that may only have IPv4 support.

Newer printers that do support DHCPv6 should have a DHCPv6 reservations (the Router Advertisement (RA) M flag should be set) so they have a well-known IPv6 address or have static IPv6 addresses with appropriate DNS AAAA records. Printers should NOT make use of SLAAC or Stateless DHCPv6 (the RA O flag set) except for specific use cases like a guest network. More details on RA flag types can be found in Chapter 3, and Chapter 9 covers DHCPv6.

All shared file storage should be accessible via IPv4 or IPv6 if the server is dual-stacked. IPv6 AAAA records must be available for UNC share names for hostname resolution. If LLMNR is not available because the client and server are not on the same subnet, then IPv6 literal names must be used to access the share. This is true for all Microsoft services that make use of UNC paths. See Chapter 8 for more information about IPv6 literal names and LLMNR.

For those who are utilizing BranchCache, realize that in distributed cache mode you can have limitations if remote site clients are a mix of IPv4 only and IPv6 only. In that deployment model clients may be unable to connect to each other if they are not utilizing the same IP version. This would result in duplicate file caching on each group of IPv4 hosts and IPv6 hosts at that branch location which defeats the purpose of what BranchCache is providing. This is not an issue for the hosted cache mode as long as the caching server is dual-stacked.

Microsoft Windows Server

Since Microsoft released Windows Server 2008, IPv6 has been native to the Windows OS. Microsoft included transition technologies in the server, specifically 6to4, ISATAP, and Teredo, to address the immediate short-term need to get customers operational with IPv6.

These transition technologies are enabled and on by default for 6to4, for ISATAP, and to a lesser degree for Teredo. Now that Windows has had several releases past its first OS introduction of native IPv6 support, it is safe to say that Microsoft has one of the best implementations (if not THE best) of IPv6 in a core server OS. See Chapter 2 for some history on IPv6 and Windows if you are interested in the details.

Microsoft Windows Server and IPv6

Microsoft Windows Server 2008, 2008R2, 2012, and 2012R2 are all capable of supporting IPv6 natively. If an AAAA record is provided via a DNS query it is important to understand that Windows Server will attempt to use IPv6 first. If a transition technology is available that will be used next, and finally the OS will fall back to IPv4. This may not seem intuitive since the OS will require IPv4 connectivity in order to make use of the transition technology. Chapter 3 covers in detail the process Windows uses to determine if IPv6 or IPv4 should be used.

Because of this ordered behavior there are use cases where having poor performing native or transition technologies via IPv6 will detrimentally impact server connectivity performance. It is possible for the host to have poor performance on IPv6 and fall back to IPv4 for things like web browsing or even file share access. These latency problems can be difficult for help desk or administrators to troubleshoot. They are often reported as complaints of "the network is slow" or the "Internet is slow."

In Windows 8, Windows 8.1, Windows Server 2012, and 2012R2 a newer method for addressing these issues was implemented. The Internet Engineering Task Force (IETF) released RFC 6555 or Happy Eyeballs, which talks about having applications or OSs implement session requests simultaneously via IPv4 and IPv6 and then using an algorithm to determine which protocol session to use and how often to retest. At this time, Windows Vista and Windows Server 2008 do not have support for RFC 6555, nor does Internet Explorer 9 (IE 9), and it is unlikely they will have support added. Microsoft also decided to do a partial implementation of RFC 6555 for Windows 8, Windows 8.1, Windows Server 2012, and 2012R2 and is utilizing Network Connectivity Status Indicator (NCSI) to perform that function. An update was released that brings Windows 7 and Windows Server 2008R2 the same NCSI functionality. More details on NCSI can be found in Chapter 10.

The limited implementation of RFC 6555 support that made it into Windows 8, Windows 8.1, Windows Server 2012, and 2012R2 works for all applications that run on the OS. An additional RFC worth looking at regarding Happy Eyeballs is RFC 6556, which is titled Testing Eyeball Happiness. An IPv6 readiness update was made available that extends NCSI functionality to Windows 7 and Windows Server 2008R2. Details can be found at http://support.microsoft.com/kb/2750841.

Microsoft Windows Server IPv6 Key Takeaways

Microsoft Windows Servers 2008 through 2012R2 are ready for the next wave of Internet growth by having robust IPv6 support. Best practices will be to dual-stack the servers so that they are able to connect to resources utilizing IPv4 and IPv6. Realize that by dual-stacking you will be showing preference for the IPv6 protocol. For Servers 2012 and 2012R2 there is a newer method for detecting IPv6 capabilities on the platform, and this function is performed by NCSI. If for some reason you need to run servers in a configuration that limits their ability to connect to the Internet, then NCSI will not function as designed. See Chapter 10 for details on NCSI so you can work around that limitation.

Microsoft Windows Client

Microsoft released Windows Vista on January 30, 2007, and IPv6 has been a part of the Windows Client ever since. Earlier versions of the Windows Client only had experimental IPv6 support for developers. When Windows XP was released there was an option to add IPv6 to the client OS. While the implementation works it is no longer RFC standards compliant and is generally not considered a supportable IPv6 client OS; therefore, I do not recommend running IPv6 on Windows XP.

In addition, on April 8, 2014, Windows XP will no longer be a supported OS version, so there is no practical reason to attempt to deploy IPv6 on Windows XP. It is assumed that enterprises that still have a large install bases of Windows XP will NOT deploy IPv6 for those clients and will leave them as IPv4 only. I also assume they will be upgrading to a modern version of Windows like Windows 8.1.

Windows Vista, 7, 8, and 8.1 all have the same transition technologies that are included in Windows Server. They also have the same tools available to manage IPv6.

Microsoft Windows Client and IPv6

Microsoft Windows Vista, 7, 8, and 8.1 all support IPv6 natively. Just like Windows Server if an AAAA record is provided via a DNS query, Windows Client will attempt to use IPv6 first. The same applies for the transition technologies. This means it has the same issue of requiring IPv4 connectivity in order to make use of the transition technology but still using IPv6 across those transition technologies before using IPv4.

Windows 8 and 8.1 are running the updated IPv6/IPv4 protocol checks with NCSI just like Windows Server 2012 and 2012R2. This means having partial RFC 6555 Happy Eyeballs behavior in the Client OS. Windows 7 does have an IPv6 readiness update available to add support for NCSI. Details can be found at the following URL: http://support.microsoft.com/kb/2750841.

Microsoft Windows Client IPv6 Key Takeaways

Best practices should be to not utilize IPv6 on Microsoft Windows XP. While it is widely deployed, it is recommended to move to Windows 7 or greater depending on where you are at with your upgrade cycle. The rollout of Windows 7, 8, or 8.1 clients will shape the timing and execution of IPv6 for the access layer. There is no reason that the Internet Edge, DMZ, network core, and server subnets could not be dual-stacked before your client deployment is complete.

As Windows XP is replaced over time (very quickly it is hoped) the remaining number of IPv4-only devices can be isolated within the network to allow better control of IPv4 traffic. As an added benefit of this method, IPv4 would only have to be enabled on resources that those devices needed to communicate with, mainly other IPv4 hosts. Remember, the long-term goal is to run an entirely native IPv6 network. At this point IPv4 is the legacy networking protocol!

Wide Area Networks

Microsoft Windows is the most widely deployed server and client operating system in enterprise and SMB networks worldwide. While most office locations leverage local area networks (LANs) that are Ethernet, almost all companies also leverage some sort of wide area network (WAN) service. WAN services allow remote offices, remote data centers, partners, and vendors to connect their hosts. WAN solutions can vary from MPLS, VPLS, Frame-Relay, T1/E1, Metro Ethernet, and VPN over Internet and more.

WAN design does have an impact on Microsoft technologies—specifically for things like AD replication, backup and recovery, high availability, and disaster recovery. IPv6 is no different because all the foregoing solutions depend on having reliable IP connectivity. As the move to IPv6 happens, it is important to reach parity with IPv4 connectivity so that no service interruption is experienced.

WAN and IPv6

For Microsoft OS platforms communicating across a WAN there should be no significant IPv6 issues outside path MTU discovery. Path MTU discovery is a critical function for IPv6 to operate correctly but is often overlooked by many administrators. It is a key difference between IPv4 and IPv6, and the rules that were used for ICMP do NOT apply for ICMPv6. This means that your firewalls and network equipment may need new rules.

While there are challenges with WAN and IPv6, they are more commonly issues for network architects to correct. There may be some overlap with WAN acceleration (for instance, if BranchCache is used), but as long as the WAN acceleration product works properly with IPv6 the issues should be limited. The great news is that IPv6 routing is just like IPv4 routing in almost all respects and therefore deployment for the WAN should be relatively painless. This doesn't mean it is not complex to design the WAN, but once the deployment is complete, operation of the network shouldn't be that dissimilar to running an IPv4 network.

WAN and IPv6 Key Takeaways

Best practices discussions around WAN for Windows typically revolve around AD and GPO replication and authentication. Within AD Sites and Services/Sites/Subnets it is necessary to have the IPv4 subnet and IPv6 prefix mappings. This will ensure that you have the correct authentication and traffic paths matching your WAN topology which was the best practice for AD and GPO deployment on IPv4 too.

Remote Offices

Remote offices have some unique challenges when addressing redundancy and high availability. While Microsoft has specific solutions for some of these issues it is important to realize that network connectivity is still a requirement in almost all cases. Since remote offices can become cut off from corporate office resources due to a WAN or VPN outage it is important that they still have basic functions available like user authentication, file and print access, and unified communications.

Remote Office and IPv6

Remote offices should not have any IPv6 issues in a dual-stack environment. If ISATAP is used and is terminated at a service block at the corporate office or data center then it is likely that IPv6 will fail at some point due to a WAN or VPN outage. This is not optimal and therefore if you deploy an ISATAP solution, some sort of highly available solution to address more WAN failure scenarios would be recommended. While outside the scope of this book, I recommend reading *IPv6 for Enterprise Networks* by Shannon McFarland, Muninder Sambi, Nikhil Sharma, and Sanjay Hooda (Cisco Press, 2011) which has a comprehensive section dedicated to ISATAP service blocks.

It is not unusual for remote offices to have local Internet access to offload WAN costs. In some cases they may only have connectivity to the corporate office via VPN over that Internet connection. Address planning should be done to determine the best IPv6 configuration to use. If a service provider is providing IPv6 addresses (PA) and the corporation also has provider independent (PI) space which do you utilize at the remote office?

When you have this situation, there needs to be a specific source address selection process. This is further complicated by the fact that there is not a good model to propagate source address selection information from the routing platforms down to the hosts.

Until that is universally solved for dual-homed non-BGP peered configurations, remote offices will have to utilize NPTv6 (RFC 6296) in order to ensure the correct prefix traffic goes out of the right gateway router if no modification of the host OS prefix policy table is possible. NPTv6 is not widely available in network devices today.

Remote Office and IPv6 Key Takeaways

Best practices for remote offices is to dual-stack and obtain native IPv6 services from their local ISP. Avoid ISATAP solutions unless absolutely necessary and if you have both PI and PA IPv6 address space you will utilize both. Some network segments will not need PA IPv6 address space because they do not need to reach anything other than what is on the corporate network (PI space). Other network segments (like your wireless guest network) might only have PA space to reach the public IPv6 Internet. Hosts that need to reach both networks would have both addresses.

At this point, you will need to utilize Group Policy, PowerShell, or netsh to manipulate the prefix policy table on the Windows clients and servers so that the correct source address is selected for the corresponding destination address. Chapter 10 provides more details on how to do that. Figure 4-19 shows an example remote office with both PI and PA IPv6 address prefix configuration.

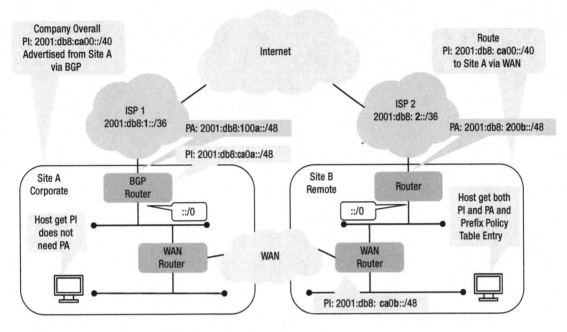

Figure 4-19. *Example remote office with IPv6*

Additional IPv6 Best Practices Resources

There are some RFCs written for service providers and application providers around IPv6 best practices. They cover guidance on deployment and best practice explicitly for those providers—see RFC 6883, for example, at http://tools.ietf.org/html/rfc6883—but these are not as useful for enterprises or SMBs trying to deploy IPv6.

The best collection of practical resources can be found at the Internet Society Deploy360 Programme web site, http://www.internetsociety.org/deploy360/. The society has current and timely information on IPv6, DNSSEC, and Routing, and its web site is a wonderful place to start if you need help on any of those topics.

## CHAPTER 5

IPv6 and PowerShell

One of the most exciting advancements in the Windows platform has been the addition of PowerShell. With the release of Windows 8 and Windows Server 2012 PowerShell is now on version 3, and with Window 8.1 and Server 2012R2 it is on version 4! The good news is the impressive enhancements made for networking in PowerShell versions 3 and 4. No longer is networking relegated to the realm of netsh commands and poorly documented registry settings!

■ **Tip**   While PowerShell versions 1 and 2 are useful tools, the real value in networking comes with the upgrade to PowerShell version 3. It cannot be understated how many cmdlets have been added. While this book is about IPv6 and covers what is possible with PowerShell, it is NOT a PowerShell book. You really want a dedicated PowerShell book to learn from. If you only get one, then I recommend *Learn Windows PowerShell3 in a Month of Lunches, 2nd Edition* by Don Jones and Jeffery Hicks (Manning, 2013). Both Don and Jeff are Microsoft PowerShell MVPs and very knowledgeable. I would also recommend *Windows PowerShell 3.0 Step by Step* by Ed Wilson (Microsoft Press, 2013).

Using PowerShell through the command line shell or with Integrated Scripting Environment (ISE) does not depend on either IPv4 or IPv6. PowerShell Remoting, however, utilizes the FQDN (Fully Qualified Domain Name) or Active Directory (AD) hostname for connecting to the remote host(s). Depending on if an AAAA record is available for that hostname, PowerShell will use either IPv6 (because it was able to resolve that hostname to an IPv6 address via the DNS AAAA record lookup) or IPv4 (because only an A record exists in the DNS [Domain Name System]). If no hostname to IP resolution is available (no IPv4 or IPv6 record is in DNS) then the OS (operating system) will attempt some other methods of name resolution like LLMNR (Link-Local Multicast Name Resolution). More details about IPv6 name resolution and DNS can be found in Chapter 8.

IPv6-Specific PowerShell Commands

Microsoft has only created two IPv6-specific PowerShell cmdlets. The remaining 279 networking cmdlets are shared between IPv4 and IPv6, which makes sense. There are also some IPv6 transition technology cmdlets that are covered later. The two IPv6-specific cmdlets are

```
Get-NetIPv6Protocol
Set-NetIPv6Protocol
```

As you can see, these two cmdlets are about working with IPv6 global protocol parameters. It is interesting to note PowerShell contains the same IPv4 command sets. It is funny that Microsoft chose to separate them even though in theory Microsoft could have simply built Get-NetIPProtocol cmdlets instead, and put a parameter field in for IP version. The IPv4 version cmdlets are (not surprisingly)

```
Get-NetIPv4Protocol
Set-NetIPv4Protocol
```

Let's dig into each IPv6 command in more detail by looking at the Get-Help commands for each.

Getting the Help Documentation

Remember, in PowerShell the best way to learn how to use a cmdlet is to use the Get-Help cmdlet and learn the syntax from the help file itself. It is also useful to use Get-<cmdlets> to pipe the cmdlets to Get-Member or its alias gm. Remember, if you want all the details of a cmdlets you would use the Get-Help <cmdlets> –full.

The –full parameter gives you the enhanced help options including the example cmdlets that are available in the help files. All of PowerShell version 3 cmdlets make use of the Internet to keep up to date, so it is handy to have an Internet connection to make sure your help files are current.

An example output of Get-Help Get-NetIPv6Protocol and Get-Help Set-NetIPv6Protocol is as follows:

```
PS C:\Windows\system32> Get-Help Get-NetIPv6Protocol

NAME
    Get-NetIPv6Protocol

SYNOPSIS
    Gets information about the IPv6 protocol configuration.

SYNTAX
    Get-NetIPv6Protocol [-AddressMaskReply <AddressMaskReply[]>] [-AsJob [<SwitchParameter>]]
 [-CimSession <CimSession[]>] [-DefaultHopLimit <UInt32[]>] [-DhcpMediaSense
    <DhcpMediaSense[]>] [-GroupForwardedFragments <GroupForwardedFragments[]>] [-IcmpRedirects
<IcmpRedirects[]>] [-MaxDadAttempts <UInt32[]>] [-MaxPreferredLifetime <TimeSpan[]>]
    [-MaxRandomTime <TimeSpan[]>] [-MaxValidLifetime <TimeSpan[]>] [-MediaSenseEventLog
<MediaSenseEventLog[]>] [-MldLevel <MldLevel[]>] [-MldVersion <MldVersion[]>]
    [-MulticastForwarding <MulticastForwarding[]>] [-NeighborCacheLimitEntries <UInt32[]>]
[-RandomizeIdentifiers <RandomizeIdentifiers[]>] [-ReassemblyLimitBytes <UInt32[]>]
    [-RegenerateTime <TimeSpan[]>] [-RouteCacheLimitEntries <UInt32[]>] [-SourceRoutingBehavior
<SourceRoutingBehavior[]>] [-ThrottleLimit <Int32>] [-UseTemporaryAddresses
    <UseTemporaryAddresses[]>] [<CommonParameters>]

DESCRIPTION
    The Get-NetIPv6Protocol cmdlet gets the global IPv6 protocol configuration for the computer.
This includes parameters such as the default hop limit, the neighbor cache limit,
    and multicast configuration.


RELATED LINKS
    Format-List
    Get-NetIPv4Protocol
```

REMARKS
    To see the examples, type: "get-help Get-NetIPv6Protocol -examples".
    For more information, type: "get-help Get-NetIPv6Protocol -detailed".
    For technical information, type: "get-help Get-NetIPv6Protocol -full".
    For online help, type: "get-help Get-NetIPv6Protocol -online"

PS C:\Windows\system32> get-help Set-NetIPv6Protocol

NAME
    Set-NetIPv6Protocol

SYNOPSIS
    Modifies information about the IPv6 Protocol configuration.

SYNTAX
    Set-NetIPv6Protocol [-AddressMaskReply <AddressMaskReply>] [-AsJob [<SwitchParameter>]]
[-CimSession <CimSession[]>] [-DefaultHopLimit <UInt32>] [-DhcpMediaSense
    <DhcpMediaSense>] [-GroupForwardedFragments <GroupForwardedFragments>] [-IcmpRedirects
<IcmpRedirects>] [-InputObject <CimInstance[]>] [-MaxDadAttempts <UInt32>]
    [-MaxPreferredLifetime <TimeSpan>] [-MaxRandomTime <TimeSpan>] [-MaxValidLifetime <TimeSpan>]
[-MediaSenseEventLog <MediaSenseEventLog>] [-MldLevel <MldLevel>] [-MldVersion
    <MldVersion>] [-MulticastForwarding <MulticastForwarding>] [-NeighborCacheLimitEntries <UInt32>]
[-PassThru [<SwitchParameter>]] [-RandomizeIdentifiers <RandomizeIdentifiers>]
    [-ReassemblyLimitBytes <UInt32>] [-RegenerateTime <TimeSpan>] [-RouteCacheLimitEntries <UInt32>]
[-SourceRoutingBehavior <SourceRoutingBehavior>] [-ThrottleLimit <Int32>]
    [-UseTemporaryAddresses <UseTemporaryAddresses>] [-Confirm [<SwitchParameter>]] [-WhatIf
[<SwitchParameter>]] [<CommonParameters>]

DESCRIPTION
    The Set-NetIPv6Protocol cmdlet modifies the global IPv6 protocol configuration for the computer.
This includes parameters such as the default hop limit, the neighbor cache
    limit, and multi-cast configuration.

RELATED LINKS
    Architectural Overview of the TCP/IP Protocol Suite on TechNet
    Get-NetIPv6Protocol

REMARKS
    To see the examples, type: "get-help Set-NetIPv6Protocol -examples".
    For more information, type: "get-help Set-NetIPv6Protocol -detailed".
    For technical information, type: "get-help Set-NetIPv6Protocol -full".
    For online help, type: "get-help Set-NetIPv6Protocol -online"

These IPv6 cmdlets are really just allowing you to set the Windows OS overall IPv6 behavior. Notice that you are
not setting interface-specific parameters but really global IPv6 settings. This means these cmdlets are really affecting
every physical and logical interface that has an IPv6 address associated to it. Notice that nowhere in the cmdlets are
there parameters for shutting off IPv6—perhaps another clue that Microsoft really doesn't want you doing that!

■ **Note**   All this happens also to be true for the IPv4 versions of the cmdlets. The cmdlets are all about global settings that affect how the Windows OS behaves overall and not specifically for a single interface.

Randomizing IPv6 Addresses for Privacy

Now let's modify some IPv6 parameters that might be useful for controlling IPv6 behavior in your network. First let's turn off the behavior to randomly generate the IPv6 address on an interface. The following commands can be used to turn that behavior off and back on:

```
# turn off privacy addressing (make it do EUI-64)
Set-NetIPv6Protocol -RandomizeIdentifiers Disabled

# turn back on privacy addressing
Set-NetIPv6Protocol -RandomizeIdentifiers Enabled
```

In the example that follows we will change the behavior and then see if it was applied to a specific adapter. In this case, we want check the Ethernet adapter which has the Interface Description of "Intel(R) 82579LM Gigabit Network Connection" and an Interface Index of 20. This interface is not active but the Set-NetAdapter parameters will still impact the link-local address of the interface.

■ **Note**   Column spacing in the following output has been tightened in order to improve the fit of the output on the printed page. You will see more whitespace between columns if you run the example commands on your own system. Similar adjustments have been made on other listings throughout this chapter.

```
PS C:\Windows\system32> Get-NetIPAddress -InterfaceIndex 20 | ft
```

ifIndex	IPAddress	PrefixLength	PrefixOrigin	SuffixOrigin	AddressState	PolicyStore
20	**fe80::5079:49a7:651c:9990**%20	64	WellKnown	Link	Deprecated	ActiveStore
20	169.254.153.144	16	WellKnown	Link	Tentative	ActiveStore

```
PS C:\Windows\system32> Get-NetAdapter -InterfaceIndex 20
```

Name	InterfaceDescription	ifIndex	Status	MacAddress	LinkSpeed
Ethernet	Intel(R) 82579LM Gigabit Net...	20	Disconnected	**F0-DE-F1-5B-B3-24**	0 bps

```
PS C:\Windows\system32> Set-NetIPv6Protocol -RandomizeIdentifiers Disabled

PS C:\Windows\system32> Get-NetIPAddress -InterfaceIndex 20 | ft
```

ifIndex	IPAddress	PrefixLength	PrefixOrigin	SuffixOrigin	AddressState	PolicyStore
20	fe80::**f2de:f1**ff:fe**5b:b324**%20	64	WellKnown	Link	Deprecated	ActiveStore
20	169.254.153.144	16	WellKnown	Link	Tentative	ActiveStore

```
PS C:\Windows\system32> Get-NetAdapter -InterfaceIndex 20

Name      InterfaceDescription        ifIndex Status       MacAddress        LinkSpeed
----      --------------------        ------- ------       ----------        ---------
Ethernet  Intel(R) 82579LM Gigabit Net...  20 Disconnected F0-DE-F1-5B-B3-24    0 bps

PS C:\Windows\system32> Get-NetIPv6Protocol

DefaultHopLimit            : 128
NeighborCacheLimit(Entries) : 256
RouteCacheLimit(Entries)    : 128
ReassemblyLimit(Bytes)      : 66185056
IcmpRedirects               : Enabled
SourceRoutingBehavior       : DontForward
DhcpMediaSense              : Enabled
MediaSenseEventLog          : Disabled
MldLevel                    : All
MldVersion                  : Version2
MulticastForwarding         : Disabled
GroupForwardedFragments     : Disabled
RandomizeIdentifiers        : Disabled
AddressMaskReply            : Disabled
UseTemporaryAddresses       : Enabled
MaxDadAttempts              : 5
MaxValidLifetime            : 7.00:00:00
MaxPreferredLifetime        : 1.00:00:00
RegenerateTime              : 00:00:05
MaxRandomTime               : 00:10:00

PS C:\Windows\system32> Set-NetIPv6Protocol -RandomizeIdentifiers Enabled

PS C:\Windows\system32> Get-NetIPAddress -InterfaceIndex 20 | ft

ifIndex IPAddress                   PrefixLength PrefixOrigin SuffixOrigin AddressState PolicyStore
------- ---------                   ------------ ------------ ------------ ------------ -----------
20      fe80::5079:49a7:651c:9990%20      64 WellKnown    Link         Deprecated   ActiveStore
20      169.254.153.144                   16 WellKnown    Link         Tentative    ActiveStore

PS C:\Windows\system32> Get-NetAdapter -InterfaceIndex 20

Name      InterfaceDescription        ifIndex Status       MacAddress        LinkSpeed
----      --------------------        ------- ------       ----------        ---------
Ethernet  Intel(R) 82579LM Gigabit Net...  20 Disconnected F0-DE-F1-5B-B3-24    0 bps

PS C:\Windows\system32> Get-NetIPv6Protocol

DefaultHopLimit            : 128
NeighborCacheLimit(Entries) : 256
RouteCacheLimit(Entries)    : 128
ReassemblyLimit(Bytes)      : 66185056
IcmpRedirects               : Enabled
```

```
SourceRoutingBehavior      : DontForward
DhcpMediaSense             : Enabled
MediaSenseEventLog         : Disabled
MldLevel                   : All
MldVersion                 : Version2
MulticastForwarding        : Disabled
GroupForwardedFragments    : Disabled
RandomizeIdentifiers       : Enabled
AddressMaskReply           : Disabled
UseTemporaryAddresses      : Enabled
MaxDadAttempts             : 5
MaxValidLifetime           : 7.00:00:00
MaxPreferredLifetime       : 1.00:00:00
RegenerateTime             : 00:00:05
MaxRandomTime              : 00:10:00
```

Controlling Temporary Addressing Behavior

Next we will manipulate the temporary addressing behavior of the adapters. In this case, we will need an active interface adapter in order to see the changes so we will use the Wi-Fi adapter which is Interface Index 19 and is named "Wi-Fi" and has an Interface Description of "Intel(R) Centrino(R) Advanced-N 6205."

```
# - turn off temporary addressing
Set-NetIPv6Protocol -UseTemporaryAddresses Disabled

# - turn back on temporary addressing
Set-NetIPv6Protocol -UseTemporaryAddresses Enabled
```

The following example shows the difference in behavior of the adapter interface. Notice that the interface has to be disabled and enabled for the changes to go into effect.

```
PS C:\Windows\System32> Get-NetAdapter -InterfaceIndex 19
```

Name	InterfaceDescription	ifIndex	Status	MacAddress	LinkSpeed
Wi-Fi	Intel(R) Centrino(R) Advanced-N 6205	19	Up	A0-88-B4-41-52-38	144 Mbps

```
PS C:\Windows\System32> Get-NetIPAddress -InterfaceIndex 19 | ft
```

ifIndex	IPAddress	PrefixLength	PrefixOrigin	SuffixOrigin	AddressState	PolicyStore
19	fe80::5ef:b5a3:2ab1:54ce%19	64	WellKnown	Link	Preferred	ActiveStore
19	2001:470:1f05:9a4:58ac:f543:d53d:bd6f	128	RouterAdv...	Random	Preferred	ActiveStore
19	2001:470:1f05:9a4:5ef:b5a3:2ab1:54ce	64	RouterAdv...	Link	Preferred	ActiveStore
19	192.168.10.160	24	Dhcp	Dhcp	Preferred	ActiveStore

```
PS C:\Windows\System32> Get-NetIPv6Protocol

DefaultHopLimit              : 128
NeighborCacheLimit(Entries)  : 256
RouteCacheLimit(Entries)     : 128
ReassemblyLimit(Bytes)       : 66185056
IcmpRedirects                : Enabled
SourceRoutingBehavior        : DontForward
DhcpMediaSense               : Enabled
MediaSenseEventLog           : Disabled
MldLevel                     : All
MldVersion                   : Version2
MulticastForwarding          : Disabled
GroupForwardedFragments      : Disabled
RandomizeIdentifiers         : Enabled
AddressMaskReply             : Disabled
UseTemporaryAddresses        : Enabled
MaxDadAttempts               : 5
MaxValidLifetime             : 7.00:00:00
MaxPreferredLifetime         : 1.00:00:00
RegenerateTime               : 00:00:05
MaxRandomTime                : 00:10:00

PS C:\Windows\System32> Set-NetIPv6Protocol -UseTemporaryAddresses Disabled

PS C:\Windows\System32> Get-NetIPAddress -InterfaceIndex 19 | ft
```

ifIndex	IPAddress	PrefixLength	PrefixOrigin	SuffixOrigin	AddressState	PolicyStore
19	fe80::5ef:b5a3:2ab1:54ce%19	64	WellKnown	Link	Preferred	ActiveStore
19	**2001:470:1f05:9a4:58ac:f543:d53d:bd6f**	**128**	**RouterAdv...**	**Random**	**Preferred**	**ActiveStore**
19	2001:470:1f05:9a4:5ef:b5a3:2ab1:54ce	64	RouterAdv...	Link	Preferred	ActiveStore
19	192.168.10.160	24	Dhcp	Dhcp	Preferred	ActiveStore

```
PS C:\Windows\System32> Disable-NetAdapter -Name "Wi-Fi" -Confirm:$false

PS C:\Windows\System32> Enable-NetAdapter -Name "Wi-Fi" -Confirm:$false

PS C:\Windows\System32> Get-NetIPAddress -InterfaceIndex 19 | ft
```

ifIndex	IPAddress	PrefixLength	PrefixOrigin	SuffixOrigin	AddressState	PolicyStore
19	fe80::5ef:b5a3:2ab1:54ce%19	64	WellKnown	Link	Preferred	ActiveStore
19	2001:470:1f05:9a4:5ef:b5a3:2ab1:54ce	64	RouterAdv...	Link	Preferred	ActiveStore
19	192.168.10.160	24	Dhcp	Dhcp	Preferred	ActiveStore

```
PS C:\Windows\System32> Get-NetIPv6Protocol

DefaultHopLimit               : 128
NeighborCacheLimit(Entries)   : 256
RouteCacheLimit(Entries)      : 128
ReassemblyLimit(Bytes)        : 66185056
IcmpRedirects                 : Enabled
SourceRoutingBehavior         : DontForward
DhcpMediaSense                : Enabled
MediaSenseEventLog            : Disabled
MldLevel                      : All
MldVersion                    : Version2
MulticastForwarding           : Disabled
GroupForwardedFragments       : Disabled
RandomizeIdentifiers          : Enabled
AddressMaskReply              : Disabled
UseTemporaryAddresses         : Disabled
MaxDadAttempts                : 5
MaxValidLifetime              : 7.00:00:00
MaxPreferredLifetime          : 1.00:00:00
RegenerateTime                : 00:00:05
MaxRandomTime                 : 00:10:00

PS C:\Windows\System32> Set-NetIPv6Protocol -UseTemporaryAddresses Enabled

PS C:\Windows\System32> Disable-NetAdapter -Name "Wi-Fi" -Confirm:$false

PS C:\Windows\System32> Enable-NetAdapter -Name "Wi-Fi" -Confirm:$false

PS C:\Windows\System32> Get-NetIPAddress -InterfaceIndex 19 | ft
```

ifIndex	IPAddress	PrefixLength	PrefixOrigin	SuffixOrigin	AddressState	PolicyStore
19	fe80::5ef:b5a3:2ab1:54ce%19	64	WellKnown	Link	Preferred	ActiveStore
19	2001:470:1f05:9a4:5ef:b5a3:2ab1:54ce	64	RouterAdv...	Link	Preferred	ActiveStore
19	**2001:470:1f05:9a4:1b9:413:7170:c1c2**	**128**	**RouterAdv...**	**Random**	**Preferred**	**ActiveStore**
19	192.168.10.160	24	Dhcp	Dhcp	Preferred	ActiveStore

```
PS C:\Windows\System32> Get-NetIPv6Protocol

DefaultHopLimit               : 128
NeighborCacheLimit(Entries)   : 256
RouteCacheLimit(Entries)      : 128
ReassemblyLimit(Bytes)        : 66185056
IcmpRedirects                 : Enabled
SourceRoutingBehavior         : DontForward
DhcpMediaSense                : Enabled
MediaSenseEventLog            : Disabled
MldLevel                      : All
MldVersion                    : Version2
MulticastForwarding           : Disabled
```

```
GroupForwardedFragments      : Disabled
RandomizeIdentifiers         : Enabled
AddressMaskReply             : Disabled
UseTemporaryAddresses        : Enabled
MaxDadAttempts               : 5
MaxValidLifetime             : 7.00:00:00
MaxPreferredLifetime         : 1.00:00:00
RegenerateTime               : 00:00:05
MaxRandomTime                : 00:10:00
```

There are many other specific IPv6 settings you can configure such as `MldVersion` or `SourceRoutingBehavior` via `Set-NetIPv6Protocol`. Some of the more important parameter options available that you might actually use are

DefaultHopLimit: The value put in the hop limit field of an outbound IPv6 packet. This value is decremented by 1 for every router that the packet passes through. When the value is 0 the packet is discarded. The default value is 128.

DhcpMediaSense: Allows an adapter to notify the Dynamic Host Control Protocol (DHCP) process if connect/disconnect events occur. For example, this allows the OS to remove routes associated with a DHCP address or to request a DHCP renewal. The default value is enabled. It is important to leave this enabled for hosts that move a lot between wireless and wired adapters.

IcmpRedirects: Determines if the OS will accept Internet Control Message Protocol (ICMP) redirects to update the path cache. The default value is enabled. If you are running in a secure network and defining static routing, then consider disabling ICMP redirects.

MaxDadAttempts: Defines how many Duplicate Address Detection attempts are tried. The default value is 5.

MaxPreferredLifetime: Defines the maximum lifetime of a temporary address. The default value is one day.

MaxValidLifetime: Defines the maximum valid lifetime of a temporary address. The default value is seven days.

MediaSenseEventLog: Allows you to log the Media Sense events for debugging purposes. The default value is disabled.

MldLevel: Allows you to set the multicast behavior. The options are All, None, and SendOnly. The default value is All.

MldVersion: Used to set the Multicast Listener Discovery (MLD) version. The default value is 2. You can set it to 1 if you need to run the older version of MLD.

MulticastForwarding: Allows you to set if the host can forward multicast traffic. The default value is disabled.

NeighborCacheLimitEntries: Allows you to set a limit on how many neighbor cache entries are kept in the OS. The default value is 256.

RandomizeIdentifiers: Defines if the OS will randomly generate an Interface Identifier (the lower 64-bits of an IPv6 address) versus using EUI-64 (based on the 48-bit MAC address.) The default value is Enabled which means it will randomly generate the Interface ID.

RegenerateTime: Defines how quickly before a temporary address is deprecated that a new address is generated. The default value is 5 seconds.

RouteCacheLimitEntries: Allows you to set a limit on how many routing cache entries are kept in the OS. The default value is 128.

SourceRoutingBehavior: Defines the source routing behavior for the host. The options are DontForward and Drop. The default value is DontForward.

UseTemporaryAddresses: Allows control over how temporary addresses work in the host. The options are Always, Counter, Disabled, and Enabled. The interesting value is Counter which allows you to generate per interface an address with the interface ID. It is designed for testing to help eliminate the random address process that an Always value will utilize. The default value is Enabled.

You can use the `-full` PowerShell parameter with `Get-Help` to find more information about all the possible configuration parameters you can set with `Set-NetIPv6Protocol`.

General Networking PowerShell Commands

Microsoft has only created two IPv6-specific PowerShell cmdlets. The remaining networking cmdlets are for IPv4 and IPv6. There are two categories of cmdlets: those that show you network parameters and those that create, define, modify, or change those parameters. The specific common networking cmdlets you should know are

```
Get-NetAdapter
Set-NetAdapter
Disable-NetAdapter
Enable-NetAdapter
Rename-NetAdapter
Restart-NetAdapter
Get-NetIPInterface
Set-NetIPInterface
Get-NetIPAddress
New-NetIPAddress
Set-NetIPAddress
Remove-NetIPAddress
Get-NetIPConfiguration
Get-NetRoute
New-NetRoute
Remove-NetRoute
Get-DnsClientServerAddress
Set-DnsClientServerAddress
```

It is important to understand what each of these cmdlets does and how they allow you to manage all aspects of networking in Windows. As mentioned earlier, there are a lot more PowerShell cmdlets for networking, but these are likely the most common ones you will utilize regularly.

Physical and Logical Interfaces

In order to manage the physical and/or logical Interfaces in Windows, the following PowerShell cmdlets are used:

```
Get-NetAdapter
Set-NetAdapter
Disable-NetAdapter
Enable-NetAdapter
Rename-NetAdapter
Restart-NetAdapter
```

You will first want to figure out what adapters you have available. You can do this by issuing

```
# - Get your network adapters' information
Get-NetAdapter
```

An example output of Get-NetAdapter is as follows. Some columns have been elided for space reasons.

```
PS C:\Windows\system32> Get-NetAdapter

Name                     InterfaceDescription                 ifIndex Status       ...
----                     --------------------                 ------- ------       ...
Ethernet                 Intel(R) 82579LM Gigabit Network Con...   21 Disconnected ...
Network Bridge           Microsoft Network Adapter Multiplexo...   30 Up           ...
vEthernet (IPv6-Demo-S... Hyper-V Virtual Ethernet Adapter #4      34 Up           ...
vEthernet (IPv6 Test)    Hyper-V Virtual Ethernet Adapter #3       28 Up           ...
vEthernet (wired-2-ext)  Hyper-V Virtual Ethernet Adapter #2       19 Up           ...
Local Area Connection 2  Cisco AnyConnect Secure Mobility Cli...   14 Not Present  ...
Local Area Connection    gogo6 Virtual Multi-Tunnel Adapter        12 Disconnected ...
Wi-Fi                    Intel(R) Centrino(R) Advanced-N 6205      20 Up           ...
```

Next you can actually do something to a specific adapter. In this case, we want to disable and then re-enable the Wi-Fi adapter which has the Interface Description of "Intel® Centrino(R) Advanced-N 6205." Following are the commands to use:

```
# - Disable the Wi-Fi adapter
Disable-NetAdapter -InterfaceDescription 'Intel(R) Centrino(R) Advanced-N 6205' -Confirm:$false

# - Enable the Wi-Fi adapter
Enable-NetAdapter -InterfaceDescription 'Intel(R) Centrino(R) Advanced-N 6205' -Confirm:$false
```

You can also use the `Rename-NetAdapter` cmdlet to do useful things like standardize the naming convention of your Wi-Fi or Ethernet ports. This is likely a more common thing to do on virtualized servers so that you can have a more uniform environment. The `Restart-NetAdapter` cmdlet does exactly what you think: it restarts the adapter and is a quicker than issuing the disable and enable commands. There are some properties that can be changed on an adapter that will not take effect until the adapter has been disabled and re-enabled, so this is a convenient way to go about doing that. The following commands rename and restart the adapter:

```
# - Rename the adapter
Rename-NetAdapter

# - Disable then Enable the adapter
Restart-NetAdapter
```

IPv4 and IPv6 Interface Management

Windows uses the same cmdlets for IPv4 and IPv6 to manage IP parameters that are available for each interface used by the OS. The PowerShell cmdlets that affect the interface are

```
Get-NetIPAddress
New-NetIPAddress
Set-NetIPAddress
Remove-NetIPAddress
Get-NetIPConfiguration
```

The `Get-NetIPAddress` cmdlet is for obtaining IP address information from the physical or logical interface in Windows. The following example script shows how the cmdlet can be used to determine the IP addresses associated with the Wi-Fi interface we were looking at in the section "Physical and Logical Interfaces."

```
# - see if any existing IP addresses are assigned to interface 20 (Wi-Fi)
Get-NetIPAddress -InterfaceIndex 20

PS C:\Windows\system32> Get-NetIPAddress -InterfaceIndex 20

IPAddress          : fe80::5ef:b5a3:2ab1:54ce%20
InterfaceIndex     : 20
InterfaceAlias     : Wi-Fi
AddressFamily      : IPv6
Type               : Unicast
PrefixLength       : 64
PrefixOrigin       : WellKnown
SuffixOrigin       : Link
AddressState       : Preferred
ValidLifetime      : Infinite ([TimeSpan]::MaxValue)
PreferredLifetime  : Infinite ([TimeSpan]::MaxValue)
SkipAsSource       : False
PolicyStore        : ActiveStore
```

```
IPAddress          : 2001:470:1f05:9a4:b5f8:7189:9783:badc
InterfaceIndex     : 20
InterfaceAlias     : Wi-Fi
AddressFamily      : IPv6
Type               : Unicast
PrefixLength       : 128
PrefixOrigin       : RouterAdvertisement
SuffixOrigin       : Random
AddressState       : Preferred
ValidLifetime      : 23:59:59
PreferredLifetime  : 03:59:59
SkipAsSource       : False
PolicyStore        : ActiveStore
IPAddress          : 2001:470:1f05:9a4:5ef:b5a3:2ab1:54ce
InterfaceIndex     : 20
InterfaceAlias     : Wi-Fi
AddressFamily      : IPv6
Type               : Unicast
PrefixLength       : 64
PrefixOrigin       : RouterAdvertisement
SuffixOrigin       : Link
AddressState       : Preferred
ValidLifetime      : 23:59:59
PreferredLifetime  : 03:59:59
SkipAsSource       : False
PolicyStore        : ActiveStore

IPAddress          : 192.168.10.160
InterfaceIndex     : 20
InterfaceAlias     : Wi-Fi
AddressFamily      : IPv4
Type               : Unicast
PrefixLength       : 24
PrefixOrigin       : Dhcp
SuffixOrigin       : Dhcp
AddressState       : Preferred
ValidLifetime      : 23:15:56
PreferredLifetime  : 23:15:56
SkipAsSource       : False
PolicyStore        : ActiveStore
```

The New-NetIPAddress cmdlet is for assigning a new IP address to a physical or logical interface in Windows. It is important to know that if an interface already has an existing IPv4 or IPv6 address assigned to the interface the cmdlet will report an error. You would use the Set-NetIPAddress cmdlet instead to specify what the IP address information should be for an interface. The last cmdlet, Remove-NetIPAddress, is used to remove IP address information from an interface. Naturally, if you are assigning IP addresses (IPv4 or IPv6) to an interface you are statically assigning a configuration to the host. There is no double checking or validating that the interface or IP address information is built out correctly, so you should test your PowerShell configuration scripts carefully before pushing them out. Loss of network connectivity for remote hosts is a difficult situation to recover from, especially for remote locations with no local console access or remote hands support.

Finally, to understand all the parameters that have been configured it is useful to have a summary reporting cmdlet and that is what Get-NetIPConfiguration provides. Think of Get-NetIPConfiguration as your PowerShell replacement for ipconfig.exe. The following code will display all the IP address information on the host:

```
# - see the existing IP address info for all interfaces
Get-NetIPConfiguration
```

The following example shows the output from Get-NetIPConfiguration:

```
PS C:\Windows\system32> Get-NetIPConfiguration

InterfaceAlias       : Network Bridge
InterfaceIndex       : 30
InterfaceDescription : Microsoft Network Adapter Multiplexor Driver
NetProfile.Name      : Unidentified network
IPv4Address          : 169.254.38.228
IPv6DefaultGateway   :
IPv4DefaultGateway   :
DNSServer            : fec0:0:0:ffff::1
                       fec0:0:0:ffff::2
                       fec0:0:0:ffff::3

InterfaceAlias       : vEthernet (IPv6-Demo-Switch)
InterfaceIndex       : 34
InterfaceDescription : Hyper-V Virtual Ethernet Adapter #4
NetProfile.Name      : Unidentified network
IPv4Address          : 169.254.73.58
IPv6DefaultGateway   :
IPv4DefaultGateway   :
DNSServer            : fec0:0:0:ffff::1
                       fec0:0:0:ffff::2
                       fec0:0:0:ffff::3

InterfaceAlias       : Wi-Fi
InterfaceIndex       : 20
InterfaceDescription : Intel(R) Centrino(R) Advanced-N 6205
NetProfile.Name      : hnet
IPv6Address          : 2001:470:1f05:9a4:5ef:b5a3:2ab1:54ce
IPv4Address          : 192.168.10.160
IPv6DefaultGateway   :
IPv4DefaultGateway   : 192.168.10.1
DNSServer            : 208.67.220.220
                       192.168.10.1

InterfaceAlias       : vEthernet (wired-2-ext)
InterfaceIndex       : 19
InterfaceDescription : Hyper-V Virtual Ethernet Adapter #2
NetProfile.Name      : Unidentified network
IPv4Address          : 169.254.247.240
IPv6DefaultGateway   :
```

```
IPv4DefaultGateway   :
DNSServer            : 2001:4860:4860::8888
                       2001:4860:4860::8844

InterfaceAlias       : Ethernet
InterfaceIndex       : 21
InterfaceDescription : Intel(R) 82579LM Gigabit Network Connection
NetAdapter.Status    : Disconnected

InterfaceAlias       : Local Area Connection
InterfaceIndex       : 12
InterfaceDescription : gogo6 Virtual Multi-Tunnel Adapter
NetAdapter.Status    : Disconnected
```

IPv4 and IPv6 Routing Management

Windows uses the same cmdlets for IPv4 and IPv6 to manage IP address routing parameters that are available for each interface used by the OS. The PowerShell cmdlets that affect IP routing are

```
Get-NetRoute
New-NetRoute
Remove-NetRoute
```

Windows utilizes a routing forwarding policy table to determine where to send IPv4 or IPv6 packets. Because each protocol is unique in how it expresses not only IP addresses but also routing destinations, a version parameter is recommended for the New-NetRoute and Remove-NetRoute cmdlets and to make the routing table easier to read for the Get-NetRoute cmdlet. The following code displays the IPv6 routing table:

```
# - see the existing IPv6 routing table
Get-NetRoute -AddressFamily IPv6
```

The following example shows an IPv6-only routing table:

```
PS C:\Windows\system32> get-netroute -AddressFamily IPv6
```

ifIndex	DestinationPrefix	NextHop	RouteMetric	PolicyStore
22	ff00::/8	::	256	ActiveStore
26	ff00::/8	::	256	ActiveStore
20	ff00::/8	::	256	ActiveStore
12	ff00::/8	::	256	ActiveStore
30	ff00::/8	::	256	ActiveStore
34	ff00::/8	::	256	ActiveStore
21	ff00::/8	::	256	ActiveStore
19	ff00::/8	::	256	ActiveStore
1	ff00::/8	::	256	ActiveStore
22	fe80::9016:6849:68c4:767/128	::	256	ActiveStore
19	fe80::689c:1135:be99:f7f0/128	::	256	ActiveStore
12	fe80::58cd:c9f6:f1a2:324c/128	::	256	ActiveStore
21	fe80::5079:49a7:651c:9990/128	::	256	ActiveStore
30	fe80::24fc:c0bd:99f6:26e4/128	::	256	ActiveStore

```
26    fe80::99e:427b:f865:ffc3/128                    ::                  256 ActiveStore
20    fe80::5ef:b5a3:2ab1:54ce/128                    ::                  256 ActiveStore
34    fe80::598:4403:b6c7:493a/128                    ::                  256 ActiveStore
22    fe80::/64                                       ::                  256 ActiveStore
26    fe80::/64                                       ::                  256 ActiveStore
20    fe80::/64                                       ::                  256 ActiveStore
12    fe80::/64                                       ::                  256 ActiveStore
30    fe80::/64                                       ::                  256 ActiveStore
34    fe80::/64                                       ::                  256 ActiveStore
21    fe80::/64                                       ::                  256 ActiveStore
19    fe80::/64                                       ::                  256 ActiveStore
32    2002::/16                                       ::                 1000 ActiveStore
20    2001:470:1f05:9a4:b5f8:7189:9783:badc/128       ::                  256 ActiveStore
20    2001:470:1f05:9a4:5ef:b5a3:2ab1:54ce/128        ::                  256 ActiveStore
20    2001:470:1f05:9a4::/64                          ::                  256 ActiveStore
1     ::1/128                                         ::                  256 ActiveStore
```

It is a simple process to add and remove a specific route into the IP routing policy table. For example,

```
# - add an IPv6 route to the routing table
New-NetRoute -DestinationPrefix 2600::/12 -InterfaceIndex 20 -NextHop fe80::5ef:b5a3:2ab1:54ce
-Publish Yes -RouteMetric 256

# - remove an IPv6 route to the routing table
Remove-NetRoute -DestinationPrefix 2600::/12 –Confirm:$false
```

Remember, in IPv6 the Windows OS uses Neighbor Discovery and specifically Router Advertisements (RAs) to determine what the default gateway is on the local area network (LAN). Chapter 3 covers Neighbor Discovery and RA in more detail. This means that DHCPv6 (covered in Chapter 9) does not provide default gateway information, nor is a default gateway needed (though I imagine many administrators will put one in regardless) for a static configuration. The following example shows the adding and removing of a route for a specific prefix and validating that state in the routing table:

```
PS C:\Windows\system32> New-NetRoute -DestinationPrefix 2600::/12 -InterfaceIndex 20 -NextHop
fe80::5ef:b5a3:2ab1:54ce -Publish Yes -RouteMetric 256

ifIndex DestinationPrefix      NextHop                      RouteMetric PolicyStore
------- -----------------      -------                      ----------- -----------
20      2600::/12              fe80::5ef:b5a3:2ab1:54ce             256 Persiste...

PS C:\Windows\system32> Get-NetRoute -AddressFamily IPv6

ifIndex DestinationPrefix                             NextHop RouteMetric PolicyStore
------- -----------------                             ------- ----------- -----------
22      ff00::/8                                      ::              256 ActiveStore
26      ff00::/8                                      ::              256 ActiveStore
20      ff00::/8                                      ::              256 ActiveStore
12      ff00::/8                                      ::              256 ActiveStore
30      ff00::/8                                      ::              256 ActiveStore
34      ff00::/8                                      ::              256 ActiveStore
```

```
21      ff00::/8                                        ::          256 ActiveStore
19      ff00::/8                                        ::          256 ActiveStore
1       ff00::/8                                        ::          256 ActiveStore
22      fe80::9016:6849:68c4:767/128                    ::          256 ActiveStore
19      fe80::689c:1135:be99:f7f0/128                   ::          256 ActiveStore
12      fe80::58cd:c9f6:f1a2:324c/128                   ::          256 ActiveStore
21      fe80::5079:49a7:651c:9990/128                   ::          256 ActiveStore
30      fe80::24fc:c0bd:99f6:26e4/128                   ::          256 ActiveStore
26      fe80::99e:427b:f865:ffc3/128                    ::          256 ActiveStore
20      fe80::5ef:b5a3:2ab1:54ce/128                    ::          256 ActiveStore
34      fe80::598:4403:b6c7:493a/128                    ::          256 ActiveStore
22      fe80::/64                                       ::          256 ActiveStore
26      fe80::/64                                       ::          256 ActiveStore
20      fe80::/64                                       ::          256 ActiveStore
12      fe80::/64                                       ::          256 ActiveStore
30      fe80::/64                                       ::          256 ActiveStore
34      fe80::/64                                       ::          256 ActiveStore
21      fe80::/64                                       ::          256 ActiveStore
19      fe80::/64                                       ::          256 ActiveStore
20      2600::/12                                       ::          256 ActiveStore
32      2002::/16                                       ::         1000 ActiveStore
20      2001:470:1f05:9a4:b5f8:7189:9783:badc/128       ::          256 ActiveStore
20      2001:470:1f05:9a4:5ef:b5a3:2ab1:54ce/128        ::          256 ActiveStore
20      2001:470:1f05:9a4::/64                          ::          256 ActiveStore
1       ::1/128                                         ::          256 ActiveStore

PS C:\Windows\system32> Remove-NetRoute -DestinationPrefix 2600::/12 –Confirm:$false

PS C:\Windows\system32> Get-NetRoute -AddressFamily IPv6

ifIndex DestinationPrefix    NextHop  RouteMetric PolicyStore
------- -----------------    -------  ----------- -----------
22      ff00::/8             ::               256 ActiveStore
26      ff00::/8             ::               256 ActiveStore
20      ff00::/8             ::               256 ActiveStore
```

IPv4 and IPv6 DNS IP Management

Windows uses the same cmdlets for IPv4 and IPv6 to manage DNS parameters that are available for the OS. The PowerShell cmdlets that affect DNS are

```
Get-DnsClientServerAddress
Set-DnsClientServerAddress
```

It is a simple process to add and remove DNS name resolution server information from the host OS using these cmdlets. The following example shows obtaining the DNS name resolvers associated with the host:

```
# - obtain the IPv6 DNS information
Get-DnsClientServerAddress -AddressFamily IPv6
```

The output shows the status for all interfaces on the OS, regardless of state.

```
PS C:\Windows\system32> Get-DnsClientServerAddress -AddressFamily IPv6

InterfaceAlias                 Interface Address ServerAddresses
                               Index     Family
---------------                --------- ------- ----------------
Local Area Connection 2           31 IPv6    {}
vEthernet (IPv6-Demo-Switch)      34 IPv6    {fec0:0:0:ffff::1,
                                              fec0:0:0:ffff::2, fec0:0:0:ffff::3}
Network Bridge                    30 IPv6    {fec0:0:0:ffff::1,
                                              fec0:0:0:ffff::2, fec0:0:0:ffff::3}
Local Area Connection* 13         26 IPv6    {fec0:0:0:ffff::1,
                                              fec0:0:0:ffff::2, fec0:0:0:ffff::3}
Local Area Connection* 11         22 IPv6    {fec0:0:0:ffff::1,
                                              fec0:0:0:ffff::2, fec0:0:0:ffff::3}
Ethernet                          21 IPv6    {}
Wi-Fi                             20 IPv6    {}
vEthernet (wired-2-ext)           19 IPv6    {2001:4860:4860::8888, 2001:4860:4860::8844}
Local Area Connection             12 IPv6    {}
Loopback Pseudo-Interface 1        1 IPv6    {fec0:0:0:ffff::1,
                                              fec0:0:0:ffff::2, fec0:0:0:ffff::3}
6TO4 Adapter                      32 IPv6    {}
```

In this particular case, we can see that the Wi-Fi interface (Index 20) has no IPv6 DNS associated with it . We will go ahead and assign it some public IPv6 DNS name resolvers. Google happens to run public and open DNS name resolvers at 2001:4860:4860::8888 and 2001:4860:4860::8844.

As a reference, Google's IPv4 public open DNS name resolvers are 8.8.8.8 and 8.8.4.4. Do you notice what Google did here? Don't be fooled. The last part of the IPv6 addresses are still HEX. The digit choices just happen to make remembering the IPv6 addresses easier.

So now here is an example of setting the public DNS name servers against the Wi-Fi interface.

```
# - set the IPv6 DNS resolvers to 2001:4860:4860::8888 and 2001:4860:4860::8844
Set-DnsClientServerAddress -InterfaceIndex 20 -ServerAddresses
("2001:4860:4860::8888","2001:4860:4860::8844")
```

And the outcome is

```
PS C:\Windows\system32> Set-DnsClientServerAddress -InterfaceIndex 20 -ServerAddresses ("2001:4860:4
860::8888","2001:4860:4860::8844")

PS C:\Windows\system32> Get-DnsClientServerAddress -AddressFamily IPv6
InterfaceAlias                 Interface Address ServerAddresses
                               Index     Family
---------------                --------- ------- ----------------
Local Area Connection 2           31 IPv6    {}
vEthernet (IPv6-Demo-Switch)      34 IPv6    {fec0:0:0:ffff::1, fec0:0:0:ffff::2, fec0:0:0:ffff::3}
Network Bridge                    30 IPv6    {fec0:0:0:ffff::1, fec0:0:0:ffff::2, fec0:0:0:ffff::3}
Local Area Connection* 13         26 IPv6    {fec0:0:0:ffff::1, fec0:0:0:ffff::2, fec0:0:0:ffff::3}
Local Area Connection* 11         22 IPv6    {fec0:0:0:ffff::1, fec0:0:0:ffff::2, fec0:0:0:ffff::3}
Ethernet                          21 IPv6    {}
Wi-Fi                             20 IPv6    {2001:4860:4860::8888, 2001:4860:4860::8844}
```

```
vEthernet (wired-2-ext)              19 IPv6    {2001:4860:4860::8888, 2001:4860:4860::8844}
Local Area Connection                12 IPv6    {}
Loopback Pseudo-Interface 1           1 IPv6    {fec0:0:0:ffff::1, fec0:0:0:ffff::2, fec0:0:0:ffff::3}
6TO4 Adapter                         32 IPv6    {}
```

And now you can see that the Wi-Fi interface has the two DNS name server IPv6 addresses applied against it. You can also use the Set-DNSClientServerAddress cmdlet to restore the name servers to what the DHCP service provided originally. You can do that with the following example code:

```
# - restore the DNS settings to what DHCP provided
Set-DnsClientServerAddress –InterfaceIndex 20 -ResetServerAddresses
```

And following are the results of setting things back to the DHCP default:

```
PS C:\Windows\system32> Set-DnsClientServerAddress –InterfaceIndex 20 -ResetServerAddresses

PS C:\Windows\system32> Get-DnsClientServerAddress -AddressFamily IPv6
```

InterfaceAlias	Interface Index	Address Family	ServerAddresses
Local Area Connection 2	31	IPv6	{}
vEthernet (IPv6-Demo-Switch)	34	IPv6	{fec0:0:0:ffff::1, fec0:0:0:ffff::2, fec0:0:0:ffff::3}
Network Bridge	30	IPv6	{fec0:0:0:ffff::1, fec0:0:0:ffff::2, fec0:0:0:ffff::3}
Local Area Connection* 13	26	IPv6	{fec0:0:0:ffff::1, fec0:0:0:ffff::2, fec0:0:0:ffff::3}
Local Area Connection* 11	22	IPv6	{fec0:0:0:ffff::1, fec0:0:0:ffff::2, fec0:0:0:ffff::3}
Ethernet	21	IPv6	{}
Wi-Fi	**20**	**IPv6**	**{}**
vEthernet (wired-2-ext)	19	IPv6	{2001:4860:4860::8888, 2001:4860:4860::8844}
Local Area Connection	12	IPv6	{}
Loopback Pseudo-Interface 1	1	IPv6	{fec0:0:0:ffff::1, fec0:0:0:ffff::2, fec0:0:0:ffff::3}
6TO4 Adapter	32	IPv6	{}

Technically, the command in the previous example is telling the interface to use the behavior it was using before any specific DNS name resolvers' IP addresses were assigned to the interface. The reason I mention this is that technically this process works for StateLess Address AutoConfiguration (SLAAC) addresses which would not necessarily use DHCPv6 at all. Chapter 3 covers SLAAC and Chapter 9 covers DHCPv6.

IPv6 Transition PowerShell Cmdlets

There are also cmdlets for transition technologies in Windows. The cmdlets are particularly important for server administrators to know so they can develop a standard transition technology template to apply to the environment they manage. Depending on the design they use for IPv6, the cmdlets described in this section may or may not need specific transition technologies operating on their servers.

The cmdlets for 6to4 are

```
Get-Net6to4Configuration
Set-Net6to4Configuration
Reset-Net6to4Configuration
```

The cmdlets for ISATAP are

```
Get-NetIsatapConfiguration
Set-NetIsatapConfiguration
Reset-NetIsatapConfiguration
```

The cmdlets for Teredo are

```
Get-NetTeredoConfiguration
Get-NetTeredoState
Set-NetTeredoConfiguration
Reset-NetTeredoConfiguration
```

Each of these cmdlets allow you to control how the Windows OS will behave in terms of utilizing IPv6 transition technologies. In fact, these are likely the most important PowerShell cmdlets you will need to know to set policies on your clients and servers regarding best practices.

In Chapter 4 we covered best practices for IPv6 deployments. As is mentioned in Chapter 4, IPv6 should still be enabled by default but for enterprise (and even most SMB and home configurations). IPv6 transition technologies should be disabled unless a specific designed solution built with them has been deployed.

The example PowerShell scripts in the subsections to follow can be used to enable various capabilities of the transition technologies. Remember that, when running PowerShell cmdlets that impose changes on the OS, you need to be running with administrator privileges or the cmdlets will not work. I have included the equivalent netsh commands in the examples (for reference) in case your platform is running PowerShell version 2, in which case the network cmdlets are not available.

6to4 IPv6 Transition Technology

Let's start with 6to4 first. You would want to know the status of the transition technology so you would run

```
# - first check the 6to4 status
Get-Net6to4Configuration

# - show the status
netsh interface ipv6 6to4 show state
```

The following output shows all the current 6to4 parameter states:

```
PS C:\Windows\system32> Get-Net6to4Configuration

Description                : 6to4 Configuration
State                      : Default
AutoSharing                : Default
RelayName                  : 6to4.ipv6.microsoft.com.
RelayState                 : Default
ResolutionIntervalSeconds  : 1440
```

Notice the state is Default which is the normal unmodified setting for 6to4. Normally you will want to turn off 6to4, especially on servers that might be in the DMZ and if the DMZ happens to use public IPv4 address space. You can turn 6to4 off using either of the following commands:

```
# - turn off 6to4
Set-Net6to4Configuration -State Disabled

# - same task with netsh for v2
netsh interface ipv6 6to4 set state disable
```

The following example sets the 6to4 state to disabled and confirms that the command worked by checking the state:

```
PS C:\Windows\system32> Set-Net6to4Configuration -State Disabled

PS C:\Windows\system32> Get-Net6to4Configuration

Description               : 6to4 Configuration
State                     : Disabled
AutoSharing               : Default
RelayName                 : 6to4.ipv6.microsoft.com.
RelayState                : Default
ResolutionIntervalSeconds : 1440
```

ISATAP IPv6 Transition Technology

For ISATAP, get the status of the transition technology by running

```
# - first check the ISATAP status
Get-NetIsatapConfiguration

# - show the status
netsh interface ipv6 isatap show state
```

You should see output as follows:

```
PS C:\Windows\system32> Get-NetIsatapConfiguration

Description               : ISATAP Configuration
State                     : Disabled
Router                    : isatap
ResolutionState           : Default
ResolutionIntervalSeconds : 60
```

Notice that the default ISATAP state is disabled. This is because in the sample environment there is no published ISATAP DNS entry or IPv4 address to trigger ISATAP to attempt to connect to an ISATAP router. If an ISATAP router entry was found, then the status of the state would determine what specifically the OS would do at that point. All the details can be found in the PowerShell cmdlets help files by issuing the following command:

```
Get-Help Get-NetIsatapConfiguration -full
```

To turn ISATAP off (as recommended in best practices), do the following:

```
# - turn off ISATAP
Set-NetIsatapConfiguration -State Disabled
Set-NetIsatapConfiguration -ResolutionState Disabled

# - same task with netsh for v2
netsh interface isatap set state disable
netsh interface isatap set router state disable
```

Here's an example, showing the new status after ISATAP is disabled.

```
PS C:\Windows\system32> Set-NetIsatapConfiguration -ResolutionState Disabled

PS C:\Windows\system32> Get-NetIsatapConfiguration

Description               : ISATAP Configuration
State                     : Disabled
Router                    : state
ResolutionState           : Disabled
ResolutionIntervalSeconds : 60
```

Teredo IPv6 Transition Technology

Teredo transition technology status can be obtained by running

```
# - Teredo status
Get-NetTeredoConfiguration
Get-NetTeredoState

# - show the status
netsh interface teredo show state
```

The Teredo status output is as follows:

```
PS C:\Windows\system32> Get-NetTeredoConfiguration

Description           : Teredo Configuration
Type                  : Default
ServerName            : teredo.ipv6.microsoft.com.
RefreshIntervalSeconds : 30
ClientPort            : 0
ServerVirtualIP       : 0.0.0.0
DefaultQualified      : False
ServerShunt           : False
```

Teredo is interesting because the default type of the transition technology is "default." However, that really means the type was unmodified and essentially the type is client. Use the Get-Help Get-NetTeredoConfiguration –full cmdlets to learn all the different types that Teredo can support.

To turn Teredo off (as recommended in best practices) do the following:

```
# - turn off teredo
Set-NetTeredoConfiguration -Type Disabled
```

```
# - same task with netsh for v2
netsh interface teredo set state type=Disabled
```

For example:

```
PS C:\Windows\system32> Set-NetTeredoConfiguration -Type Disabled

PS C:\Windows\system32> Get-NetTeredoConfiguration

Description             : Teredo Configuration
Type                    : Disabled
ServerName              : teredo.ipv6.microsoft.com.
RefreshIntervalSeconds  : 30
ClientPort              : 0
ServerVirtualIP         : 0.0.0.0
DefaultQualified        : False
ServerShunt             : False
```

As a general rule of thumb all three transition services should be disabled. If you have no specific solution in place that uses these technologies TURN THEM OFF! Do make careful note that if you are doing a Microsoft DirectAccess solution, you may indeed be using one of these. If so, you will need to make sure its configuration on your platform OS matches the requirements for the deployment. The Get-NetTeredoState will not display any output unless the Teredo state is active. This is how you can quickly verify if a Windows client is utilizing Teredo.

IPv6 IPsec PowerShell Cmdlets

There are also cmdlets specifically for IPsec technologies in Windows. IPsec setup and configuration parameters are the most common work that would be managed by PowerShell, so the examples in this section focus on those. Do realize there are 58 PowerShell cmdlets for IPsec alone, so these are only a fraction of what is possible to do. IPsec is not unique to IPv6; though it was always included in the original specifications for IPv6, it was back-ported to IPv4. Also, the original RFCs indicate that IPsec be mandatory for IPv6, but that may change due to the fact that some mobile and sensor networking stacks do not need it but have to include it in their very limited space constraints on code size and memory. This section assumes the reader is already familiar with IPsec and therefore some of the specific terms and parameters that are used in IPsec are not covered in detail.

The cmdlets to review are

```
Show-NetIPsecRule
Get-NetIPsecRule
Enable-NetIPsecRule
Disable-NetIPsecRule
New-NetIPsecRule
Remove-NetIPsecRule
Set-NetIPsecRule
```

Building IPv6 IPsec Tunnels

Building out an IPv6 IPsec configuration would start with the New-NetIPsecRule cmdlets. It is important to remember that while you can build out the IPsec rules, you will still have to do routing entries to change how the network traffic forwarding works. We will not cover that since it was covered earlier in the IPv4 and IPv6 Routing Management section; just realize you need to create the IPsec configurations first before modifying the routing rules.

Figure 5-1 shows a simple typical site-to-site IPsec deployment that will be used to show the building parameters required to get an IPsec configuration started utilizing IPv6.

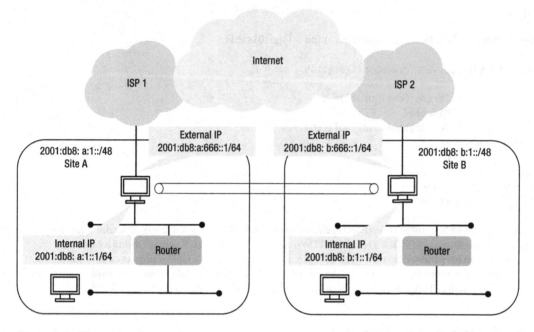

Figure 5-1. *IPsec network example*

There are a lot of other things to consider in the configuration of IPsec parameters such as authentication and encryption types, key lengths, and dynamic versus static peering. Recommended best practices for these are outside the scope of this book and I would advise reviewing some of the excellent security books and technical articles available to determine the best parameter settings.

PowerShell, unlike the netsh command sets for IPsec, will require you to define some object variables that you will pass to the PowerShell cmdlet at the time you execute. The nice thing about this is that you can reuse those in your scripting environment to update specific IPsec parameters over time if required.

Building IPv6 IPsec Tunnel from New-NetIPsecRule cmdlets

In this section I leverage the example files from New-NetIPsecRule in order to build out an IPv6 IPsec tunnel. I hope by doing this it will make it easier to follow along as to how to adapt IPv4 examples to build out IPv6 PowerShell cmdlets.

The New-NetIPsecRule cmdlet has a help example file. We use Example 3 from that help file as the template for our example configuration but instead utilize IPv6 parameters. The Example 3 sample configuration file looks as follows:

```
EXAMPLE 3

PS C:\> $qMProposal = New-NetIPsecQuickModeCryptoProposal -Encapsulation ESP -ESPHash SHA1
-Encryption DES3
```

```
    PS C:\> $qMCryptoSet = New-NetIPsecQuickModeCryptoSet -DisplayName "esp:sha1-des3" -Proposal
$qMProposal

    PS C:\> New-NetIPSecRule -DisplayName "Tunnel from HQ to Dallas Branch" -Mode Tunnel
-LocalAddress 192.168.0.0/16 -RemoteAddress 192.157.0.0/16 -LocalTunnelEndpoint 1.1.1.1
    -RemoteTunnelEndpoint 2.2.2.2 -InboundSecurity Require -OutboundSecurity Require
-QuickModeCryptoSet $qMCryptoSet.Name
```

This example creates an IPsec tunnel that routes traffic from a private network at
192.168.0.0/16 through an interface on the local computer at 1.1.1.1 attached to a public
network to a second computer through a public interface at 2.2.2.2 to another private network at
192.157.0.0/16. All traffic through the tunnel is integrity checked using ESP/SHA1, and encrypted
using ESP/DES3.

Starting with the first part, notice the example is defining the Phase 1 parameters for IPsec. In this case we are
going to use the exact same configuration as it is universal for IPv4 or IPv6. Second, the example defines the Phase 2
crypto parameters, and again, these are universal for IPv4 or IPv6 so we use the exact same configuration. Finally, the
actual New-NetIPsecRule cmdlet is shown. Here is where we replace the parameters with those shown in Figure 5-1.

The example with the modified IPv6 configuration ends up as

```
# - build new IPsec rule on site A edge server
$qMProposal = New-NetIPsecQuickModeCryptoProposal -Encapsulation ESP -ESPHash SHA1 -Encryption DES3
$qMCryptoSet = New-NetIPsecQuickModeCryptoSet -DisplayName "esp:sha1-des3" -Proposal $qMProposal
New-NetIPsecRule -DisplayName "Tunnel from Site A to Site B" -Mode Tunnel -LocalAddress
2001:db8:a:1::/64 -RemoteAddress 2001:db8:b:1::/64 -LocalTunnelEndpoint 2001:db8:a:666::1
-RemoteTunnelEndpoint 2001:db8:b:666::1 -InboundSecurity Require -OutboundSecurity Require
-QuickModeCryptoSet $qMCryptoSet.Name

    # - build new IPsec rule on site B edge server
$qMProposal = New-NetIPsecQuickModeCryptoProposal -Encapsulation ESP -ESPHash SHA1 -Encryption DES3
$qMCryptoSet = New-NetIPsecQuickModeCryptoSet -DisplayName "esp:sha1-des3" -Proposal $qMProposal
New-NetIPsecRule -DisplayName "Tunnel from Site B to Site A" -Mode Tunnel -LocalAddress
2001:db8:b:1::/64 -RemoteAddress 2001:db8:a:1::/64 -LocalTunnelEndpoint 2001:db8:b:666::1
-RemoteTunnelEndpoint 2001:db8:a:666::1 -InboundSecurity Require -OutboundSecurity Require
-QuickModeCryptoSet $qMCryptoSet.Name
```

Results are as follows when executed and validated on the local machine:

```
PS C:\Windows\system32> $qMProposal = New-NetIPsecQuickModeCryptoProposal -Encapsulation ESP
-ESPHash SHA1 -Encryption DES3
$qMCryptoSet = New-NetIPsecQuickModeCryptoSet -DisplayName "esp:sha1-des3" -Proposal $qMProposal
New-NetIPsecRule -DisplayName "Tunnel from Site A to Site B" -Mode Tunnel -LocalAddress
2001:db8:a:1::/64 -RemoteAddress 2001:db8:b:1::/64 -LocalTunnelEndpoint 2001:db8:a:666::1
-RemoteTunnelEndpoint 2001:db8:b:666::1 -InboundSecurity Require -OutboundSecurity Require
-QuickModeCryptoSet $qMCryptoSet.Name

IPsecRuleName        : {8b9a7e29-1ed0-4711-a210-cbd7a48c8a49}
DisplayName          : Tunnel from Site A to Site B
Description          :
DisplayGroup         :
Group                :
```

```
Enabled               : True
Profile               : Any
Platform              : {}
Mode                  : Tunnel
InboundSecurity       : Require
OutboundSecurity      : Require
QuickModeCryptoSet    : {d1293465-aca1-46e9-8e57-8b251781392f}
Phase1AuthSet         : Default
Phase2AuthSet         : Default
KeyModule             : Default
AllowWatchKey         : False
AllowSetKey           : False
LocalTunnelEndpoint   : {2001:db8:a:666::1}
RemoteTunnelEndpoint  : {2001:db8:b:666::1}
RemoteTunnelHostname  :
ForwardPathLifetime   : 0
EncryptedTunnelBypass : False
RequireAuthorization  : False
User                  : Any
Machine               : Any
PrimaryStatus         : OK
Status                : The rule was parsed successfully from the store. (65536)
EnforcementStatus     : NotApplicable
PolicyStoreSource     : PersistentStore
PolicyStoreSourceType : Local

PS C:\Windows\system32> Show-NetIPsecRule

$_ | Get-NetFirewallAddressFilter
    LocalAddress          : 2001:db8:a:1::/64
    RemoteAddress         : 2001:db8:b:1::/64

$_ | Get-NetFirewallInterfaceTypeFilter
    InterfaceType         : Any

$_ | Get-NetFirewallInterfaceFilter
    InterfaceAlias        : Any

$_ | Get-NetFirewallPortFilter
    Protocol              : Any
    LocalPort             : Any
    RemotePort            : Any
    IcmpType              : Any
    DynamicTransport      : Any

$_ | Get-NetQuickModeCryptoSet
    Name                  : {d1293465-aca1-46e9-8e57-8b251781392f}
    DisplayName           : esp:sha1-des3
    Description           :
    DisplayGroup          :
    Group                 :
```

```
Proposal                  : {
                          : 0 : Encapsulation: ESP
                          :   : EspHash: SHA1
                          :   : Encryption: DES3
                          :   : MaxLifetimeKilobytes: 100000
                          :   : MaxLifetimeMinutes: 60
                          : }
PfsGroup                  : None
PrimaryStatus             : OK
Status                    : The rule was parsed successfully from the store. (65536)
EnforcementStatus         :
PolicyStoreSource         : PersistentStore
PolicyStoreSourceType     : Local
```
WARNING: The default object NetPhase1AuthenticationSet(MSFT_NetIKE1AuthSet) is not present in the current store. To find this object, execute the query against the ActiveStore.

WARNING: The default object NetPhase2AuthenticationSet(MSFT_NetIKEP2AuthSet) is not present in the current store. To find this object, execute the query against the ActiveStore.

There are some warnings in the output having to do with not querying against the ActiveStore, but otherwise everything built out as expected. We next remove the IPsec rule and modify the configuration to utilize preshared keys which are the most common (perhaps not the most secure, but I leave that for others to debate) deployment of IPsec.

Execute the following command to remove the IPsec rule we just built:

```
# - remove the IPsec rule on the site A edge server
Remove-NetIPsecRule -DisplayName "Tunnel from Site A to Site B"
```

For example:

```
PS C:\Windows\system32> Remove-NetIPsecRule -DisplayName "Tunnel from Site A to Site B"

PS C:\Windows\system32> Get-NetIPsecRule

PS C:\Windows\system32>
```

Building IPv6 IPsec Tunnel with Preshared Keys

The next logical step is to use some sort of preshared key option with the IPsec tunnel configuration to secure things. The preshared key is used in Phase 1 to authenticate the initial seed key building so there is a secure authentication tunnel to build out Phase 2. We specify our new preshared key variation of the PowerShell configuration using the following:

```
# - now lets modify this a bit and create a preshared key example for site A edge server
$Site2SitePSK = New-NetIPsecAuthProposal -Machine -PreSharedKey IPv6isAwesome
$Site2SiteAuthSET = New-NetIPsecPhase1AuthSet -Displayname "Site A to Site B PSK Auth Set for IPv6"
-Proposal $Site2SitePSK
New-NetIPsecRule -DisplayName "Tunnel from Site A to Site B Network Rule" -Enabled True -Profile Any
-Mode Tunnel -LocalAddress 2001:db8:a:1::/64 -RemoteAddress 2001:db8:b:1::/64 -LocalTunnelEndpoint
2001:db8:a:666::1 -RemoteTunnelEndpoint 2001:db8:b:666::1 -InboundSecurity Require -OutboundSecurity
Require -Phase1AuthSet $Site2SiteAuthSet.name
```

```
# - now lets modify this a bit and create a preshared key example for site B edge server
$Site2SitePSK = New-NetIPsecAuthProposal -Machine -PreSharedKey IPv6isAwesome
$Site2SiteAuthSET = New-NetIPsecPhase1AuthSet -Displayname "Site B to Site A PSK Auth Set for IPv6"
-Proposal $Site2SitePSK
New-NetIPsecRule -DisplayName "Tunnel from Site B to Site A Network Rule" -Enabled True -Profile Any
-Mode Tunnel -LocalAddress 2001:db8:b:1::/64 -RemoteAddress 2001:db8:a:1::/64 -LocalTunnelEndpoint
2001:db8:b:666::1 -RemoteTunnelEndpoint 2001:db8:a:666::1 -InboundSecurity Require -OutboundSecurity
Require -Phase1AuthSet $Site2SiteAuthSet.name
```

Following is the output and validated configuration of the IPsec rule. You can see that the rule was built out as expected.

```
PS C:\Windows\system32> $Site2SitePSK = New-NetIPsecAuthProposal -Machine -PreSharedKey
IPv6isAwesome
$Site2SiteAuthSET = New-NetIPsecPhase1AuthSet -Displayname "Site A to Site B PSK Auth Set for IPv6"
-Proposal $Site2SitePSK
New-NetIPsecRule -DisplayName "Tunnel from Site A to Site B Network Rule" -Enabled True -Profile Any
-Mode Tunnel -LocalAddress 2001:db8:a:1::/64 -RemoteAddress 2001:db8:b:1::/64 -LocalTunnelEndpoint
2001:db8:a:666::1 -RemoteTunnelEndpoint 2001:db8:b:666::1 -InboundSecurity Require -OutboundSecurity
Require -Phase1AuthSet $Site2SiteAuthSet.name

IPsecRuleName         : {e57d727c-bbdb-40fc-886c-f4c2f444ade4}
DisplayName           : Tunnel from Site A to Site B Network Rule
Description           :
DisplayGroup          :
Group                 :
Enabled               : True
Profile               : Any
Platform              : {}
Mode                  : Tunnel
InboundSecurity       : Require
OutboundSecurity      : Require
QuickModeCryptoSet    : Default
Phase1AuthSet         : {ec024c4f-c8f5-4e4d-8c72-1c2371b2f5d8}
Phase2AuthSet         : Default
KeyModule             : Default
AllowWatchKey         : False
AllowSetKey           : False
LocalTunnelEndpoint   : {2001:db8:a:666::1}
RemoteTunnelEndpoint  : {2001:db8:b:666::1}
RemoteTunnelHostname  :
ForwardPathLifetime   : 0
EncryptedTunnelBypass : False
RequireAuthorization  : False
User                  : Any
Machine               : Any
PrimaryStatus         : OK
Status                : The rule was parsed successfully from the store. (65536)
EnforcementStatus     : NotApplicable
PolicyStoreSource     : PersistentStore
PolicyStoreSourceType : Local
```

```
PS C:\Windows\system32> Show-NetIPsecRule

$_ | Get-NetFirewallAddressFilter
     LocalAddress        : 2001:db8:a:1::/64
     RemoteAddress       : 2001:db8:b:1::/64

$_ | Get-NetFirewallInterfaceTypeFilter
     InterfaceType       : Any

$_ | Get-NetFirewallInterfaceFilter
     InterfaceAlias      : Any

$_ | Get-NetFirewallPortFilter
     Protocol            : Any
     LocalPort           : Any
     RemotePort          : Any
     IcmpType            : Any
     DynamicTransport    : Any
```

WARNING: The default object NetQuickModeCryptoSet(MSFT_NetIKEQMCryptoSet) is not present in the current store. To find this object, execute the query against the ActiveStore.

```
$_ | Get-NetIPsecPhase1AuthSet
     Name                : {ec024c4f-c8f5-4e4d-8c72-1c2371b2f5d8}
     DisplayName         : Site A to Site B PSK Auth Set for IPv6
     Description         :
     DisplayGroup        :
     Group               :
     Proposal            : {
                         : 0 : PreSharedKey
                         :   : PreSharedKey: IPv6isAwesome
                         : }
     PrimaryStatus       : OK
     Status              : The rule was parsed successfully from the store. (65536)
     EnforcementStatus   :
     PolicyStoreSource   : PersistentStore
     PolicyStoreSourceType : Local
```

WARNING: The default object NetPhase2AuthenticationSet(MSFT_NetIKEP2AuthSet) is not present in the current store. To find this object, execute the query against the ActiveStore.

As you can see, we still have the default object Phase 1 and Phase 2 errors because we didn't query against the ActiveStore. Let's do that now, and see if the output changes. You can query against the ActiveStore by issuing

```
# - check the IPsec rule
Show-NetIPsecRule -PolicyStore ActiveStore
```

And the output shows

```
PS C:\Windows\system32> Show-NetIPsecRule -PolicyStore ActiveStore

$_ | Get-NetFirewallAddressFilter
     LocalAddress        : 2001:db8:a:1::/64
     RemoteAddress       : 2001:db8:b:1::/64
```

```
$_ | Get-NetFirewallInterfaceTypeFilter
      InterfaceType          : Any

$_ | Get-NetFirewallInterfaceFilter
      InterfaceAlias         : Any

$_ | Get-NetFirewallPortFilter
      Protocol               : Any
      LocalPort              : Any
      RemotePort             : Any
      IcmpType               : Any
      DynamicTransport       : Any

$_ | Get-NetQuickModeCryptoSet
      Name                   : {E5A5D32A-4BCE-4e4d-B07F-4AB1BA7E5FE2}
      DisplayName            : Service Hardcoded Default Phase2 CryptoSet
      Description            : Service Hardcoded Default Phase2 CryptoSet
      DisplayGroup           :
      Group                  :
      Proposal               : {
                             : 0 : Encapsulation: ESP
                             :   : EspHash: SHA1
                             :   : MaxLifetimeKilobytes: 100000
                             :   : MaxLifetimeMinutes: 60
                             : 1 : Encapsulation: ESP
                             :   : EspHash: SHA1
                             :   : Encryption: AES128
                             :   : MaxLifetimeKilobytes: 100000
                             :   : MaxLifetimeMinutes: 60
                             : 2 : Encapsulation: ESP
                             :   : EspHash: SHA1
                             :   : Encryption: DES3
                             :   : MaxLifetimeKilobytes: 100000
                             :   : MaxLifetimeMinutes: 60
                             : 3 : Encapsulation: AH
                             :   : AhHash: SHA1
                             :   : MaxLifetimeKilobytes: 100000
                             :   : MaxLifetimeMinutes: 60
                             : }
      PfsGroup               : None
      PrimaryStatus          : OK
      Status                 : The rule was parsed successfully from the store. (65536)
      EnforcementStatus      :
      PolicyStoreSource      : No Policy Store (Hardcoded)
      PolicyStoreSourceType  : Hardcoded

$_ | Get-NetIPsecPhase1AuthSet
      Name                   : {ec024c4f-c8f5-4e4d-8c72-1c2371b2f5d8}
      DisplayName            : Site A to Site B PSK Auth Set for IPv6
      Description            :
      DisplayGroup           :
      Group                  :
```

```
    Proposal               : {
                           : 0 : PreSharedKey
                           :   : PreSharedKey: IPv6isAwesome
                           : }
    PrimaryStatus          : OK
    Status                 : The rule was parsed successfully from the store. (65536)
    EnforcementStatus      :
    PolicyStoreSource      : PersistentStore
    PolicyStoreSourceType  : Local

$_ | Get-NetIPsecPhase2AuthSet
    Name                   : {E5A5D32A-4BCE-4e4d-B07F-4AB1BA7E5FE4}
    DisplayName            : Service Hardcoded Default Phase2 AuthSet
    Description            : Service Hardcoded Default Phase2 AuthSet
    DisplayGroup           :
    Group                  :
    Proposal               : {
                           : }
    PrimaryStatus          : OK
    Status                 : The rule was parsed successfully from the store. (65536)
    EnforcementStatus      :
    PolicyStoreSource      : No Policy Store (Hardcoded)
    PolicyStoreSourceType  : Hardcoded
```

There we go; everything is good on Site A, and you would simply follow the same procedure for Site B with the local and remote portions of the configuration reversed.

If you need to disable or enable the IPsec rule (say, for maintenance reasons), then you have several different options. You can execute something like

```
# - disable the IPsec rule
Set-NetIPsecRule -DisplayName "Tunnel from Site A to Site B Network Rule" -Enabled False

# - display the IPsec rule to validate it is disabled
Get-NetIPsecRule -DisplayName "Tunnel from Site A to Site B Network Rule" -PolicyStore ActiveStore
```

And the following output shows that this works:

```
PS C:\Windows\system32> Set-NetIPsecRule -DisplayName "Tunnel from Site A to Site B Network Rule"
-Enabled False
Get-NetIPsecRule -DisplayName "Tunnel from Site A to Site B Network Rule" -PolicyStore ActiveStore


IPsecRuleName          : {e57d727c-bbdb-40fc-886c-f4c2f444ade4}
DisplayName            : Tunnel from Site A to Site B Network Rule
Description            :
DisplayGroup           :
Group                  :
Enabled                : False
Profile                : Any
Platform               : {}
Mode                   : Tunnel
InboundSecurity        : Require
```

```
OutboundSecurity      : Require
QuickModeCryptoSet    : Default
Phase1AuthSet         : {ec024c4f-c8f5-4e4d-8c72-1c2371b2f5d8}
Phase2AuthSet         : Default
KeyModule             : Default
AllowWatchKey         : False
AllowSetKey           : False
LocalTunnelEndpoint   : {2001:db8:a:666::1}
RemoteTunnelEndpoint  : {2001:db8:b:666::1}
RemoteTunnelHostname  :
ForwardPathLifetime   : 0
EncryptedTunnelBypass : False
RequireAuthorization  : False
User                  : Any
Machine               : Any
PrimaryStatus         : Inactive
Status                : The rule was parsed successfully from the store. (65536)
EnforcementStatus     : {ProfileInactive, Disabled}
PolicyStoreSource     : PersistentStore
PolicyStoreSourceType : Local
```

The other option is to execute the specific cmdlets to do the same operation.

```
# - enable the IPsec rule
Enable-NetIPsecRule -DisplayName "Tunnel from Site A to Site B Network Rule" -Confirm:$false

# - check the IPsec rule
Get-NetIPsecRule -DisplayName "Tunnel from Site A to Site B Network Rule" -PolicyStore ActiveStore
```

As you can see, executing these cmdlets enables the IPsec rule as expected.

```
PS C:\Windows\system32> # - enable the IPsec rule
Enable-NetIPsecRule -DisplayName "Tunnel from Site A to Site B Network Rule" -Confirm:$false
# - check the IPsec rule
Get-NetIPsecRule -DisplayName "Tunnel from Site A to Site B Network Rule" -PolicyStore ActiveStore


IPsecRuleName         : {e57d727c-bbdb-40fc-886c-f4c2f444ade4}
DisplayName           : Tunnel from Site A to Site B Network Rule
Description           :
DisplayGroup          :
Group                 :
Enabled               : True
Profile               : Any
Platform              : {}
Mode                  : Tunnel
InboundSecurity       : Require
OutboundSecurity      : Require
QuickModeCryptoSet    : Default
Phase1AuthSet         : {ec024c4f-c8f5-4e4d-8c72-1c2371b2f5d8}
Phase2AuthSet         : Default
KeyModule             : Default
AllowWatchKey         : False
```

```
AllowSetKey             : False
LocalTunnelEndpoint     : {2001:db8:a:666::1}
RemoteTunnelEndpoint    : {2001:db8:b:666::1}
RemoteTunnelHostname    :
ForwardPathLifetime     : 0
EncryptedTunnelBypass   : False
RequireAuthorization    : False
User                    : Any
Machine                 : Any
PrimaryStatus           : OK
Status                  : The rule was parsed successfully from the store. (65536)
EnforcementStatus       : {ProfileInactive, Enforced}
PolicyStoreSource       : PersistentStore
PolicyStoreSourceType   : Local
```

The nice thing about the Enable-NetIPsecRule and Disable-NetIPsecRule cmdlets is the fact that you can use them without accidentally modifying parameters of the IPsec rule, which you could potentially do with the Set-NetIPsecRule cmdlet which is open to change any parameter of the IPsec rule. So let's confirm this by disabling and validating the same operation.

```
# - disable the IPsec rule
Disable-NetIPsecRule -DisplayName "Tunnel from Site A to Site B Network Rule" -Confirm:$false

# - check the IPsec rule
Get-NetIPsecRule -DisplayName "Tunnel from Site A to Site B Network Rule" -PolicyStore ActiveStore
```

And the output shows it is working as expected.

```
PS C:\Windows\system32> # - disable the IPsec rule
Disable-NetIPsecRule -DisplayName "Tunnel from Site A to Site B Network Rule" -Confirm:$false
# - check the IPsec rule
Get-NetIPsecRule -DisplayName "Tunnel from Site A to Site B Network Rule" -PolicyStore ActiveStore
```

```
IPsecRuleName           : {e57d727c-bbdb-40fc-886c-f4c2f444ade4}
DisplayName             : Tunnel from Site A to Site B Network Rule
Description             :
DisplayGroup            :
Group                   :
Enabled                 : False
Profile                 : Any
Platform                : {}
Mode                    : Tunnel
InboundSecurity         : Require
OutboundSecurity        : Require
QuickModeCryptoSet      : Default
Phase1AuthSet           : {ec024c4f-c8f5-4e4d-8c72-1c2371b2f5d8}
Phase2AuthSet           : Default
KeyModule               : Default
AllowWatchKey           : False
AllowSetKey             : False
LocalTunnelEndpoint     : {2001:db8:a:666::1}
RemoteTunnelEndpoint    : {2001:db8:b:666::1}
```

```
RemoteTunnelHostname   :
ForwardPathLifetime    : 0
EncryptedTunnelBypass  : False
RequireAuthorization   : False
User                   : Any
Machine                : Any
PrimaryStatus          : Inactive
Status                 : The rule was parsed successfully from the store. (65536)
EnforcementStatus      : {ProfileInactive, Disabled}
PolicyStoreSource      : PersistentStore
PolicyStoreSourceType  : Local
```

Finally, we can clear up and remove the IPsec rule using the Remove-NetIPsecRule cmdlet. Remember, this completely removes the IPsec rule, so if you have any plans to use the IPsec rule again later, simply disable the rule instead. The commands to do that are

```
# - remove the IPsec rule on the site A edge server
Remove-NetIPsecRule -DisplayName "Tunnel from Site A to Site B Network Rule"

# - confirm there are no rules
Show-NetIPsecRule
```

After disabling the rule, we are back to our original state with no IPsec rules.

```
PS C:\Windows\system32> Remove-NetIPsecRule -DisplayName "Tunnel from Site A to Site B Network Rule"

PS C:\Windows\system32> Show-NetIPsecRule

PS C:\Windows\system32>
```

Obviously there is a lot more that goes into debugging IPsec rules and the traffic payloads between machines. You can do a simple search in PowerShell for the appropriate cmdlets that would be helpful by using the Get-Help cmdlet and the wildcard * parameter. It would be something like

```
get-help *ipsec*
```

There are a tremendous amount of cmdlets related to IPsec so please refer to Microsoft's TechNet pages that maintain that information at http://technet.microsoft.com/en-us/library/jj554906%28v=wps.620%29.aspx.

IPv6 VPN PowerShell Cmdlets

There are also cmdlets specifically for VPN in Windows. VPN is not unique to IPv6 and the cmdlets will take DNS or IP-specific parameters. VPN configuration through PowerShell makes automating VPN access to third-party networks much easier since a .ps1 file can be distributed with the correct syntax to ensure it will build properly the first time.

The cmdlets to review are

```
Get-VpnConnection
Add-VpnConnection
Remove-VpnConnection
Set-VpnConnection
Set-VpnConnectionProxy
```

The Get-VpnConnection cmdlet allows you to see the status of current VPN connections. A connection has to be set up or this cmdlet will have no output.

```
# - to get current VPN Connection status
Get-VpnConnection
```

It is a simple process to add and remove a specific VPN connection. The following configuration will build out an example VPN configuration and remove it. In this case we are using the ServerAddress parameter as vpn.example. com which could be resolved with either an A or AAAA record.

```
# - generate EAP configuration
$EAPConf = New-EapConfiguration -UseWinlogonCredential

# - generate new VPN
Add-VpnConnection -Name "TestVPN" -ServerAddress "vpn.example.com" -TunnelType Ikev2
-EncryptionLevel Required -AuthenticationMethod Eap -SplitTunneling -EapConfigXmlStream
$EAPConf.EapConfigXmlStream
```

And the output shows it is working as expected.

```
PS C:\Windows\system32> # - generate EAP configuration
$EAPConf = New-EapConfiguration -UseWinlogonCredential
# - generate new VPN
Add-VpnConnection -Name "TestVPN" -ServerAddress "vpn.example.com" -TunnelType Ikev2
-EncryptionLevel Required -AuthenticationMethod Eap -SplitTunneling -EapConfigXmlStream
$EAPConf.EapConfigXmlStream
```

The configuration can be confirmed by running the Get-VpnConnection cmdlet after adding the VPN connection. The output shows that the VPN connection configuration was built out.

```
PS C:\Windows\system32> Get-VpnConnection

Name                   : TestVPN
ServerAddress          : vpn.example.com
AllUserConnection      : False
Guid                   : {E3E4F5BB-9F53-4910-AE53-82C6AB2AA44F}
TunnelType             : Ikev2
AuthenticationMethod   : {Eap}
EncryptionLevel        : Required
L2tpIPsecAuth          :
UseWinlogonCredential  : False
EapConfigXmlStream     : #document
ConnectionStatus       : Disconnected
NapState               : NotConnected
RememberCredential     : False
SplitTunneling         : True
```

You can remove the VPN connection from the host with

```
# - remove the VPN named "TestVPN"
Remove-VpnConnection -Name "TestVPN" -Force
```

The output should be confirmed with a Get-VpnConnection as shown.

```
PS C:\Windows\system32> Remove-VpnConnection -Name "TestVPN" -Force

PS C:\Windows\system32> Get-VpnConnection
```

Finally, you can change the VPN Connection parameters without having to remove and rebuild the configuration. You can do this with the Set-VpnConnection and Set-VpnConnectionProxy cmdlets as shown.

```
# -  change the VPN parameters of TestVPN
Set-VpnConnection -Name "TestVPN" -ServerAddress "[2001:db8:cafe:a::1]"

# - set up a proxy VPN
Set-VpnConnectionProxy -Name "TestVPN" -ProxyServer "[2001:db8:cafe:a::1]:8080" -BypassProxyForLocal
```

The output shows the changes.

```
PS C:\Windows\system32> Set-VpnConnection -Name "TestVPN" -ServerAddress "[2001:db8:cafe:a::1]"

PS C:\Windows\system32> Set-VpnConnectionProxy -Name "TestVPN" -ProxyServer
"[2001:db8:cafe:a::1]:8080" -BypassProxyForLocal

PS C:\Windows\system32> Get-VpnConnection

Name                  : TestVPN
ServerAddress         : [2001:db8:cafe:a::1]
AllUserConnection     : False
Guid                  : {E3E4F5BB-9F53-4910-AE53-82C6AB2AA44F}
TunnelType            : Ikev2
AuthenticationMethod  : {Eap}
EncryptionLevel       : Required
L2tpIPsecAuth         :
UseWinlogonCredential : False
EapConfigXmlStream    : #document
ConnectionStatus      : Disconnected
NapState              : NotConnected
RememberCredential    : False
SplitTunneling        : True
```

Conclusion

This chapter provided IPv6 PowerShell information on configuring network interfaces, the IPv6 transition technologies, IPsec, and VPN. Some of the biggest challenges in deploying IPv6 are understanding some of the options you have for configuring the protocol and, additionally, the tools that you need to manipulate them. The goal is to give you the framework of the PowerShell cmdlets you need so that you can properly manage and manipulate your IPv6 configuration in your Windows environment. With the adoption of cloud computing and automation, understanding how to use PowerShell is a critical skill and, we hope, this chapter has outlined the cmdlets you need to know to properly manage and deploy IPv6.

## CHAPTER 6

IPv6 and the Windows Firewall

When Microsoft took the opportunity to rewrite the networking protocol stack for Windows it also chose to build out a robust and very advanced firewall. Windows Firewall with Advanced Security (WFAS) has many capabilities that far exceed the industry standard in terms of programmatic controls and extensibility. One of the key differences is the ability to utilize PowerShell and Group Policy to control what happens in the firewall.

Microsoft also added IPv6 controls side by side with IPv4, allowing the firewall to perform functions for either network protocol. In addition, Microsoft enabled advanced management of QoS (quality of service) and virtual private network (VPN), also allowing them to be managed via Group Policy, netsh, and PowerShell. Microsoft has built into the server and client operating system (OS) the most robust remotely administrative firewall and advanced security solution available for Windows.

■ **Note** This chapter reinforces the importance of learning PowerShell. Not only are general network settings capable of being managed and controlled by PowerShell, but the firewall and all its associated features and functions can be managed as well. At this point you should realize that PowerShell is a must-*know* tool, and a skill you need to develop. There are third-party firewalls that are available for use with Windows; however, they do not have the same integration and extensibility that the Windows firewall has built in. Third-party firewalls were very popular with Windows XP, likely due to some of the vulnerabilities in the OS. It is no longer necessary or even recommended to use a third-party firewall with Windows. Anti-malware and anti-virus are another matter and not covered though those products can impact the firewall behavior.

PowerShell Transport Layer Filters

Windows Server 2008, 2008R2, 2012, and 2012R2 have the ability to manage Transmission Control Protocol (TCP) characteristics per destination network. This allows us to control specific behavior of a TCP session so that it is tuned to what is required to reach a specific destination. We do this via transport layer filters.

A transport layer filter is only concerned with the TCP protocol itself. Transport layers allow you to control TCP characteristics based on the networks a host is trying to reach and to apply those parameters based on the network filter information. The cmdlets for managing transport filters are

```
Get-NetTCPSetting
Get-NetTransportFilter
New-NetTransportFilter
Remove-NetTransportFilter
```

The following is an example showing what TCP settings the host currently has and also what the transport filter looks like:

```
# - next show all the specific TCP settings and what Transport filter options are available
Get-NetTCPSetting

# - next show the Transport filters
Get-NetTransportFilter
```

The output from executing these cmdlets is as follows:

```
PS C:\Windows\system32> Get-NetTCPSetting

SettingName                     : Automatic
MinRto(ms)                      :
InitialCongestionWindow(MSS)    :
CongestionProvider              :
CwndRestart                     :
DelayedAckTimeout(ms)           :
MemoryPressureProtection        :
AutoTuningLevelLocal            :
AutoTuningLevelGroupPolicy      :
AutoTuningLevelEffective        :
EcnCapability                   :
Timestamps                      :
InitialRto(ms)                  :
ScalingHeuristics               :
DynamicPortRangeStartPort       :
DynamicPortRangeNumberOfPorts   :

SettingName                     : Custom
MinRto(ms)                      : 20
InitialCongestionWindow(MSS)    : 4
CongestionProvider              : DCTCP
CwndRestart                     : True
DelayedAckTimeout(ms)           : 10
MemoryPressureProtection        : Disabled
AutoTuningLevelLocal            : Normal
AutoTuningLevelGroupPolicy      : NotConfigured
AutoTuningLevelEffective        : Local
EcnCapability                   : Disabled
Timestamps                      : Disabled
InitialRto(ms)                  : 3000
ScalingHeuristics               : Disabled
DynamicPortRangeStartPort       : 49152
DynamicPortRangeNumberOfPorts   : 16384

SettingName                     : Compat
MinRto(ms)                      : 300
InitialCongestionWindow(MSS)    : 2
CongestionProvider              : Default
CwndRestart                     : False
```

```
DelayedAckTimeout(ms)            : 200
MemoryPressureProtection         : Disabled
AutoTuningLevelLocal             : Normal
AutoTuningLevelGroupPolicy       : NotConfigured
AutoTuningLevelEffective         : Local
EcnCapability                    : Disabled
Timestamps                       : Disabled
InitialRto(ms)                   : 3000
ScalingHeuristics                : Disabled
DynamicPortRangeStartPort        : 49152
DynamicPortRangeNumberOfPorts    : 16384

SettingName                      : Datacenter
MinRto(ms)                       : 20
InitialCongestionWindow(MSS)     : 4
CongestionProvider               : DCTCP
CwndRestart                      : True
DelayedAckTimeout(ms)            : 10
MemoryPressureProtection         : Disabled
AutoTuningLevelLocal             : Normal
AutoTuningLevelGroupPolicy       : NotConfigured
AutoTuningLevelEffective         : Local
EcnCapability                    : Disabled
Timestamps                       : Disabled
InitialRto(ms)                   : 3000
ScalingHeuristics                : Disabled
DynamicPortRangeStartPort        : 49152
DynamicPortRangeNumberOfPorts    : 16384

SettingName                      : Internet
MinRto(ms)                       : 300
InitialCongestionWindow(MSS)     : 4
CongestionProvider               : CTCP
CwndRestart                      : False
DelayedAckTimeout(ms)            : 50
MemoryPressureProtection         : Disabled
AutoTuningLevelLocal             : Normal
AutoTuningLevelGroupPolicy       : NotConfigured
AutoTuningLevelEffective         : Local
EcnCapability                    : Disabled
Timestamps                       : Disabled
InitialRto(ms)                   : 3000
ScalingHeuristics                : Disabled
DynamicPortRangeStartPort        : 49152
DynamicPortRangeNumberOfPorts    : 16384

PS C:\Windows\system32> Get-NetTransportFilter

SettingName       : Internet
Protocol          : TCP
LocalPortStart    : 0
```

```
LocalPortEnd      : 65535
RemotePortStart   : 0
RemotePortEnd     : 65535
DestinationPrefix : *
```

Transport filters are not something that is commonly deployed unless you need to tune TCP settings in your environment. More important, they are designed to be used only on a Windows server and cannot be used on Windows client at all.

The following examples simply define the destination prefixes (both IPv4 and IPv6) that require the prebuilt Datacenter settings (which are shown above). This redefining will force the OS to apply the Datacenter TCP parameters to anything going to those destinations.

```
# - you can create a custom Transport filter using
New-NetTransportFilter -SettingName Datacenter -DestinationPrefix 10.0.0.0/8
New-NetTransportFilter -SettingName Datacenter -DestinationPrefix
2001:db8:cafe:10::/64
# - confirm the new Transport filters were added
Get-NetTransportFilter
```

The scripts output is as follows:

```
PS C:\> New-NetTransportFilter -SettingName Datacenter -DestinationPrefix 10.0.0.0/8
SettingName       : Datacenter
Protocol          : TCP
LocalPortStart    : 0
LocalPortEnd      : 65535
RemotePortStart   : 0
RemotePortEnd     : 65535
DestinationPrefix : 10.0.0.0/8
PS C:\> New-NetTransportFilter -SettingName Datacenter -DestinationPrefix 2001:db8:cafe:10::/64
SettingName       : Datacenter
Protocol          : TCP
LocalPortStart    : 0
LocalPortEnd      : 65535
RemotePortStart   : 0
RemotePortEnd     : 65535
DestinationPrefix : 2001:db8:cafe:10::/64
PS C:\> Get-NetTransportFilter
SettingName       : Automatic
Protocol          : TCP
LocalPortStart    : 0
LocalPortEnd      : 65535
RemotePortStart   : 0
RemotePortEnd     : 65535
DestinationPrefix : *
SettingName       : Datacenter
Protocol          : TCP
LocalPortStart    : 0
LocalPortEnd      : 65535
RemotePortStart   : 0
RemotePortEnd     : 65535
DestinationPrefix : 2001:db8:cafe:10::/64
```

```
SettingName      : Datacenter
Protocol         : TCP
LocalPortStart   : 0
LocalPortEnd     : 65535
RemotePortStart  : 0
RemotePortEnd    : 65535
DestinationPrefix : 10.0.0.0/8
```

To remove a transport filter, you would do the following:

```
# - remove the custom Transport filters - you can add -confirm:$false if you want to avoid
# - the interactive confirmation prompts from PowerShell
Remove-NetTransportFilter -SettingName Datacenter -DestinationPrefix 10.0.0.0/8
Remove-NetTransportFilter -SettingName Datacenter -DestinationPrefix 2001:db8:cafe:10::/64
# - check the status to confirm they have been removed
Get-NetTransportFilter
```

The output from removing looks as follows:

```
PS C:\> Remove-NetTransportFilter -SettingName Datacenter -DestinationPrefix 10.0.0.0/8
PS C:\> Remove-NetTransportFilter -SettingName Datacenter -DestinationPrefix 2001:db8:cafe:10::/64
PS C:\> Get-NetTransportFilter
SettingName      : Automatic
Protocol         : TCP
LocalPortStart   : 0
LocalPortEnd     : 65535
RemotePortStart  : 0
RemotePortEnd    : 65535
DestinationPrefix : *
```

That's pretty much all there is to managing transport filters. If you are using a Windows server in your Datacenter then transport filters might be a useful tool to help insure you get the performance and parameters correct between Datacenter locations. PowerShell makes quick work of what needs to be done. Once again, I can't underscore strongly enough the benefits from learning PowerShell. It is well worth your time to learn.

Understanding Profiles

Windows makes use of several types of profiles: wireless network profiles and firewall profiles just to name a few. These two profile types can be related and slightly confusing, so let's review them quickly. Let's first define wireless network profiles and how firewall profiles are mapped to them.

Wireless Network Profiles

Wireless network profiles allow the client OS to remember standard wireless configurations and have different preference rules (order of operation) for joining a wireless network. Also, wireless network profiles can be added and removed from the OS; however, firewall profiles are permanent. Realistically, wireless network profiles will have a firewall profile associated with them based on the parameters you give the OS upon joining a new wireless network. The firewall profiles are detailed in the next section. If you indicate that you want to look for network shares, printers or TVs, for example, then Windows assumes you are on a private or domain (work) network as defined by the Public Domain profile. It can determine the domain-joined network automatically. If you indicate you don't want to share anything, then it assumes you are on a public network.

■ **Caution**   Wireless network profiles often are referenced in a similar way to firewall profiles and it is easy to confuse the two. More details can be found at `http://windows.microsoft.com/en-US/windows-8/manage-wireless-network-profiles`, which covers network profiles specifically.

Figure 6-1 shows the standard Windows 8.1 dialog prompt you get after joining a new wireless network for the first time. In this example I have joined the wireless network "HOWFUNKY" and you can see that the option clearly is prompting to determine what firewall profile to assign to this wireless connection.

Figure 6-1. *Wireless firewall profile prompt*

Each wireless network the Windows client OS joins will establish a wireless network profile. For Windows Vista and Windows 7 these profiles could be managed more directly through the graphical user interface (GUI), but in Windows 8 and Windows 8.1 they are hidden away from the end user and managed dynamically. You can utilize netsh to get more information and to remove wireless network profiles if needed. Some example netsh commands to manage wireless networks are

```
# - to clear the wireless key for profile HOWFUNKY
netsh wlan show profile name="HOWFUNKY" key=clear
# - to delete the profile named HOWFUNKY
netsh wlan delete profile name="HOWFUNKY"
# - to set the connection mode from "automatic" to "manual" for wifi association
netsh wlan set profileparameter name="HOWFUNKY" connectionmode=manual
```

A netsh example of displaying the HOWFUNKY profile information from the wireless connection from Figure 6-1 is

```
PS C:\> netsh wlan show profile name="HOWFUNKY"
Profile HOWFUNKY on interface Wi-Fi:
=======================================================================
Applied: All User Profile
Profile information
-------------------
    Version             : 1
    Type                : Wireless LAN
    Name                : HOWFUNKY
    Control options     :
        Connection mode    : Connect manually
        Network broadcast  : Connect only if this network is broadcasting
        AutoSwitch         : Do not switch to other networks

Connectivity settings
---------------------
    Number of SSIDs     : 1
    SSID name           : "HOWFUNKY"
    Network type        : Infrastructure
    Radio type          : [ Any Radio Type ]
    Vendor extension      : Not present
Security settings
-----------------
    Authentication      : WPA2-Personal
    Cipher              : CCMP
    Security key        : Present
Cost settings
-------------
    Cost                : Unrestricted
    Congested           : No
    Approaching Data Limit : No
    Over Data Limit     : No
    Roaming             : No
    Cost Source         : Default
```

I am not aware of any specific PowerShell cmdlets that are capable of providing the same functionality that the previous netsh commands provide. If you require scripted managing of the wireless connection profiles, then utilizing Group Policy to run a remote script with netsh is likely the best practice today.

Firewall Profiles

One of the unique aspects of the Windows OS is the concept of firewall profiles. The Windows OS utilizes firewall profiles to define what the OS should utilize (two are named Public and Private, for instance) for a security posture to have while connected to that network.

When you first connect to a network with Windows Vista, Windows 7, Windows 8, or Windows 8.1 the OS will prompt you to indicate if you want to share resources (are you on a home private network, for instance) and trust resources on that network or not. The wireless or wired interface will have an associated firewall profile that is built out. The options for the connection profiles are Public (Internet), Private and DomainAuthenticated. These are the only firewall profiles available; you cannot create new ones or delete them.

Let's get back to firewall profiles and how they impact the Windows firewall. Firewall profiles happen to align with the Windows firewall in that each firewall profile has associated firewall rules. You can use the following PowerShell cmdlets to control the Windows firewall profiles:

```
Get-NetFirewallProfile
Set-NetFirewallProfile
```

The first cmdlet of Get-NetFirewallProfile will output all the existing firewall profiles on the host (unfortunately it will not tell you which interfaces it is associated with). The following example output shows by default what is set in Windows 8.1:

```
PS C:\> Get-NetFirewallProfile
Name                            : Domain
Enabled                         : True
DefaultInboundAction            : NotConfigured
DefaultOutboundAction           : NotConfigured
AllowInboundRules               : NotConfigured
AllowLocalFirewallRules         : NotConfigured
AllowLocalIPsecRules            : NotConfigured
AllowUserApps                   : NotConfigured
AllowUserPorts                  : NotConfigured
AllowUnicastResponseToMulticast : NotConfigured
NotifyOnListen                  : True
EnableStealthModeForIPsec       : NotConfigured
LogFileName                     : %systemroot%\system32\LogFiles\Firewall\pfirewall.log
LogMaxSizeKilobytes             : 4096
LogAllowed                      : False
LogBlocked                      : False
LogIgnored                      : NotConfigured
DisabledInterfaceAliases        : {NotConfigured}
Name                            : Private
Enabled                         : True
DefaultInboundAction            : NotConfigured
DefaultOutboundAction           : NotConfigured
AllowInboundRules               : NotConfigured
AllowLocalFirewallRules         : NotConfigured
AllowLocalIPsecRules            : NotConfigured
AllowUserApps                   : NotConfigured
AllowUserPorts                  : NotConfigured
AllowUnicastResponseToMulticast : NotConfigured
NotifyOnListen                  : True
EnableStealthModeForIPsec       : NotConfigured
LogFileName                     : %systemroot%\system32\LogFiles\Firewall\pfirewall.log
LogMaxSizeKilobytes             : 4096
LogAllowed                      : False
LogBlocked                      : False
LogIgnored                      : NotConfigured
DisabledInterfaceAliases        : {NotConfigured}
Name                            : Public
Enabled                         : True
DefaultInboundAction            : NotConfigured
DefaultOutboundAction           : NotConfigured
```

```
AllowInboundRules                 : NotConfigured
AllowLocalFirewallRules           : NotConfigured
AllowLocalIPsecRules              : NotConfigured
AllowUserApps                     : NotConfigured
AllowUserPorts                    : NotConfigured
AllowUnicastResponseToMulticast   : NotConfigured
NotifyOnListen                    : True
EnableStealthModeForIPsec         : NotConfigured
LogFileName                       : %systemroot%\system32\LogFiles\Firewall\pfirewall.log
LogMaxSizeKilobytes               : 4096
LogAllowed                        : False
LogBlocked                        : False
LogIgnored                        : NotConfigured
DisabledInterfaceAliases          : {NotConfigured}
```

To determine the interface to which you should apply the firewall profile, use the Get-NetConnectionProfile cmdlets. The follow example shows the output of the cmdlets:

```
PS C:\> Get-NetConnectionProfile

Name              : Unidentified network
InterfaceAlias    : Network Adapter VMnet1
InterfaceIndex    : 20
NetworkCategory   : Public
IPv4Connectivity  : NoTraffic
IPv6Connectivity  : NoTraffic

Name              : Unidentified network
InterfaceAlias    : Network Adapter VMnet6
InterfaceIndex    : 22
NetworkCategory   : Public
IPv4Connectivity  : NoTraffic
IPv6Connectivity  : NoTraffic

Name              : Unidentified network
InterfaceAlias    : Network Adapter VMnet8
InterfaceIndex    : 21
NetworkCategory   : Public
IPv4Connectivity  : NoTraffic
IPv6Connectivity  : NoTraffic

Name              : HOWFUNKY
InterfaceAlias    : Wi-Fi
InterfaceIndex    : 4
NetworkCategory   : Private
IPv4Connectivity  : Internet
IPv6Connectivity  : Internet
```

As you can see, each profile has parameter settings and a status. If we want to modify the firewall profile we could do so using the Set-NetFirewallProfile cmdlet and define appropriate parameters. In this example I will simply turn off the domain firewall on the host OS and then turn it back on. I have removed some of the PowerShell output in the example and emphasized the salient parameters.

```
PS C:\> Set-NetFirewallProfile -profile domain -Enabled False
PS C:\> get-netfirewallprofile -profile domain
Name                        : Domain
Enabled                     : False
DefaultInboundAction        : NotConfigured
DefaultOutboundAction       : NotConfigured
<...>
PS C:\> Set-NetFirewallProfile -profile domain -Enabled True
PS C:\> get-netfirewallprofile -profile domain
Name                        : Domain
Enabled                     : True
DefaultInboundAction        : NotConfigured
DefaultOutboundAction       : NotConfigured
<...>
```

You can turn on all the firewall profiles (which is best practice and the default setting of Windows) by doing
`Set-NetFirewallProfile -Profile Domain,Public,Private -Enabled True`.

Firewall profiles are not something you will typically modify much except to perhaps enable or disable them when troubleshooting and also to apply them to the correct wireless network profile to have appropriate firewall rules applied.

PowerShell Advanced Firewall Rules

Beyond the transport filters and the firewall profiles are the standard firewall rules that impact most administrators. When deploying firewall rules there are two general approaches that make the most sense. You should build a generic set of firewall rules that are applied to all hosts in your environment, or alternately build rule sets that are specific for client hosts (Windows 7, 8, or 8.1, for instance) and another for your server hosts. The reality is that your server firewall rules should likely be more restrictive because you know all the specific services and connection requests that host should be making (in theory). You will need to determine if these rules apply to all the firewall profile types (Private, Public and Domain) or only to a subset.

You will want to apply these rules utilizing your favorite deployment method. You can find details on how to utilize a Group Policy Object (GPO) for this function at `http://technet.microsoft.com/en-us/library/cc753955%28v=WS.10%29.aspx` and I will cover PowerShell next to show how flexible Windows is in manipulating the firewall.

Do realize, it is also possible to do much of the same work utilizing netsh commands. Microsoft outlines how to do that at `http://technet.microsoft.com/en-us/library/cc771920%28WS.10%29.aspx` and it makes sense to review that site if you are limited to netsh as a deployment option.

■ **Note** Microsoft has made available information about the WFAS design process and it is a worthwhile read if you plan on implementing specific security policies within your environment. It can be found at `http://technet.microsoft.com/en-us/library/jj721516.aspx`.

The common PowerShell cmdlets for the Advanced Firewall are

```
Get-NetFirewallRule
New-NetFirewallRule
Disable-NetFirewallRule
Enable-NetFirewallRule
Remove-NetFirewallRule
```

```
Copy-NetFirewallRule
Rename-NetFirewallRule
Show-NetFirewallRule
```

These cmdlets are capable of building rules for IPv4, IPv6, ICMPv4, and ICMPv6 along with several other protocol types in addition to TCP and UDP (User Datagram Protocol), which are the most commonly used. You can also leverage netsh commands if PowerShell is not available on the Windows OS version you are attempting to change firewall rules on. Some netsh command examples for the firewall are

```
netsh advfirewall firewall show rule name=all
netsh advfirewall firewall add rule name="Block ICMPv6 Outbound" dir=out protocol=icmpv6
action=block
netsh advfirewall firewall show rule name="Block ICMPv6 Outbound"
netsh advfirewall firewall delete rule name="Block ICMPv6 Outbound"
```

To learn all the syntax for the netsh commands simply use the "?" after the command to determine the parameters and syntax format required. This example output shows what parameters are available for rule:

```
PS C:\> netsh advfirewall firewall show rule ?
Usage: show rule name=<string>
        [profile=public|private|domain|any[,...]]
        [type=static|dynamic]
        [verbose]
Remarks:
- Displays all matching rules as specified by name and optionally,
        profiles and type. If verbose is specified all matching rules are
        displayed.
Examples:
        Display all dynamic inbound rules:
        netsh advfirewall firewall show rule name=all dir=in type=dynamic
        Display all the settings for all inbound rules called
        "allow browser":
        netsh advfirewall firewall show rule name="allow browser" verbose
```

Often you first need to know what firewall rules you have on your Windows host. You do this by utilizing the Get-NetFirewallRule cmdlet. This will display all the firewall rules (the example output has been shortened because the typical output is very long).

```
PS C:\> Get-NetFirewallRule
Name                 : vm-monitoring-icmpv6
DisplayName          : Virtual Machine Monitoring (Echo Request - ICMPv6-In)
Description          : Echo Request messages are sent as ping requests to other nodes.
DisplayGroup         : Virtual Machine Monitoring
Group                : @vmicres.dll,-700
Enabled              : False
Profile              : Any
Platform             : {}
Direction            : Inbound
Action               : Allow
EdgeTraversalPolicy  : Block
LooseSourceMapping   : False
```

```
LocalOnlyMapping      : False
Owner                 :
PrimaryStatus         : OK
Status                : The rule was parsed successfully from the store. (65536)
EnforcementStatus     : NotApplicable
PolicyStoreSource     : PersistentStore
PolicyStoreSourceType : Local
Name                  : vm-monitoring-rpc
DisplayName           : Virtual Machine Monitoring (RPC)
Description           : Allow Task Scheduler service to be remotely managed via RPC/TCP.
DisplayGroup          : Virtual Machine Monitoring
Group                 : @vmicres.dll,-700
Enabled               : False
Profile               : Any
Platform              : {}
Direction             : Inbound
Action                : Allow
EdgeTraversalPolicy   : Block
LooseSourceMapping    : False
LocalOnlyMapping      : False
Owner                 :
PrimaryStatus         : OK
Status                : The rule was parsed successfully from the store. (65536)
EnforcementStatus     : NotApplicable
PolicyStoreSource     : PersistentStore
PolicyStoreSourceType : Local
Name                  : vm-monitoring-icmpv4
DisplayName           : Virtual Machine Monitoring (Echo Request - ICMPv4-In)
Description           : Echo Request messages are sent as ping requests to other nodes.
DisplayGroup          : Virtual Machine Monitoring
Group                 : @vmicres.dll,-700
Enabled               : False
Profile               : Any
Platform              : {}
Direction             : Inbound
Action                : Allow
EdgeTraversalPolicy   : Block
LooseSourceMapping    : False
LocalOnlyMapping      : False
Owner                 :
PrimaryStatus         : OK
Status                : The rule was parsed successfully from the store. (65536)
EnforcementStatus     : NotApplicable
PolicyStoreSource     : PersistentStore
PolicyStoreSourceType : Local
<...>
```

As you can see, the `Get-NetFirewallRule` cmdlet provides all sorts of useful information, but it is more typical that you would want the number of active or enabled rules. For example,

```
PS C:\> Get-NetFirewallRule -Enabled true | measure
Count    : 183
<...>
```

If you just want to see the private firewall profile then you can issue `Get-NetFirewallProfile -name Private |`
`Get-NetFirewallRule`.

This outputs only the firewall rules that are involved in the private firewall profile on the host. Using these PowerShell cmdlets you can determine what firewall rules are being enforced. The next challenge is to add and remove rules that you many want to apply.

You should be aware of some key items for the PowerShell that is used in building new firewall rules. By default, if no profile (firewall profile) is assigned in the cmdlet then the firewall rule is applied to all the profiles. This is likely *not* the behavior you want. It is best practice to explicitly define the profile you would like to apply the rules to or the combination of profiles.

The following PowerShell cmdlets examples are used for demonstrate the firewall rules cmdlets:

```
# - example of creating a new firewall rule
# - blocking the telnet application (not just a port)
New-NetFirewallRule -DisplayName "Block Outbound Telnet" -Direction Outbound -Program %SystemRoot%\
System32\tlntsvr.exe -Protocol TCP -LocalPort 23 -Action Block

# - remove the firewall rule
Remove-NetFirewallRule -DisplayName "Block Outbound Telnet"
```

When executed in PowerShell the output looks as follows:

```
PS C:\> New-NetFirewallRule -DisplayName "Block Outbound Telnet" -Direction Outbound -Program
%SystemRoot%\System32\tlntsvr.exe -Protocol TCP -LocalPort 23 -Action Block

Name                 : {dc21d241-13f8-4e9d-a081-da9fbf685704}
DisplayName          : Block Outbound Telnet
Description          :
DisplayGroup         :
Group                :
Enabled              : True
Profile              : Any
Platform             : {}
Direction            : Outbound
Action               : Block
EdgeTraversalPolicy  : Block
LooseSourceMapping   : False
LocalOnlyMapping     : False
Owner                :
PrimaryStatus        : OK
Status               : The rule was parsed successfully from the store. (65536)
EnforcementStatus    : NotApplicable
PolicyStoreSource    : PersistentStore
PolicyStoreSourceType : Local
PS C:\> Get-NetFirewallRule -DisplayName "Block Outbound Telnet"
Name                 : {dc21d241-13f8-4e9d-a081-da9fbf685704}
```

```
DisplayName            : Block Outbound Telnet
Description            :
DisplayGroup           :
Group                  :
Enabled                : True
Profile                : Any
Platform               : {}
Direction              : Outbound
Action                 : Block
EdgeTraversalPolicy    : Block
LooseSourceMapping     : False
LocalOnlyMapping       : False
Owner                  :
PrimaryStatus          : OK
Status                 : The rule was parsed successfully from the store. (65536)
EnforcementStatus      : NotApplicable
PolicyStoreSource      : PersistentStore
PolicyStoreSourceType  : Local
PS C:\> Remove-NetFirewallRule -DisplayName "Block Outbound Telnet"
PS C:\>
```

The next example shows how to block 6to4 for the public firewall profile. Alternately, you could set the profile parameter to Any and it would apply it to all the firewall profiles, or if the parameter value was left out it would default to applying it to all. The example includes both the PowerShell and netsh commands to compare them.

```
# - example of blocking a specific IPv4 address to prevent 6to4
New-NetFirewallRule -DisplayName "Block 6to4 Outbound" -Direction Outbound -Protocol 41
-RemoteAddress 192.88.99.1 -Action Block -Profile Public

# - you can do the same command with netsh with
netsh advfirewall firewall add rule name="Block 6to4 Outbound" dir=out protocol=41
remoteip=192.88.99.1 action=block profile=public
# - to display the firewall rule use
Get-NetFirewallRule -DisplayName "Block 6to4 Outbound"
# - and to display the firewall rule with netsh
netsh advfirewall firewall show rule name="Block 6to4 Outbound"
# - finally to remove the rule with PowerShell
Remove-NetFirewallRule -DisplayName "Block 6to4 Outbound"
# - and to remove it with netsh
netsh advfirewall firewall delete rule name="Block 6to4 Outbound"
```

Windows client and server have numerous existing firewall rules for each profile type in addition to any you choose to implement separately. It can be daunting to review all the existing firewall policy rules that are in place, so some PowerShell reporting might make things a bit easier to understand. To capture all the firewall policy rules you can use something like Get-NetFirewallRule | Out-File C:\firewall.out.file.txt.

Alternately, you can utilize the export cmdlet and get the firewall rules into an Excel spreadsheet to allow easier auditing. It is possible to also export it as html or xml. This might be something you would want to do against your Windows servers on a regular basis to audit them for changes.

```
Get-NetFirewallRule | Export-Csv C:\ firewall.out.file.csv
```

Best practice is to utilize PowerShell and PowerShell remoting to handle pushing firewall rules and updates across your Windows servers and client devices. If that is not an option due to OS version issues or lack of PowerShell remoting support then utilizing netsh commands as a script via Group Policy is the next best solution.

Individual Server Firewall Management

It is possible on a Windows server to use the WFAS GUI to manage all the inbound and outbound rules for the firewall. Figure 6-2 is a screenshot showing each of the rule types (inbound, outbound, and connection security) and additionally the profiles (domain, private, public).

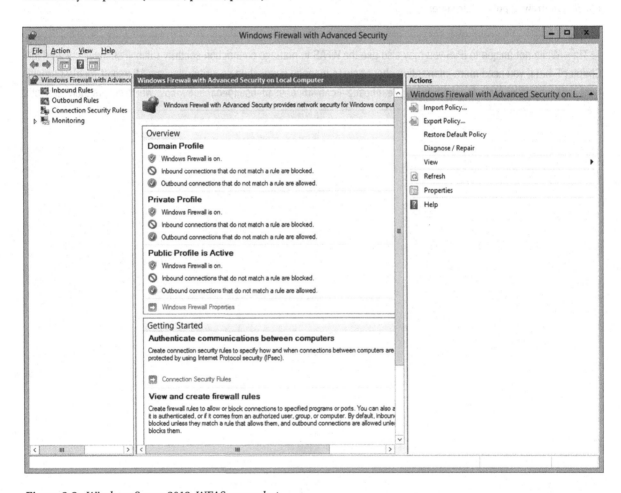

Figure 6-2. *Windows Server 2012, WFAS screenshot*

One nice feature is the ability to import and export policy rules, but be extremely careful when doing this. If you import new firewall policy rules they completely replace existing ones so you will lose all changes if they are not in the new imported rules. There are also options on where to keep log files along with options for setting up IPsec (Internet protocol security) parameters.

If you will be managing more than one firewall configuration on a server I do not recommend the WFAS GUI as your primary management method. It is much easier to utilize PowerShell to do the same repeatable tasks and know that they are easy to roll back also. This would principally apply to non–domain-joined Windows hosts, for instance, if you are running standalone instances of a Windows server in Windows Azure.

Finally, if you are managing Windows server and client hosts and need to apply firewall policy rules then Group Policy with netsh is your best option if you do not have Windows 8 and 8.1 or Windows 2012 and 2012R2 domain-joined hosts. It will ensure you have the broadest support for Windows hosts for now. If you are not domain-joined but fortunate to be able to utilize all PowerShell I recommend doing so as it will be much easier to maintain going forward. Microsoft recommends managing all domain-joined Windows servers and clients with Group Policy, regardless of the tool you are using to execute the firewall rules; it keeps your Windows hosts in a more consistent firewall policy rule state.

■ **Tip**   While not unique to IPv6 you may also use the WFAS to manage connection security rules. IPsec was covered in Chapter 5 but if you need more information about how to manage connection security rules see Microsoft TechNet article http://technet.microsoft.com/library/e36be3e2-6cab-4b06-984d-b5649e04eb66.aspx, which covers them in depth.

■ ■ ■

## CHAPTER 7

IPv6 in Hyper-V and Virtual Networking

Some of the most transformative changes happening in information technology (IT) today are in virtualization. It is what enables large-scale cloud automation, multi-tenant solutions running on shared hardware, and efficiencies in scale for deploying services.

It is likely that at some point you will deploy (if you have not already) virtualization in your environment. Microsoft has its virtualization hypervisor, called Hyper-V, and additionally it has a virtual networking solution which leverages Network Virtualization Generic Routing Encapsulation (NVGRE) as the protocol to move packets from one virtualization host to another without needing complicated network hardware solutions. Both solutions are integrated tightly within the Microsoft server operating system (OS) and different OS versions have different levels of support and interoperability. The principal concern is what hypervisor the guest virtual machines are operating on. To gain all the newest features Windows Server 2012 R2 is required; however, Windows Server 2008 and greater have many of the same features, the exception being NVGRE which was first introduced with Windows Server 2012.

It is important to cover how each technology utilizes IPv6 and also if there are any specific constraints or concerns you might have to address in your design if you wish to run and use IPv6 in your network.

Let's discuss Hyper-V first and how IPv6 fits into what Microsoft has built into its hypervisor.

Hyper-V and IPv6

Microsoft first released its hypervisor as a beta for Windows Server 2008 and in the second half of 2008 it was automatically made available via a Windows update for all. It has been updated for Windows Server 2008 R2, Server 2012, and Server 2012 R2. It was also made available as a standalone OS hypervisor (Microsoft Hyper-V Server 2008, 2008R2, 2012, and 2012R2) and as a role on Windows server platforms. The hypervisor was extended to the client OS with the release of Windows 8 Pro where Hyper-V could be run as a role too. The standalone free version of Hyper-V Server is available at http://www.microsoft.com/en-us/server-cloud/hyper-v-server/default.aspx and has no licensing requirement.

Hyper-V is a fully functional and high-performance hypervisor that has some unique feature capabilities relative to some of the other hypervisors available in the marketplace. Microsoft has made huge investments in Hyper-V around storage, compute, and, most important for this book, networking. Hyper-V has all the capabilities of the Windows OS in terms of administrative controls (PowerShell remoting for instance) but also gains all its capabilities for IPv6. In fact, Hyper-V has the most robust IPv6 support of all hypervisors in the industry today, mainly due to being able to leverage all the work that was done for Windows.

So what specific features does Hyper-V support relating to IPv6 and what potential impact will that have when attempting to run guest virtual machines (VMs) on those platforms? Because Hyper-V is leveraging the network stack of Windows it is able to run all the same transition technologies that Windows server and client have presently for IPv6. Specifically, 6to4, ISATAP, and Teredo can all be run and administered in the same way they are with Windows. There are some caveats: if your Hyper-V deployments are standalone or the free Hyper-V server version (in a workgroup and not domain joined) then you will not be able to leverage Group Policy to manage those Hyper-V hosts, but netsh and PowerShell are still available.

Also, the firewall is available to manage and control in the same fashion but the same caveats apply for managing the rules. You will also limit the capabilities of the Hyper-V instance if you are running on the free Hyper-V Server until you join it to a domain. You can domain join it via PowerShell or from the interactive menu that is provided after you log into the Hyper-V server.

While all the functionality is in Hyper-V server, the management interface for the free Hyper-V Server 2008 and newer does not necessarily allow you the same capabilities initially to set up the Hyper-V server. Because of this let's cover the two separately.

Microsoft Hyper-V Server 2008 Through Hyper-V Server 2012 R2

Microsoft makes the Hyper-V server product available for free. There is no license key required to run the product and all the versions of Hyper-V server support IPv6. As you can see in Figure 7-1 the management interface for the free version of Hyper-V server is different from the Windows server. In this case, the screenshot is of Hyper-V Server 2012 and it shows that you utilize a menu selection initially to set the parameters of the Hyper-V server.

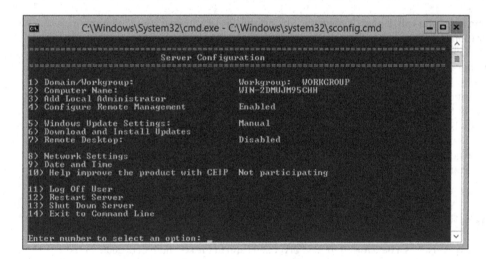

Figure 7-1. *Hyper-V Server 2012 setup*

Next is Figure 7-2, which shows the prompts when selecting option 8 ("Network Settings") from the menu.

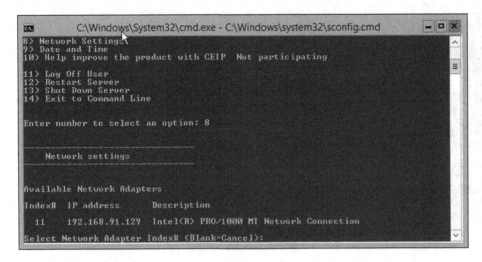

Figure 7-2. *Hyper-V Server 2012 network setting*

Then we come to Figure 7-3, which shows the prompts when selecting the Network Adapter Index (which is 11 in this case) from the menu. Figure 7-3 shows the Hyper-V Server 2012 Network Adapter Index (ZoneID or ScopeID).

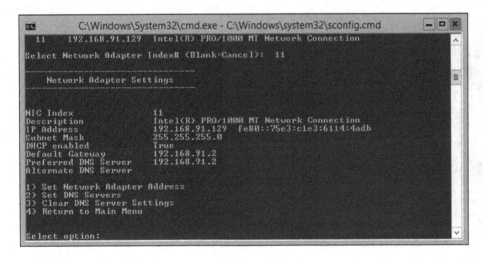

Figure 7-3. *Hyper-V Server 2012 Network Adapter Index*

You will need to select option 1 to set the network adapter address, as shown in Figure 7-4. You will be asked if you are doing a static or Dynamic Host Configuration Protocol (DHCP) configuration for the host. In this case I chose to statically assign the Internet protocol (IP) address for the host.

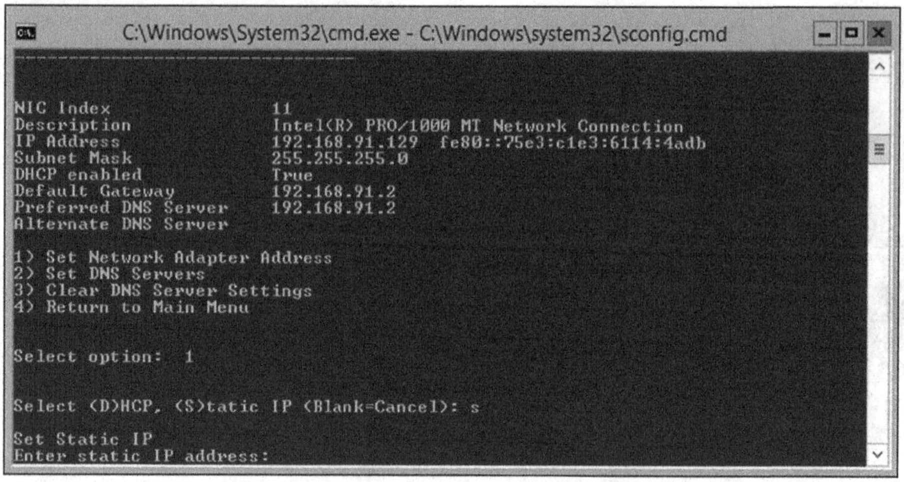

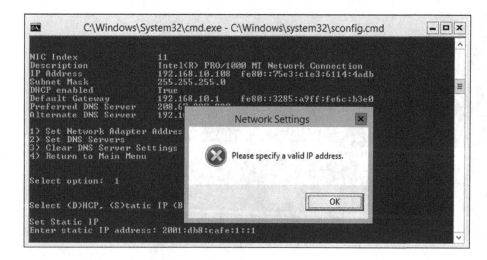

Figure 7-4. *Hyper-V Server 2012 setting network adapter address*

Unfortunately, it seems that the Hyper-V Server 2008 through 2012R2 configuration menu does NOT allow you to statically set any IPv6 address information; as shown in Figure 7-5, you can only input IPv4 information.

Figure 7-5. *Hyper-V Server 2012 with static IPv6 error*

The interesting part is that because Hyper-V Server 2008 through 2012 R2 have full support for IPv6, if you enable the Hyper-V server on a network that already has IPv6 enabled (SLAAC or DHCPv6) it will obtain an IPv6 address as expected and will utilize it. Figure 7-6 shows Hyper-V Server 2012 displaying the IPv4 and link-local IPv6 information in the menu screen.

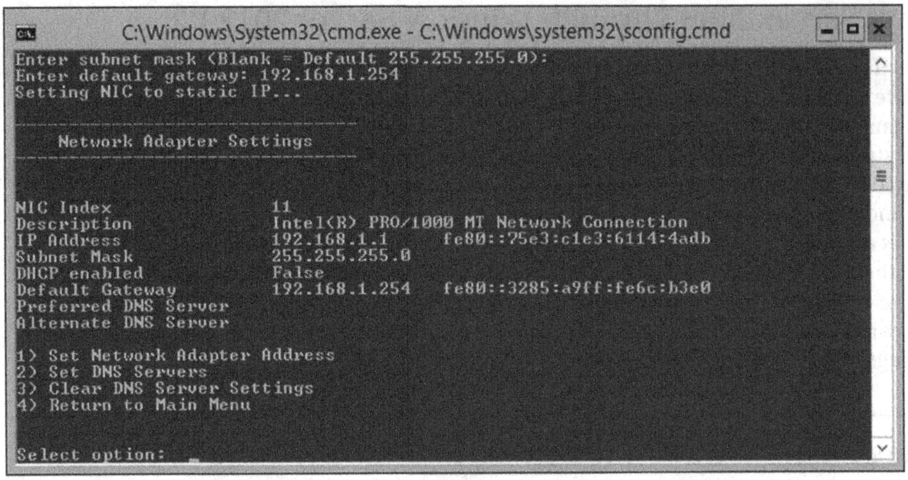

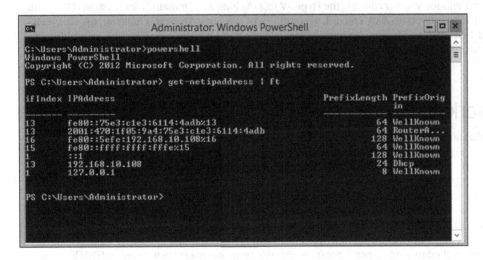

Figure 7-6. *Hyper-V Server 2012 with IPv6 information displayed*

Unfortunately, this output does NOT display the global unicast IPv6 address the host obtained. In order to determine that you must jump into PowerShell and use the Get-NetIPAddress cmdlet to display all the information about the IPv4 and IPv6 addresses that the host has per adapter. Figure 7-7 shows the Hyper-V Server 2012 R2 output.

Figure 7-7. *Hyper-V Server 2012 R2 displaying IP address information*

While it is unfortunate that the interactive menu does not support configuring IPv6 from scratch you can domain join and alternately run PowerShell remoting to reconfigure the Hyper-V server to have whatever network configuration you require. You can also manage the Hyper-V server from System Center or Server Manager which can also be leveraged to build out the adapter and IP address information for each Hyper-V server within your environment. For similar deployments simply use the local console and PowerShell to reconfigure the host as required. Once again, we see how important PowerShell is becoming for managing all aspects of a Windows host.

Microsoft Windows Server 2008 Through Window Server 2012 R2

Unlike Hyper-V Server 2008 through Hyper-V Server 2012 R2, the Windows server family has a more robust initial configuration option because of the full graphical user interface (GUI) Windows has available. If you require the full GUI it is installed by default or if you wish to run a more limited graphical interface you have the option of using minimal server interface (a stripped-down GUI version of Windows server), and finally, no GUI is available for server core. Regardless of which option you choose you will still be using System Center, PowerShell, or Server Manager to administer and run your Windows servers either locally or remotely.

If your Windows servers are domain joined then System Center with Virtual Machine Manager is likely the best solution to manage all the IPv6 parameters of the Hyper-V hosts. Those hosts' configuration parameters can be specified for IPv4 and/or IPv6 and you can leverage Group Policy, PowerShell, netsh, or the registry to set all the other IPv6-specific settings you wish to have on your Hyper-V hosts. You can refer to Chapters 3, 5, and 6 for specific details on managing all those settings.

■ **Tip**   There is a difference in setting Hyper-V host IPv6 settings versus the guest OS IPv6 settings. It is unlikely that you need to spend a lot of time on the Hyper-V host configurations if you already have DHCPv6 set up for the Hyper-V host server network. The most you will want to do is make sure the transition technologies are off. This recommendation matches the best practices for Windows server outlined in Chapter 4.

System Center, PowerShell, Group Policy, and Server Manager all will make use of IPv6 to remotely connect to a remote Hyper-V server or a Windows server running the Hyper-V role. As long as a Domain Name System (DNS) entry is available that resolves to an appropriate AAAA record, everything will just work. The only challenge you will likely find is in environments where you need to leverage network virtualization and determining how your guest VMs will behave with regard to IPv6 network behavior. So let's jump into network virtualization and what Microsoft has built to support that function.

Hyper-V Network Virtualization and IPv6

Hyper-V Network Virtualization (HNV) was first introduced in Windows Server 2012. Microsoft has invested heavily into making HNV a critical element in its Private Cloud solution. Details about HNV can be found at `http://technet.microsoft.com/en-us/library/jj134230.aspx` and details about Microsoft's Private Cloud solution can be found at `http://technet.microsoft.com/en-us/cloud/private-cloud.aspx`.

A key aspect to HNV is how IP traffic is forwarded from one Hyper-V guest on a specific Hyper-V host to another Hyper-V guest in the same or separate IP subnet. It is worth reviewing quickly what HNV actually does from a high level and how that impacts (if at all) IPv6.

HNV leverages NVGRE (Network Virtualization with Generic Routing) in order to allow Hyper-V hosts to have an appropriate encapsulation method to send Hyper-V guest OS IP traffic from one guest OS to another. HNV leverages System Center Virtual Machine Manager (SCVMM) to control the IP (IPv4 and IPv6) forwarding table updates that have to be maintained on all the Hyper-V hosts. SCVMM is able to do this because it knows about all the guest VMs that are operating on the Hyper-V hosts and therefore knows their IP, MAC, and other information required to make such a global decision.

While there are a lot of details and nuances about how NVGRE and SCVMM do the actual process we will simplify it to what is shown in Figure 7-8—a blue tenant (guest) network, along with a red tenant network, and how guest VMs forward traffic from one host to the other on the same tenant network.

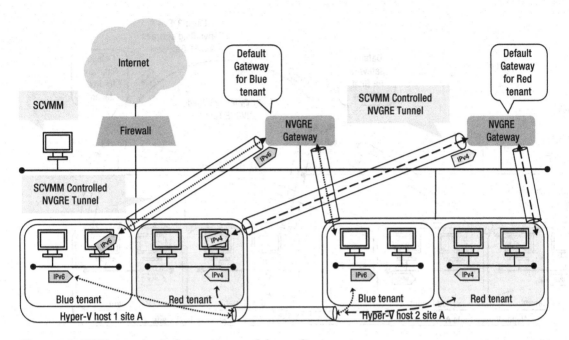

Figure 7-8. *HNV example, single-tenant network forwarding*

Figure 7-8 and the upcoming Figure 7-9 simplify what SCVMM does, but effectively it creates NVGRE tunnel configurations from one Hyper-V host to another. It also indicates what tenant switch packet forwarding should occur to move an IPv6 packet from one Hyper-V host to another for the guest VMs that are present on that Hyper-V host. In order for a tenant to move an IPv6 packet from its isolated tenant network (blue, for example) to another tenant network (red) it needs to make use of a gateway.

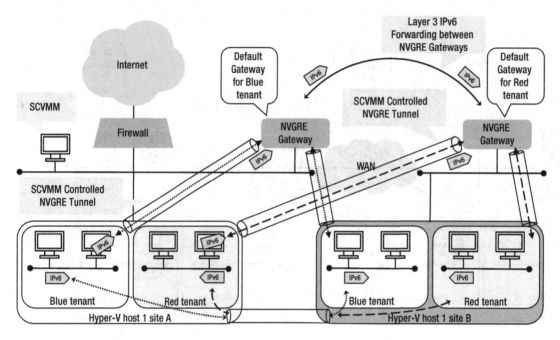

Figure 7-9. *HNV example, multiple tenant network forwarding across a wide area network*

These gateways in Server 2012 R2 are software defined and can be run on Windows Server 2012 R2 directly or can be a third-party hardware appliance. The gateway functions as the Layer 3 network port that connects to the physical infrastructure. In fact, you could create your own gateway if you wanted by simply running the Routing and Remote Access Server (RRAS) role on a Windows server and put in the correct routing rules to forward the correct IPv6 prefix to that RRAS. The NVGRE gateway removes the need to do all the work to maintain that and simplifies the process by leveraging SCVMM to orchestrate everything. Effectively, SCVMM becomes a virtual network controller that is in charge of knowing how to forward packets inside the private cloud network.

Figure 7-9 shows how the blue tenant network forwards traffic to the red tenant network. What is important to note is that SCVMM and NVGRE do not care if the underlying physical network (Microsoft calls this network the Provider) is running IPv6 or not in order to transport IPv6 blue tenant traffic to the NVGRE gateway. Only from the blue NVGRE gateway to the red NVGRE gateway do we require IPv6. This physical network in this particular case is called the underlay network and in Microsoft terminology uses provider address space.

■ **Caution** Microsoft's use of the provider address (PA) term does NOT correspond to the IPv6 community use of the provider assigned (PA) term. Do not be confused, PA as Microsoft uses it in reference to NVGRE is that the network infrastructure that the hosting provider maintains has an address space (IPv4 or IPv6) associated with it and that address space is different from the customer address (CA) that is used by the tenants.

The blue tenant network would be an overlay network just as the red tenant network would also be an overlay network. Neither the blue nor the red network can see each other unless they forward traffic to each other via their NVGRE gateways.

One of the interesting aspects of the CA space (or the overlay network) is that the IP address space could be identical to that of another customer on the same Hyper-V environment and they would not have any issues or see each other's traffic. This is a more salient point for those using IPv4 since it is common to utilize RFC 1918 address space in these sort of deployments. While technically it is possible for two separate tenants to run the same IPv6 address space, it makes no sense to do so. There is no shortage of unique IPv6 addresses. It also reduces the number of functions the NVGRE gateway has to perform. For IPv6 it only has to do IPv6 forwarding. For IPv4 it must forward and likely also perform some sort of stateful NAT.

At this time, through SCVMM it is only possible to have IPv4 or IPv6 available as an overlay (CA) network. It is not possible to specify both an IPv4 and an IPv6 network for the same overlay. This means that through SCVMM it is not possible to build out a dual-stack overlay network solution. It is possible to utilize PowerShell to reconfigure the overlay network to support dual-stack. This is not a trivial task and I am hopeful that Microsoft will update SCVMM to accommodate a dual-stack option when creating the overlay network.

Virtualizing Windows

When utilizing Hyper-V or some other hypervisor to host a Windows server or client guest OS, you should address some best practices for networking, and specifically for IPv6. Those who use gold images of the Windows OS in order to build VMs will need to take additional steps: they will need to make sure to remove the existing DHCPv6 Unique Identifiers (DUID) from the OS build. This prevents duplicate DUIDs appearing on the network which causes problems for the DHCPv6 process.

You can solve the duplicate DUID of a Windows host by simply utilizing the sysprep process. If you run the sysprep command without the /generalize option to build the operating system then the duplicate DUID issue occurs. If you run the sysprep command with the /generalize option then a DHCP client application programming interface (API) process is run that clears out the value of the DUID.

■ **Note** Windows Deployment Services, System Center Virtual Machine Manager, and Configuration Manager are important tools to use in the process of deploying virtual machines. There are PowerShell cmdlets along with API functions to make deployment of VMs more efficient and scalable. For deployment services with PowerShell see http://technet.microsoft.com/en-us/library/dn283416%28v=wps.630%29.aspx and for System Center Virtual Machine Manager see http://technet.microsoft.com/en-us/library/jj613358.aspx

---

Alternately, you can remove a DUID from the Windows host using a manual process. You will have to delete the following registry key HKEY_LOCAL_MACHINE\SYSTEM\CurrentControlSet\services\TCPIP6\Parameters\Dhcpv6DUID and reboot the computer. Perform the following steps to remove this registry key value:

1. Open the Registry Editor (regedit.exe from the command line window that has administrative privileges will work)

2. Navigate to HKEY_LOCAL_MACHINE\SYSTEM\CurrentControlSet\services\TCPIP6\Parameters

3. Right click and delete the DWORD value named 'Dhcpv6DUID'

4. Reboot the computer

Figure 7-10 shows the registry key value that you must delete.

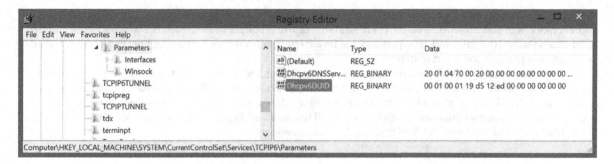

Figure 7-10. *Removing the DHCPv6 DUID value*

For Windows 7 and Windows Server 2008R2 this issue was addressed with an update. You can find details at `http://support.microsoft.com/kb/2763523`. For Windows 8 and Windows Server 2012 this issue was also addressed with an update and details for that one can be found at `http://support.microsoft.com/kb/2770917`.

Best practice is to utilize sysprep to avoid the duplicate DUID issue. If you get errors in your DHCPv6 log regarding duplicate DUIDs then you likely are not using sysprep properly for the Windows guest OS build. You will need to find the Windows guest OSs that are having DUID conflicts and use the previously discussed process to reset their DUID configuration. If you continue to get duplicate DUID errors in the DHCPv6 logs then you might have more than one guest VM build from that original gold image and you will need to track them all down to resolve the problem.

In summary, the IPv6 implementation in Microsoft Hyper-V Server and Hyper-V Network Virtualization are both robust and ready to run production workloads. Microsoft was able to leverage its work in Windows server and extend the same IPv6 functionality into these technologies. It is exciting to see broad IPv6 support in the software-defined network solution that Microsoft is bringing to market.

CHAPTER 8

■ ■ ■

IPv6 and DNS

The Internet requires some fundamental network services to work. These include network connectivity, routing, a shared networking protocol (IPv4 and IPv6), an address allocation process (StateLess Address Auto Configuration, or SLAAC, and Dynamic Host Configuration Protocol, or DHCP), and a name resolution process called Domain Name System (DNS). DNS is the way we resolve unique Fully Qualified Domain Names (FQDNs) to IPv4 or IPv6 addresses. DNS is not unique to Windows because all Internet systems need to use it to operate. Apple's OSX, Linux, and BSD all make use of BIND, the widely used DNS implementation.

Microsoft chose to implement its own DNS service in Windows. DNS is installed on Windows server as a new role and can be run as a standalone DNS server or can function as Active Directory-Integrated DNS. The advantage of Active Directory-Integrated DNS is that Active Directory Domain Services (AD DS) storage is leveraged for replication of DNS zone databases. This means that DNS servers that participate in AD and are set up as integrated do not operate in the same way that classic Bind DNS servers would.

While IPv4 and IPv6 are very different from a network protocol basis there really isn't any functional difference in how they leverage DNS. So we should jump in and see how DNS handles IPv4 versus how it handles IPv6.

How Is DNS Different for IPv6?

There are only two items that are different for IPv4 versus IPv6 in regard to DNS record types. They are

- A new record type—AAAA, which is used to represent a FQDN to IPv6 mapping, and

- A new reverse record domain name—ip6.arpa, which is used to represent an IPv6 address to a FQDN mapping.

While DNS did not have to change significantly to support IPv6, some operational issues may differ depending on need requirements. I cover those in the section "Operationally Managing IPv6 DNS."

You can read more about DNS extensions to support IPv6 in RFC 3596, which can be found at http://tools.ietf.org/html/rfc3596.

IPv6 DNS-Specific Records

As mentioned, we have a new IPv6 record type which is called a quad-A record and is represented as AAAA. Since an IPv4 address is 32 bits and represented by a single A, the IETF in RFC 3596 chose to represent an IPv6 address which is 128 bits as 4 As, which is sort of clever. The Internet Assigned Numbers Authority (IANA) value for an AAAA record type is 28 (decimal). The data format is 128 bits and holds the actual IPv6 address.

A query against a FQDN that results in multiple AAAA records will provide them all to the query host which is the expected behavior as this matches what happens with IPv4. Effectively, all the best practices you utilize for DNS while operating with IPv4 apply when operating DNS on IPv6. In fact, best practices are to simply dual-stack your existing

DNS server with static IPv4 and static IPv6 addresses. The Windows server will answer IPv4 or IPv6 queries on either network protocol for either record type (A or AAAA) by default. See the section "Operationally Managing IPv6 DNS" to learn how to modify some of this behavior.

IPv6 rDNS Domain

While both IPv4 A and IPv6 AAAA records are relatively well known DNS record types, the less frequently used PTR record type is not. A PTR record is a pointer record and allows someone to query against two special domain names in order to determine what FQDN is associated with a particular IPv4 or IPv6 address. IPv4 uses the in-addr.arpa domain name and IPv6 uses the ip6.arpa domain name to host the same information. These domain names do a specific mapping process to allow network operators to delegate the hosting of the zones for public IPv4 and IPv6 address blocks. In the case of IPv6 the address is broken up on nibble boundaries and the value for each nibble is a single HEX value. Each nibble must be represented fully and the address format is reversed. That is because IPv6 (and IPv4 for that matter) get more specific left to right whereas DNS FQDNs get more specific right to left. Thus, in order to map the IPv6 address information into DNS the address format was reversed. It is easiest to see all this with an example so here are two standard IPv6 address and the associated reverse DNS entry that is built out for it.

```
2001:db8:1f05:d37:202c:7674:c4c2:4fa8
2001:db8:1f05:d37::1
```

First, we need to remove zero compression and leading zeros since we need every nibble. The addresses will look as follows:

```
2001:0db8:1f05:0d37:202c:7674:c4c2:4fa8
2001:0db8:1f05:0d37:0:0:0:1
```

We still need every nibble to be included so it must be fully expanded so the addresses look as follows:

```
2001:0db8:1f05:0d37:202c:7674:c4c2:4fa8
2001:0db8:1f05:0d37:0000:0000:0000:0001
```

With this final format we can build out the reverse entry in the IP6.ARPA zone. It will end up looking like the following:

```
8.a.f.4.2.c.4.c.4.7.6.7.c.2.0.2.7.3.d.0.5.0.f.1.8.b.d.0.1.0.0.2.IP6.ARPA.
1.0.0.0.0.0.0.0.0.0.0.0.0.0.0.0.0.0.7.3.d.0.5.0.f.1.8.b.d.0.1.0.0.2.IP6.ARPA.
```

I have highlighted the zero compression and leading zero areas in the reverse entries to show how easy it is to miss them. This is yet another reason you will want to make use of a DNS, DHCP, and IP Address Management (DDI) solution so you are not attempting to do any of this administration by hand. It is very easy to make a simple typo, and missing or swapping out a nibble value is incredibly easy to do. To avoid this problem I recommend using the create PTR reverse record option when you are building out A or AAAA forward record entries (IPv4 or IPv6).

Installing Windows DNS

There are two main methods for installing the DNS role on a Windows server:

- Use the server manager graphic user interface (GUI) to set up the role on the server.
- Utilize PowerShell to do the same.

I will cover doing both of these for a standalone Windows server configuration. You can alternately install and set up the DNS role via System Center; however, this makes more sense for domain-joined Windows servers. The only difference is that in domain joined you can run DNS as AD integrated.

DNS Server Manager GUI Installation

When performing an install in standard Windows Server 2012 and 2012R2 (not server core installs), Server Manager is automatically launched at initial logon. To install the DNS server role you will select the Manage tab from the Server Manager Dashboard screen as shown in Figure 8-1. Next select the "Add Roles and Features" option which will launch a new wizard screen (see Figure 8-2 showing some of the options that are available from this wizard).

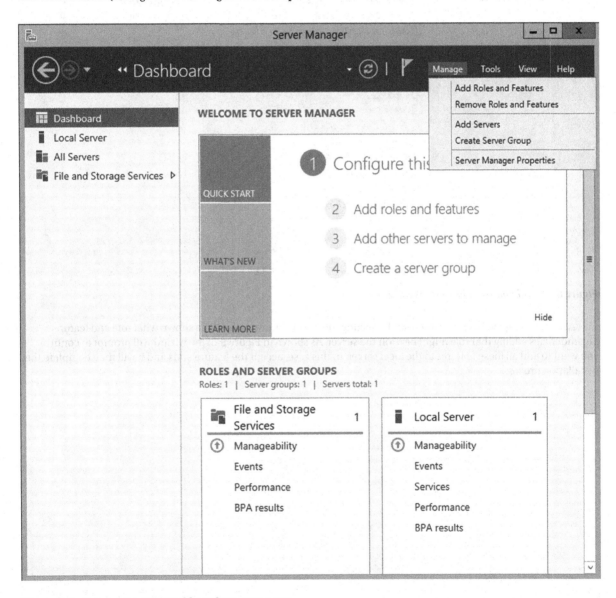

Figure 8-1. *Server Manager Dashboard manage menu*

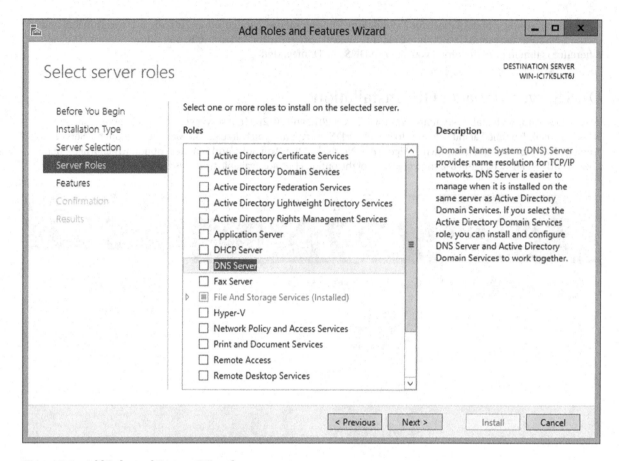

Figure 8-2. *Add Roles and Features Wizard*

After selecting the DNS server role and selecting the "Next" button you will be shown what role and feature dependencies adding that role might have on the server. As shown in Figure 8-3, the wizard will prompt to confirm you want to add all these features to the local server. In this case, accept the feature adds and it will then complete the installation process.

Figure 8-3. Add features confirmation

At this point you will be back at the Server Manager Dashboard. There will be a new sub-role section in the dashboard now. Figure 8-4 shows the new DNS role that has been installed.

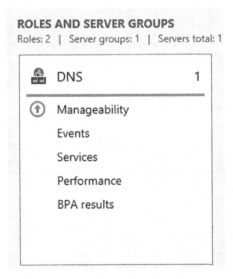

Figure 8-4. Server Manager Dashboard with DNS role

From the Server Manager Dashboard you will want to select the Tools menu, as shown in Figure 8-5, and under that select "DNS" which will launch the DNS Manager as shown in Figure 8-6.

Figure 8-5. *Server Manager Dashboard Tools menu*

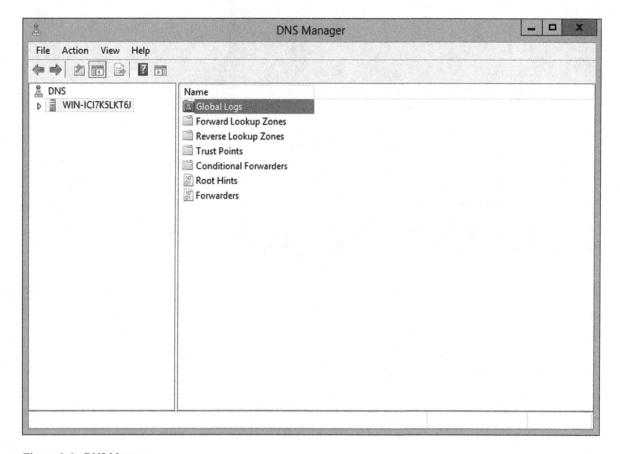

Figure 8-6. *DNS Manager*

At this point you can now manage specific parameters about DNS from the GUI as DNS is set up and ready to use. For instance, you can build forward and reverse zones and then records in those zones or modify the Root Hints entries.

DNS Server PowerShell Installation

Unlike using Server Manager to install Windows DNS role, it is relatively easy to get the initial setup for DNS working with a simple PowerShell cmdlet. That being said, you will still need to do all the configuration work post installation, and regardless of the installation method that work can be done with PowerShell or via the GUI. Given the importance of PowerShell I cover the management of DNS via PowerShell here. The installation of PowerShell can be done by executing the following:

```
Add-WindowsFeature DNS
```

As you can see, this cmdlet has limited parameter requirements since it is a simple Windows role on the server being installed. On a clean Windows Server 2012R2 installation the example PowerShell output is

```
PS C:\> Add-WindowsFeature DNS
WARNING: The following recommended condition is not met for DNS:
No static IP addresses were found on this computer. If the IP
address changes, clients might not be able to contact this server.
Please configure a static IP address on this computer before
installing DNS Server.
Success Restart Needed Exit Code      Feature Result
------- -------------- ---------      --------------
True    No             Success        {DNS Server}
WARNING: Windows automatic updating is not enabled. To ensure that
your newly-installed role or feature is automatically updated,
turn on Windows Update.
```

You can confirm the status of the installation by using

```
Get-WindowsFeature DNS
```

And the output on the server shows

```
PS C:\> Get-WindowsFeature DNS
Display Name                           Name
Install State
------------                           ----            -------------
[X] DNS Server                         DNS
Installed
```

Finally, if you want to modify the DNS listener IP addresses you will need to modify the XML output from the Get-DnsServer cmdlet and import that back in using the Set-DnsServer cmdlet. You can export to the XML using the following example PowerShell snippet:

```
Get-DnsServer | Export-Clixml -Path "c:\DnsServerConfig1.xml"
```

Once you have modified the XML (search for listener to find the appropriate section of the XML) then you can import the new XML back in using

```
$x = Import-Clixml "c:\DnsServerConfig1.xml"
Set-DnsServer -InputObject $x
```

Unfortunately, Windows Hyper-V Server does not allow the DNS server role to be installed. To gain all the benefits of DNS (and DHCP for that matter) on Windows you will need to run Windows Server 2008 through 2012R2. Best practices for the DNS role installation would be to have a static IPv4 and/or IPv6 address on the server already.

Managing IPv6 DNS Records

After getting the DNS role installed, your next major task is to actually manage DNS records. There are two sides to this process—the DNS server itself and the DNS clients that make use of that DNS server to register records dynamically. In this section I cover both, so let's start with the DNS server configuration.

IPv6 DNS Resource Entries

The most efficient way to add entries to the DNS server is to do so via PowerShell. While it is possible to build out entries with the GUI when you are administering a lot of servers you will want to leverage PowerShell to complete the task. After installing the DNS role, new PowerShell cmdlets are made available. The common cmdlets you will want to utilize are

```
Add-DnsServerPrimaryZone
Add-DnsServerResourceRecordAAAA
Remove-DnsServerResourceRecord
```

To get started we first need to have an actual zone to put host resource records into. In this case we will use the Add-DnsServerPrimaryZone cmdlet to build out the example.com zone.

```
Add-DnsServerPrimaryZone -Name "example.com" -ZoneFile
"example.com.dns"
```

To build out a specific AAAA record type for a server we would execute

```
Add-DnsServerResourceRecordAAAA -Name "ipv6host" -ZoneName "example.com" -CreatePtr -AllowUpdateAny
-IPv6Address "2001:db8:a::1" -TimeToLive 08:00:00
```

Alternatively, you can invoke the other cmdlet

```
Add-DnsServerResourceRecord -AAAA -Name "ipv6host" -ZoneName
"example.com" -CreatePtr -AllowUpdateAny -IPv6Address
"2001:db8:a::1" -TimeToLive 08:00:00
```

The following example shows adding a zone for example.com and then adding an AAAA record type into a server and the output to confirm the entry and how to remove both the AAAA record and the zone itself:

```
PS C:\> Add-DnsServerPrimaryZone -Name "example.com" -ZoneFile
"example.com.dns"
```

```
PS C:\> Get-DnsServerZone -Name "example.com"
ZoneName       ZoneType      IsAutoCreated   IsDsIntegrated   IsReverseLookupZone   IsSigned
--------       --------      -------------   --------------   -------------------   --------
example.com    Primary       False           False            False                 False
PS C:\> Add-DnsServerResourceRecordAAAA -Name "ipv6host" -ZoneName
"example.com" -AllowUpdateAny -IPv6Address "2001:db8:a::1" -
TimeToLive 08:00:00
PS C:\> Get-DnsServerResourceRecord -RRType AAAA -ZoneName
"example.com"

HostName       RecordType    Timestamp     TimeToLive     RecordData
--------       ----------    ---------     ----------     ----------
ipv6host       AAAA          0             08:00:00       2001:db8:a::1

PS C:\> Remove-DnsServerResourceRecord -name "ipv6host" -ZoneName
"example.com" -RRType AAAA -Force
PS C:\> Get-DnsServerResourceRecord -RRType AAAA -ZoneName
"example.com"
```

Because no entry exists, there is no resource record type displayed. At this point you are ONLY checking for AAAA record types; it is possible that an A record type exists in the zone but it will not be displayed by the cmdlet the example executes.

Removing the zone simply utilizes the Remove-DNSServerZone cmdlet; however, the output to confirm the removal is more verbose in explaining that the zone no longer exists and is not on the server. Following is some sample output:

```
PS C:\> Remove-DNSServerZone -Name "example.com" -Force
PS C:\> Get-DnsServerZone -Name "example.com"
Get-DnsServerZone : The zone example.com was not found on server WIN-ICI7K5LKT6J.
At line:1 char:1
+ Get-DnsServerZone -Name "example.com"
+ ~~~~~~~~~~~~~~~~~~~~~~~~~~~~~~~~~~~~~~
    + CategoryInfo          : ObjectNotFound:
(example.com:root/Microsoft/...S_DnsServerZone) [Get-DnsServerZone],
CimException
    + FullyQualifiedErrorId : WIN32 9601,Get-DnsServerZone
```

As you can see, any of the standard DNS functions you would do with the GUI you can do equally as well with PowerShell, and in this particular case we are narrowing down what we are managing to IPv6-specific cmdlets; however, you can do all the same functions for IPv4.

DNS Role IPv6 PowerShell cmdlets

Besides IPv6 functions, some additional DNS role PowerShell cmdlets are worth reviewing—specifically, they may impact IPv6 transition services or DNS management. Take, for instance, the deployment of ISATAP (Intra-Site Automatic Tunnel Addressing Protocol). Recall from Chapter 3 that ISATAP requires DNS to function properly and that the ISATAP FQDN is reserved. You can see how Windows DNS reserves the namespace by using the

Get-DnsServerGlobalQueryBlockList cmdlet. As you can see from the following output from a Windows Server 2012R2 host, Microsoft protects the ISATAP keyword by blocking it globally:

```
PS C:\> Get-DnsServerGlobalQueryBlockList
Enable : True
List   : {wpad, isatap}
```

Because Microsoft has added ISATAP to the global query block list by default, if you are not deploying ISATAP then you do not have to do anything. It is possible to modify the list using the Set-DnsServerGlobalQueryBlockList cmdlets. If you do plan to implement ISATAP then you will need to change the block list so ISATAP will function as expected.

There are also key cmdlets like

```
Get-DnsServerRootHint
Import-DnsServerRootHint
Add-DnsServerRootHint
Remove-DnsServerRootHint
```

The output for the Get-DnsServerRootHint cmdlet is shown next. The root level nameservers with IPv6 addresses are in bold.

```
PS C:\> Get-DnsServerRootHint | sort-object -property
{$_.NameServer.RecordData.NameServer} -Unique
```

NameServer	IPAddress
a.root-servers.net.	{198.41.0.4, 198.41.0.4, 2001:503:ba3e::2:30}
b.root-servers.net.	{192.228.79.201, 192.228.79.201}
c.root-servers.net.	{192.33.4.12, 192.33.4.12}
d.root-servers.net.	{199.7.91.13, 128.8.10.90, 2001:500:2d::d}
e.root-servers.net.	{192.203.230.10, 192.203.230.10}
f.root-servers.net.	{192.5.5.241, 192.5.5.241, 2001:500:2f::f}
g.root-servers.net.	{192.112.36.4, 192.112.36.4}
h.root-servers.net.	{128.63.2.53, 128.63.2.53, 2001:500:1::803f:235}
i.root-servers.net.	{192.36.148.17, 192.36.148.17, 2001:7fe::53}
j.root-servers.net.	{192.58.128.30, 192.58.128.30, 2001:503:c27::2:30}
k.root-servers.net.	{193.0.14.129, 193.0.14.129, 2001:7fd::1}
l.root-servers.net.	{199.7.83.42, 199.7.83.42, 2001:500:3::42}
m.root-servers.net.	{202.12.27.33, 202.12.27.33, 2001:dc3::35}

If you want to input a new root hints file entry (which you should not have to do all that often) then you would use the Add-DnsServerRootHint cmdlet. If you want to redo the Root Hint file to only do IPv6, for example, you could change the entries using the Remove-DnsServerRootHint cmdlet and Add-DnsServerRootHint cmdlet. So, if we wanted to make the a.root-servers.net to only have the IPv6 address of 2001:503:ba3e::2:30 then you would do

```
Remove-DnsServerRootHint -NameServer "a.root-servers.net"
Add-DnsServerRootHint -NameServer "a.root-servers.net" -IPAddress 2001:503:ba3e::2:30
```

To check the output you would issue

```
Get-DnsServerRootHint | Where-Object
{$_.NameServer.RecordData.NameServer -EQ "a.root-servers.net."} |
Sort-Object -Unique
```

The following example shows this command being executed on a Server 2012R2 host. Minor formatting changes to the output were done to make it fit on the page.

```
PS C:\> Remove-DnsServerRootHint -NameServer "a.root-servers.net" -Force
PS C:\> Add-DnsServerRootHint -NameServer "a.root-servers.net" - IPAddress 2001:503:ba3e::2:30
PS C:\> Get-DnsServerRootHint | Where-Object
{$_.NameServer.RecordData.NameServer -EQ "a.root-servers.net."} | Sort-Object -Unique
NameServer          IPAddress
----------          ---------

a.root-servers.net.  2001:503:ba3e::2:30
```

As you can see, you can manage all the DNS root hint file entries using simple PowerShell cmdlets. Additional DNS specific PowerShell cmdlets related to IPv6 would be

```
Get-DnsServerSetting
Test-DnsServer
```

The Get-DnsServerSetting cmdlet displays all the DNS server settings on the host specified and an example output would look as follows:

```
PS C:\> Get-DnsServerSetting
ComputerName      : WIN-ICI7K5LKT6J
MajorVersion      : 6
MinorVersion      : 2
BuildNumber       : 9200
IsReadOnlyDC      : False
EnableDnsSec      : True
EnableIPv6        : True
ListeningIPAddress : {fe80::b97c:4d15:3bae:a4ca, 192.168.91.128}
AllIPAddress       : {fe80::b97c:4d15:3bae:a4ca, 192.168.91.128}
```

Next, if you need to test your DNS server at all for specific zone functionality then you will use the Test-DnsServer cmdlet. An example would be to check if a zone record was created properly as shown.

```
PS C:\> Test-DnsServer -IPAddress ::1 -ZoneName "example.com"
IPAddress    Result                  RoundTripTime    TcpTried    UdpTried
---------    ------                  -------------    --------    --------
::1          NotAuthoritativeForZone 00:00:00         False       True

PS C:\> Add-DnsServerPrimaryZone -Name "example.com" -ZoneFile
"example.com.dns"
PS C:\> Test-DnsServer -IPAddress ::1 -ZoneName "example.com"
IPAddress    Result                  RoundTripTime    TcpTried    UdpTried
---------    ------                  -------------    --------    -------
::1          Success                 00:00:00         False       True
```

To see all the PowerShell cmdlets associated with the DNS module simply use the `Get-Command` cmdlet. Simply issue

```
Get-Command -Module DNSServer
```

The output is too long to display in its entirety, but a partial output of the cmdlet would look as follows:

```
PS C:\> Get-Command -Module DNSServer
CommandType     Name                                        ModuleName
-----------     ----                                        ----------
Alias           Export-DnsServerTrustAnchor                 DNSServer
Function        Add-DnsServerConditionalForwarderZone       DNSServer
Function        Add-DnsServerDirectoryPartition             DNSServer
Function        Add-DnsServerForwarder                      DNSServer
Function        Add-DnsServerPrimaryZone                    DNSServer
Function        Add-DnsServerResourceRecord                 DNSServer
Function        Add-DnsServerResourceRecordA                DNSServer
Function        Add-DnsServerResourceRecordAAAA             DNSServer
...
```

That covers the majority of IPv6 cmdlets that DNS would utilizes with IPv6. There obviously is much more you can do with PowerShell and DNS so spend some time exploring the cmdlets.

How to Change Windows Client DNS Settings

It is not uncommon to want to change the DNS settings of a Windows host. Specifically, you may want to change the DNS resolvers that the host is using to resolve DNS queries. This would be true for Windows Server 2008 through 2012R2 hosts as well as Windows Vista, 7, 8, and 8.1 hosts. Luckily, we have PowerShell cmdlets to manage all of that behavior and also to test the DNS settings.

Before we begin it is useful to know what DNS servers your host is using. You use the `Get-DnsClientServerAddress` cmdlet to perform this function. Specify the parameter -AddressFamily if you only want to the see the IPv4 or IPv6 values. This will display the information for all your interfaces, including the tunnel interface. If you want narrow things down to keep the output shorter, it is possible to do that by specifying the interface explicitly.

The following example PowerShell session shows *all* the DNS server information on a host:

```
PS C:\> Get-DnsClientServerAddress
InterfaceAlias                Interface  Address  ServerAddresses
                              Index      Family
-------------                 ---------  -------  ---------------
Local Area Connection             10     IPv4     {208.67.220.220, 192.168.10.1}
Local Area Connection             10     IPv6     {}
Local Area Connection* 3           7     IPv4     {}
Local Area Connection* 3           7     IPv6     {fec0:0:0:ffff::1, fec0:0:0:ffff::2, fec0:0:0:ffff::3}
Bluetooth Network Connection       6     IPv4     {}
Bluetooth Network Connection       6     IPv6     {fec0:0:0:ffff::1, fec0:0:0:ffff::2, fec0:0:0:ffff::3}
Wi-Fi                              4     IPv4     {208.67.220.220, 192.168.10.1}
Wi-Fi                              4     IPv6     {2001:470:20::2, 2001:4860:4860::8888}
VMware Network Adapter V...1      15     IPv4     {}
VMware Network Adapter V...1      15     IPv6     {fec0:0:0:ffff::1, fec0:0:0:ffff::2,fec0:0:0:ffff::3}
VMware Network Adapter V...8      16     IPv4     {}
VMware Network Adapter V...8      16     IPv6     {fec0:0:0:ffff::1, fec0:0:0:ffff::2, fec0:0:0:ffff::3}
```

```
isatap.{BB8BD59D-21C9-44D...        12 IPv4    {}
isatap.{BB8BD59D-21C9-44D...        12 IPv6    {fec0:0:0:ffff::1, fec0:0:0:ffff::2, fec0:0:0:ffff::3}
Loopback Pseudo-Interface 1          1 IPv4    {}
Loopback Pseudo-Interface 1          1 IPv6    {fec0:0:0:ffff::1, fec0:0:0:ffff::2, fec0:0:0:ffff::3}
isatap.home.howfunky.com             8 IPv4    {}
isatap.home.howfunky.com             8 IPv6    {}
isatap.{3474A072-9FB4-44C...        33 IPv4    {}
isatap.{3474A072-9FB4-44C...        33 IPv6    {}
```

If we only want to see the IPv6 information we can do

```
PS C:\> Get-DnsClientServerAddress -AddressFamily IPv6
InterfaceAlias                  Interface Address  ServerAddresses
                                Index     Family
--------------                  --------- -------  ----------------------------------------------------
Local Area Connection              10 IPv6    {}
Local Area Connection* 3            7 IPv6    {fec0:0:0:ffff::1, fec0:0:0:ffff::2, fec0:0:0:ffff::3}
Bluetooth Network Connection        6 IPv6    {fec0:0:0:ffff::1, fec0:0:0:ffff::2, fec0:0:0:ffff::3}
Wi-Fi                               4 IPv6    {2001:470:20::2, 2001:4860:4860::8888}
VMware Network Adapter V...1       15 IPv6    {fec0:0:0:ffff::1, fec0:0:0:ffff::2, fec0:0:0:ffff::3}
VMware Network Adapter V...8       16 IPv6    {fec0:0:0:ffff::1, fec0:0:0:ffff::2, fec0:0:0:ffff::3}
isatap.{BB8BD59D-21C9-44D...       12 IPv6    {fec0:0:0:ffff::1, fec0:0:0:ffff::2, fec0:0:0:ffff::3}
Loopback Pseudo-Interface 1         1 IPv6    {fec0:0:0:ffff::1, fec0:0:0:ffff::2, fec0:0:0:ffff::3}
isatap.home.howfunky.com            8 IPv6    {}
isatap.{3474A072-9FB4-44C...       33 IPv6    {}
```

The first thing we want to do is be able to set the specific DNS server IP address used. The Set-DnsClientServerAddress cmdlet will let us set that specific parameter. In the following example code we are setting the nameservers to be two public IPv6 nameservers from Google. The two are addressed as 2001:4860:4860::8888 and 2001:4860:4860::8844, respectively.

```
Set-DnsClientServerAddress -InterfaceIndex 4 -ServerAddresses
("2001:4860:4860::8888","2001:4860:4860::8844")
```

Next, you will want check the changes and then test to make sure you can resolve against those nameservers. You would do that by using the Resolve-DnsName cmdlet. For instance, to check www.cav6tf.org we would do

```
Get-DnsClientServerAddress -InterfaceIndex 4 -AddressFamily IPv6
Resolve-DnsName -Name www.cav6tf.org -Type AAAA
```

And the output would show

```
PS C:\> Get-DnsClientServerAddress -InterfaceIndex 4 - AddressFamily IPv6

InterfaceAlias                  Interface Address  ServerAddresses
                                Index     Family
--------------                  --------- -------  ---------------------------------------
Wi-Fi                               4 IPv6    {2001:470:20::2, 2001:4860:4860::8888}

PS C:\> Set-DnsClientServerAddress -InterfaceIndex 4 - ServerAddresses ("2001:4860:4860::8888","200
```

```
1:4860:4860::8844")

PS C:\> Get-DnsClientServerAddress -InterfaceIndex 4 - AddressFamily IPv6

InterfaceAlias                  Interface Address ServerAddresses
                                Index     Family
--------------                  --------- ------- --------------------------------------------
Wi-Fi                                   4 IPv6    {2001:4860:4860::8888, 2001:4860:4860::8844}

PS C:\> Resolve-DnsName -Name www.cav6tf.org -Type AAAA

Name                            Type  TTL    Section   NameHost
----                            ----  ---    -------   --------
www.cav6tf.org                  CNAME 84015  Answer    cav6tf.org

Name        : cav6tf.org
QueryType   : AAAA
TTL         : 84015
Section     : Answer
IP6Address  : 2001:470:0:11a::403e:a5c5
```

As you can see, the host is able to resolve the AAAA record request. However, this does not necessarily mean that the host actually did the resolution over IPv6. One of the nice things about DNS is that it is just as happy to operate over IPv4 as IPv6. You should do a specific test against the server to determine if you can actually connect to the DNS server via IPv6. To do this use the -Server parameter. When you do this it will make the specific request using that server. For example:

```
PS C:\> Resolve-DnsName -Name www.cav6tf.org -Type AAAA -Server 2001:4860:4860::8888
Name                            Type  TTL    Section   NameHost
----                            ----  ---    -------   --------
www.cav6tf.org                  CNAME 2014   Answer    cav6tf.org
Name        : cav6tf.org
QueryType   : AAAA
TTL         : 2014
Section     : Answer
IP6Address  : 2001:470:0:11a::403e:a5c5
```

If the IPv6 server is not available you will get output like the following:

```
PS C:\> Resolve-DnsName -Name www.cav6tf.org -Type AAAA -Server 2001:4860:4860::8888
Resolve-DnsName : www.cav6tf.org : This operation returned because the timeout period expired
At line:1 char:1
+ Resolve-DnsName -Name www.cav6tf.org -Type AAAA -Server 2001:4860:4860::8888
+ ~~~~~~~~~~~~~~~~~~~~~~~~~~~~~~~~~~~~~~~~~~~~~~~~~~~~~~~~~~~~~~~~~~~~~~~~~~~~~~~
    + CategoryInfo          : OperationTimeout: (www.cav6tf.org:String) [Resolve-DnsName], Win32Exception
    + FullyQualifiedErrorId : ERROR_TIMEOUT,Microsoft.DnsClient.Commands.ResolveDnsName
```

So you can now change the settings for the DNS servers on a host and test them to confirm you can resolve names.

How Windows Clients Chose Which IPv6 to Register in DNS

Once a Windows host has an IPv6 address, how does it determine if it should register that address in DNS dynamically (called Dynamic DNS or DDNS)? Because Windows makes use of these transition technologies, the method of registration will vary a bit depending on your specific deployment. The general rule for DDNS registration, though, is that a Windows server or client will only register its IPv6 address if that address is defined as being global unicast or a unique local address (ULA). If you are using ISATAP with a global unicast prefix or a unique local prefix those will also be registered in DNS.

The upshot is that addresses that are temporary, 6to4, Teredo, loopback, and link-local, by default do not register dynamically in DNS. This does not mean you couldn't add them yourself, but doing so is not a recommended best practice. Some specific use cases, such as DirectAccess will modify this behavior and register address types in DNS that are used for the DA client. This means if DA leverages Teredo or IP-HTTPS it will register those IPv6 addresses dynamically.

Operationally Managing IPv6 DNS

DNS is a great service to trial dual-stack with since it is a very forgiving application, which has to do with how DNS behaves. DNS naturally falls back to IPv4 services as part of how the protocol functions if IPv6 is not available. It is possible to build all sorts of interesting configurations involving DNS. However, one of the things that may come up is the desire to have an IPv6-only DNS server.

You can set the DNS server to only listen on IPv6. Begin by right clicking on the DNS server and selecting Properties from the dropdown menu. Figure 8-7 shows the Interfaces tab which allows us to control what Interface IP address the DNS server will listen on.

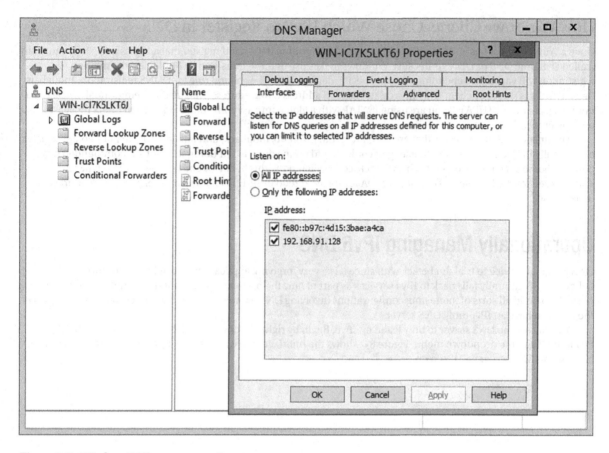

Figure 8-7. *Windows DNS server properties*

Windows 8.1 and Server 2012R2 have some additional functionality related to determining how a Windows host is reaching a specific destination, and you can leverage DNS to do some useful things in that process. For instance, we can use the `Resolve-DnsName` cmdlet to resolve the AAAA record to an IPv6 address and then pass that value to see which interface is used to reach that destination. Do that as follows:

```
$rn = Resolve-DnsName -name www.cav6tf.org -type AAAA
Find-NetRoute -RemoteIPAddress $rn.ip6address
```

And the example output of this gives us

```
PS C:\> $rn = Resolve-DnsName -name www.cav6tf.org -type AAAA
PS C:\> $rn
Name                      Type  TTL    Section    NameHost
----                      ----  ---    -------    --------
www.cav6tf.org            CNAME 85974  Answer     cav6tf.org
Name       : cav6tf.org
QueryType  : AAAA
TTL        : 85974
Section    : Answer
IP6Address : 2001:470:0:11a::403e:a5c5
```

```
PS C:\> Find-NetRoute -RemoteIPAddress $rn.ip6address
IPAddress          : 2001:470:1f05:9a4:6085:be82:8442:9b54
InterfaceIndex     : 4
InterfaceAlias     : Wi-Fi
AddressFamily      : IPv6
Type               : Unicast
PrefixLength       : 64
PrefixOrigin       : RouterAdvertisement
SuffixOrigin       : Link
AddressState       : Preferred
ValidLifetime      : 23:59:59
PreferredLifetime  : 03:59:59
SkipAsSource       : False
PolicyStore        : ActiveStore

Caption            :
Description        :
ElementName        :
InstanceID         : DD9:55>55poB:DD=<B?DkCppDpo@mDl=o:55;
AdminDistance      :
DestinationAddress :
IsStatic           :
RouteMetric        : 256
TypeOfRoute        : 3
AddressFamily      : IPv6
DestinationPrefix  : ::/0
InterfaceAlias     : Wi-Fi
InterfaceIndex     : 4
NextHop            : fe80::3285:a9ff:fe6c:b3e0
PreferredLifetime  : 00:00:29
Protocol           : NetMgmt
Publish            : No
Store              : ActiveStore
ValidLifetime      : 00:00:29
PSComputerName     :
ifIndex            : 4
```

Clearly this can be very useful when trying to debug how an application is actually reaching a resources. It is telling you what IPv6 address and interface the host is using.

Other Types of Name Resolution

DNS is not the only way to perform name resolution in Windows. Microsoft also leverages Link Local Multicast Name Resolution (LLMNR) and IPv6 literals to resolve names. While LLMNR is not IPv6 specific (it works on IPv4 too) it is something to be aware of for those who operate home or workgroup networks.

LLMNR

LLMNR is defined in RFC 4795 (http://tools.ietf.org/html/rfc4795) and is part of the Zeroconf effort in the IETF (Internet Engineering Task Force). LLMNR effectively allows the host to resolve names when a DNS server is not present on the network or is not reachable. Ad hoc wireless and wired networks are a good example of when this might happen. LLMNR leverages most of the work done in DNS for message types, but it utilizes a different port.

LLMNR sends Name Query Request messages to UDP port 5355 and receives a Name Query Response message to UDP port 5355. These messages have a specific IPv6 multicast address of ff02::1:3 and all IPv6 hosts will listen on that multicast address if they want to leverage LLMNR. If DNS servers are configured on a Windows host and they are operational the host will use those. If the Windows host is unable to resolve names it will fall back the LLMNR by default.

▪ **Note**   For more information on Zeroconf see http://en.wikipedia.org/wiki/Zero-configuration_networking which covers LLMNR along with Apple's Bonjour mDNS implementation.

IPv6 Literals

Windows Server 2008 through 2012R2 and Windows Vista, 7, 8, and 8.1 all support IPv6 literals. IPv6 literals is an easy way to specify a hostname and have the Windows host resolve it to an IPv6 address. It is very simple: you take an IPv6 address and replace the "`:`" delimiter with a "`-`" and append `ipv6-literal.net` to the end.

For example, say that we have the IPv6 address of

```
2001:470:0:11a::403e:a5c5
Then the IPv6 literal name would be:
2001-470-0-11a--403e-a5c5.ipv6-literal.net
```

Here is an example of both pinging the actual IPv6 address and then using the IPv6 literal name.

```
PS C:\> ping 2001:470:0:11a::403e:a5c5
Pinging 2001:470:0:11a::403e:a5c5 with 32 bytes of data:
Reply from 2001:470:0:11a::403e:a5c5: time=26ms
Reply from 2001:470:0:11a::403e:a5c5: time=17ms
Reply from 2001:470:0:11a::403e:a5c5: time=17ms
Reply from 2001:470:0:11a::403e:a5c5: time=19ms
Ping statistics for 2001:470:0:11a::403e:a5c5:
    Packets: Sent = 4, Received = 4, Lost = 0 (0% loss),
Approximate round trip times in milli-seconds:
    Minimum = 17ms, Maximum = 26ms, Average = 19ms
PS C:\> ping 2001-470-0-11a--403e-a5c5.ipv6-literal.net
Pinging 2001:470:0:11a::403e:a5c5 with 32 bytes of data:
Reply from 2001:470:0:11a::403e:a5c5: time=17ms
Reply from 2001:470:0:11a::403e:a5c5: time=17ms
Reply from 2001:470:0:11a::403e:a5c5: time=21ms
Reply from 2001:470:0:11a::403e:a5c5: time=18ms
Ping statistics for 2001:470:0:11a::403e:a5c5:
    Packets: Sent = 4, Received = 4, Lost = 0 (0% loss),
Approximate round trip times in milli-seconds:
    Minimum = 17ms, Maximum = 21ms, Average = 18ms
```

As you can see, even zero compression works as expected. If you need to make use of the zone ID (remember, that is % used to separate the IPv6 address from the interface ID) you can use an "**s**" to replace the "**%**" so, for instance, on a link-local address you would have

```
fe80::6085:be82:8442:9b54%4
 And the IPv6 literal name would be:
fe80--6085-be82-8442-9b54s4.ipv6-literal.net
```

So, why would Windows need IPv6 literals? Windows does not support colons in UNC pathnames which makes an IPv6 address illegal to put into a UNC path (unlike IPv4). Microsoft solved this for Windows by registering the ipv6-literal.net domain name (so it could legitimately use the FQDN) and then building out a transcription of the IPv6 literal name to the actual IPv6 address. This allows the use of UNC paths with IPv6 addresses if you do not have a DNS server available to do name resolution.

Name Resolution Policy Table

The Name Resolution Policy Table (NRPT) is a name resolution function to allow special handling of name resolution requests. NRPT allows the domain administrator to define specific DNS servers for individual DNS namespaces (zones) so that they can control how FQDNs resolve. NRPT is a feature utilized by DirectAccess and DNSSEC solutions but also can be used for any other policy-based name resolution routing. For DirectAccess specifically (which is the most common use case of NRPT) it is used to route name resolution requests for the internal corporate namespace to the DirectAccess server, while routing all other name resolution requests to the DNS servers defined on the network adapter. It is not IPv6 specific, but I mention it briefly so you know there is an additional process that can be involved in changing the IPv6 name resolution process.

IPv6 DNS Challenges

There are some challenges with DNS and IPv6 and they have more to do with Internet policy and trying to keep the Internet working properly. One of the issues that comes up often is when a host (Windows or another operating system, or OS) has a global unicast IPv6 address but actually doesn't have a routable way to get out to the IPv6 Internet. How should the host behave? Should it attempt to connect to IPv6 addresses it is able to resolve via an IPv4 DNS request? Should a DNS server respond with an AAAA resource record type back to a host that is requesting the information via IPv4?

As you can see, these are really policy and administrative practices and have little to do with the ability of the OS to do that function. At one point Google was operating a DNS whitelist to limit those that could resolve AAAA record types unless they were from an approved IPv6 prefix range. This reduced the number of IPv6 networks that could work with Google services but also insured that those that were doing IPv6 were serious because they had to make the effort to request to be on the whitelist.

With the rapid growth of IPv6 recently, it is difficult to maintain such a list and not have an impact on those who might want or need those services. There were also other companies such as Yahoo! that were considering doing similar policy enforcements. After the World IPv6 Launch on June 6, 2012, Google switched from a whitelist approach to a blacklist approach making its IPv6 DNS records open for all. This is a much easier policy for the Internet at large and likely the one that will be used going forward.

■ **Note** Details about IPv6 brokenness and DNS whitelisting can be found at `http://en.wikipedia.org/wiki/IPv6_brokenness_and_DNS_whitelisting`

CHAPTER 9

■ ■ ■

IPv6 and DHCP

Dynamic Host Configuration Protocol (DHCP) is just as much a fundamental service for the Internet to work as DNS (Domain Name System). For IPv6 this means leveraging DHCPv6 to handle IPv6 address allocations. DHCPv6 is the way modern networks allocate IPv6 addresses on a LAN (local area network) and DHCP is what has been traditionally used for IPv4 addresses in the past. DHCP and DHCPv6 are not unique to Windows because all modern Internet systems use DHCP to do the address allocation function. Apple's OSX, Linux, and BSD all make use of their own implementations of DHCP and DHCPv6 servers which are principally based on the code from Internet Systems Consortium (ISC).

How Is DHCP Different for IPv6?

DHCP has traditionally been used in IPv4 networks to allocate IP addresses to hosts that may move networks on a regular basis (like a laptop or other mobile device) and for client access devices like wireless access points, voice over Internet Protocol (VoIP) handsets, video end points, printers, scanners, and client workstations. It may also be leveraged for server networks and virtual private network (VPN) clients.

Traditionally DHCP has allowed Windows administrators to control the following standard IPv4 configuration information:

- Network
- Subnet
- Default gateway
- DNS server(s)
- NTP (Network Time Protocol) server(s)
- Option code(s)

What is unique about DHCPv6 is the fact that the IPv6 protocol behaves differently and therefore requires some fundamental changes in how DHCPv6 behaves. First I want to cover what DHCPv6 still provides control for in terms of IPv6 configuration information. DHCPv6 allows you to configure

- Network prefix
- DNS server(s)
- NTP servers(s)
- Option code(s)

As you can see, absent from the list is the default gateway because the local router(s) handle the process of router advertisement (RAs). RAs indicate which local router is available as a default gateway, making this function redundant. See Chapter 3 for more information about RAs. A singular network prefix value is given instead of a combined network and subnet value and for IPv6 this will be a /64. In fact, the DHCPv6 relay message process identifies link and peer addresses and these are both 16-byte fields which result in 64-bit fields. This means that proxy DHCPv6 servers will not provide a relay message format other than a /64 for allocating a prefix to a requesting DHCPv6 client device.

The remaining configuration information stays the same for all practical purposes. Technically some of the option codes and other parameters are different, but the functional way it works and what is included in DHCPv6 are the same as DHCP for IPv4.

In addition to actual DHCPv6 server parameter functions being different, the DHCPv6 client is slightly different from DHCP. DHCPv6 does not use the MAC address of the client like DHCP and instead leverages the DHCP Unique Identifier (DUID) and the Interface Association Identifier (IAID). Chapter 3 covers more details about the DUID, but this is a different enough behavior from what IPv4 does that it should be noted. The DUID is unique per host and the IAID is unique per interface so the combination of them is a unique value pair that DHCPv6 can use to assign out IPv6 addresses.

When you make IPv6 address reservations in DHCPv6 you will need to know the DUID and the IAID of the client device and NOT its MAC address as you do with IPv4. Because you are likely going to dual-stack your network, you will actually need to know the MAC, IAID, and DUID to build reservations for both protocols. This is where a DNS, DHCP, and IP Address Management (DDI) solutions become very useful because those products can do client correlation between IPv4 and IPv6.

DHCPv6-Specific Attributes

RFC 3315 (http://tools.ietf.org/html/rfc3315) defines how DHCPv6 works and is worth reading to learn how DHCPv6 actually functions. For those that have run DHCP for IPv4, however, there are really only a handful of differences to be aware of that might cause some confusion. The first is that DHCPv6 has two operating modes, stateful and stateless. These were covered in Chapter 3 under the DHCPv6 section, but I'll cover them again here.

DHCPv6 Stateful

Chapter 3 covered RAs and the flag options that are available in RAs that are used to indicate to hosts how to configure their addresses. For DHCPv6 stateful it requires that the M (Managed Address Configuration flag) and the O (Other Stateful Configuration flag) be set to 1 in the RA. If you want your client operating system (OS) to use only DHCPv6 for obtaining an address you will also need to set the A flag to 0. If you are using Windows Server 2012R2 or earlier as a router unfortunately this is not an option.

The impact of not being able to turn off the A flag is that your host will obtain two IPv6 addresses—one from the prefix advertisement defined in the router and another from the DHCPv6 server itself. These prefixes do not have to match (which introduces even more confusion) because the link-local router defines to the host that the next hop for the default gateway is the link-local address of the router itself and not a global unicast address or unique local address (ULA) that the router might support on that link-local network segment.

It is recommended that enterprise networks run DHCPv6 Stateful and that they also turn off the A flag advertisements on their routers. Doing this requires all devices on that network to have support for DHCPv6; otherwise, they will only obtain an IPv4 address if they are dual-stacked. In addition, it may be desirable to turn off temporary addresses, which forces the hosts to use the address that DHCPv6 assigns out to the host to source traffic.

Remember, if you plan on using DHCPv6 reservations in a network prefix then you will require the DUID and the IAID. In order to specify that host IPv6 requirement while building out the reservation, the DUID and IAID combination will need to be unique, similar to the way the MAC address is unique. These reservations will be for global unicast and ULA and not typically for link-local addresses.

If you deploy DHCPv6 in a stateful manner this most closely matches a standard DHCP IPv4 deployment. Realize that the default gateway information will be handled by the router via RAs.

DHCPv6 Stateless

The difference between stateful and stateless really comes from the fact that the DHCPv6 server does not provide any IPv6 address information in the stateless configuration. It only provides "Other" information, which is why the O flag is set to 1 and the M flag is set to 0. The main purpose of this configuration is to allow Stateless Address Autoconfiguration (SLAAC) hosts the ability to find additional IPv6 resource information.

The most obvious additional information is DNS server IP address information, but the DHCPv6 server can also provide other option code information such as to identify NTP (Network Time Protocol) servers and TFTP (Trivial File Transfer Protocol) servers. DHCPv6 can also provide basically any other information that is typically provided via option codes.

DHCPv6 options are covered later in the section on "DHCPv6 Scopes", but DHCPv6 stateless is typically deployed with SLAAC. It can also be used with static or manually assigned hosts to provide them with DHCPv6 option information. Best practice is to use DHCPv6 stateless with SLAAC in network segments where you may have hosts that do not have DHCPv6 clients. This still allows the host to obtain an IPv6 address, but it will leverage the DHCP IPv4 option codes (in a dual-stack configuration) to do IPv6 AAAA DNS name resolution. This is far from ideal; however, it is a common deployment in guest wireless networks.

Installing Windows DHCPv6

Just as with DNS, there are two main methods for installing the DHCP role on a Windows server: you can use the Server Manager graphic user interface (GUI) to set up the role on the server or you can utilize PowerShell. As I did with DNS, I will cover doing both of these for a standalone Windows server configuration. You can alternately install and set up the DHCP role via System Center; however, this makes more sense for domain-joined Windows servers. Really, the end result is the same as a standalone with the exception if it is AD integrated.

DHCPv6 Server Manager GUI Installation

When you perform standard Windows Server 2012 and 2012R2 installs (not server core installs), Server Manager is automatically launched at initial logon. To install the DHCP server role you will select the Manage tab from the Server Manager Dashboard screen as shown in Figure 9-1. Next select the "Add Roles and Features" option which will launch a new wizard screen (see Figure 9-2 showing some of the options that are available from this wizard).

Figure 9-1. *Server Manager Dashboard manage menu*

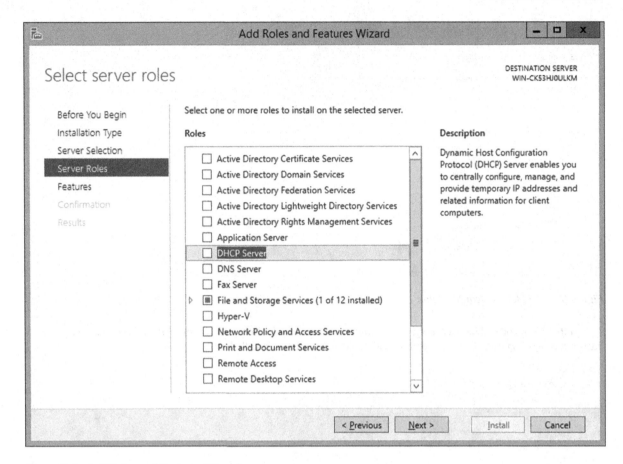

Figure 9-2. *Add Roles and Features Wizard*

After selecting the DHCP Server role and selecting the "Next" button you will be shown what role and feature dependencies adding that role might have on the server. As shown in Figure 9-3, it will prompt to confirm you want to add all these features to the local server. In this case, accept the feature adds and it will then complete the installation process.

Figure 9-3. *Add features confirmation*

At this point you will be back at the Server Manager Dashboard. There will be a new sub-role section in the dashboard now. Figure 9-4 shows the new DHCP role that has been installed.

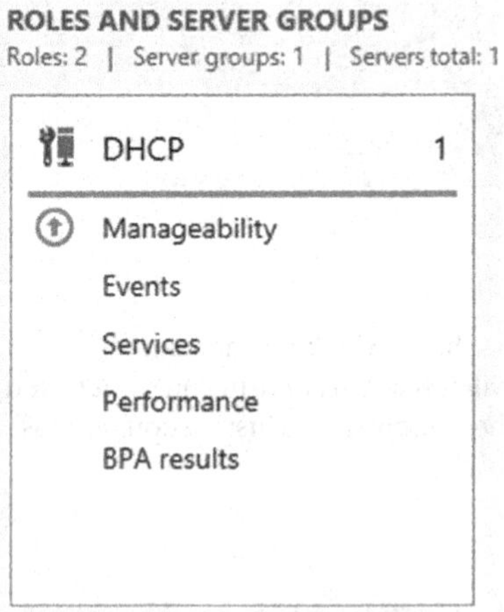

ROLES AND SERVER GROUPS
Roles: 2 | Server groups: 1 | Servers total: 1

📶 DHCP	1
⬆ Manageability	
Events	
Services	
Performance	
BPA results	

Figure 9-4. *Server Manager Dashboard with DHCP role*

From the Server Manager Dashboard you will want to select the Tools menu, as shown in Figure 9-5, and under that select "DHCP" which will launch the DHCP Manager as shown in Figure 9-6.

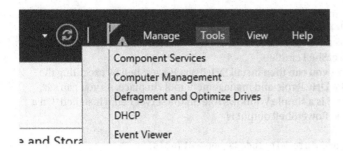

Figure 9-5. *Server Manager Dashboard Tools menu*

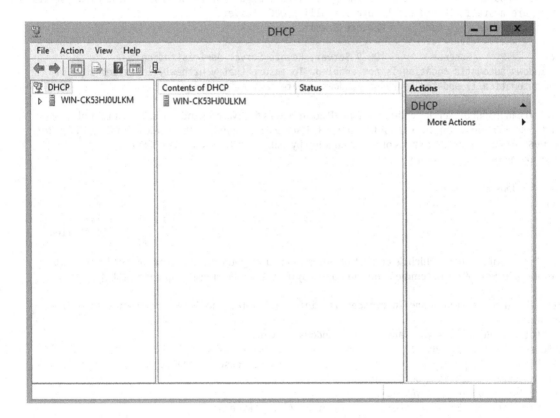

Figure 9-6. *DHCP Manager*

At this point you can now manage specific parameters of the DHCP server from the GUI as the basic functions for DHCP are set up and ready to use.

DHCPv6 Server PowerShell Installation

Unlike using Server Manager to install Windows DHCP role, it is relatively easy to get the initial setup for DHCP working with a simple PowerShell cmdlet. One of the differences of the DHCP service from that of DNS is that the DHCP role requires that the server have a static IPv4 and/or IPv6 address assigned depending on your planned use of the DHCP service. That being said, you will still need to do all the configuration work post installation, and regardless of the installation method that work can be done with PowerShell or via the GUI. Given the importance of PowerShell, I principally cover the management of DHCP via PowerShell here. First you will want to statically set up an IPv6 address on the host using the New-NetIPAddress PowerShell cmdlets.

After you have set up a static address on the server you can then install DHCP via PowerShell by executing the following Add-WindowsFeature DHCP cmdlets to get the DHCP role and management tools in place. As you can see, this cmdlet has limited parameter requirements since it is a simple Windows role on the server being installed. On a clean Windows Server 2012R2 installation the example PowerShell output is

```
PS C:\> Add-WindowsFeature DHCP -IncludeAllSubFeature -IncludeManagementTools
WARNING: The following recommended condition is not met for DHCP: No static IP addresses were
found on this computer. If the IP address changes, clients might not be able to contact this server.
Please configure a static IP address before installing DHCP Server.
Success Restart Needed Exit Code      Feature Result
------- -------------- ---------      --------------
True    No             Success        {DHCP Server, Remote Server Administration...
WARNING: Windows automatic updating is not enabled. To ensure that your newly-installed role or
feature is automatically updated, turn on Windows Update.
```

Clearly you can install the service without a static IP addresses as this warning indicates. You can simply assign a static IP address after you set this up and confirm the DHCP service is listening on that static IP address. This is true for IPv4 or IPv6. You can confirm the status of the installation by using Get-WindowsFeature DHCP.

And the output on the server shows

```
PS C:\> Get-WindowsFeature DHCP
Display Name                                      Name                      Install State
------------                                      ----                      -------------
[X] DHCP Server                                   DHCP                          Installed
```

Finally, if you want to modify which listener IPv6 addresses are used you will need to modify the binding order from the Set-DhcpServerv6Binding cmdlet. You can do this by using the following example PowerShell snippet:

```
# determine the InterfaceIndex and InterfaceAlias information for the Adapter you want to modify
Get-NetAdapter
# set the static IPv6 address you want on the Windows Server
New-NetIPAddress -InterfaceIndex 12 -IPAddress <IPv6 Address> -PrefixLength 64
# disable the use of temporary addresses on the server just in case someone enabled it - it is off
by default on Server which is a best practice
Set-NetIPv6Protocol -UseTemporaryAddresses Disabled
Set-DhcpServerv6Binding -BindingState $true -InterfaceAlias "Ethernet"
```

Following is an example of executing this on a Windows 2012R2 Server with the DHCP role installed already:

```
PS C:\> New-NetIPAddress -InterfaceIndex 12 -IPAddress 2001:470:1f05:9a4::2 -PrefixLength 64

IPAddress         : 2001:470:1f05:9a4::2
InterfaceIndex    : 12
InterfaceAlias    : Ethernet
AddressFamily     : IPv6
Type              : Unicast
PrefixLength      : 64
PrefixOrigin      : Manual
```

```
SuffixOrigin        : Manual
AddressState        : Tentative
ValidLifetime       : Infinite ([TimeSpan]::MaxValue)
PreferredLifetime   : Infinite ([TimeSpan]::MaxValue)
SkipAsSource        : False
PolicyStore         : ActiveStore

IPAddress           : 2001:470:1f05:9a4::2
InterfaceIndex      : 12
InterfaceAlias      : Ethernet
AddressFamily       : IPv6
Type                : Unicast
PrefixLength        : 64
PrefixOrigin        : Manual
SuffixOrigin        : Manual
AddressState        : Invalid
ValidLifetime       : Infinite ([TimeSpan]::MaxValue)
PreferredLifetime   : Infinite ([TimeSpan]::MaxValue)
SkipAsSource        : False
PolicyStore         : PersistentStore

PS C:\> Set-DhcpServerv6Binding -BindingState $true -InterfaceAlias "Ethernet"

PS C:\> Get-DhcpServerv6Binding
InterfaceAlias                          IPAddress              BindingState
--------------                          ---------              ------------
Ethernet                                2001:470:1f05:9a4::2 True
```

Figure 9-7 shows the confirmed binding configuration via the GUI which matches the PowerShell cmdlet output, as it should.

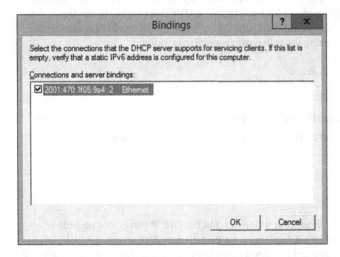

Figure 9-7. *DHCPv6 bind order information*

Unfortunately, Window Hyper-V Server does not allow the DHCP server role to be installed. To gain all the benefits of DHCP on Windows you will need to run Windows Server 2008 through 2012R2. Best practices for the DHCP role installation would be to have a static IPv4 and/or IPv6 address on the server already.

You can confirm the status of the installation by using Get-WindowsFeature DHCP.

And the output on the server shows

```
PS C:\> Get-WindowsFeature DHCP
Display Name                                      Name            Install State
------------                                      ----            -------------
[X] DHCP Server                                   DHCP                Installed
```

As a side note on installation of DHCP for the purpose of IPv6 only, when doing the install even if you have set up a static IPv6 address on the Windows server it will still give the following error:

```
PS C:\> Add-WindowsFeature DHCP -IncludeAllSubFeature -IncludeManagementTools
WARNING: The following recommended condition is not met for DHCP: No static IP addresses were found
on this computer. If the IP address changes, clients might not be able to contact this server.
Please configure a static IP address before installing DHCP Server.
```

This is due to the fact that you do not have an IPv4 address statically assigned to the server. The cmdlet is only checking IPv4 and not IPv6 so you can safely ignore the error. If you are deploying for IPv4 and IPv6 (dual-stack) then you should set up a static IPv4 address and modify the binding to use that static IPv4 address.

If you want your DHCP server to be AD integrated you will want to execute the Add-DhcpServerInDC PowerShell cmdlet to give it permissions. The DHCP server role should be installed on an AD joined server for this to work and will require the Fully Qualified Domain Name (FQDN) of the server. For example,

```
Add-DhcpServerInDC -DnsName "dhcp-server.example.com"
```

This would work for the DHCP server named dhcp-server.example.com. Alternately you can use the IPv6 address of the server also.

Finally, it is best practice to shut off the DHCPv6 client process on the DHCP server; otherwise, if it is providing DHCP on a locally attached server, it will obtain an IPv6 address for itself from the DHCPv6 service. While technically there is nothing wrong with this, there is no reason to add to the confusion by having multiple IPv6 addresses on the DHCPv6 server host. You can turn off this behavior by using the following PowerShell cmdlet:

```
Set-NetIPInterface -InterfaceIndex <#> -Dhcp Disabled
```

■ **Tip** In summary, the DHCP server should have a static IPv6 address, it should not run the DHCP client in the same interface as the listening interface of the DHCP server, and it should have a binding to the static IPv6 address.

DHCPv6 Scopes

After getting DHCP installed you will need to configure IP address scopes so that the DHCP server can provide IP addresses to DHCP clients. This is true for both IPv4 and IPv6. I will cover setting up new IPv6 scopes. The section "Operationally Managing DHCPv6" covers adding and removing scopes along with looking for specific information in a scope.

New Scope Creation

To add a new scope with PowerShell you will use the Add-DHCPServerv6Scope cmdlet. The following example PowerShell shows how to do this:

```
Add-DHCPServerv6Scope -Prefix 2001:db8:cafe:10:: -name test1-ipv6 -state Active
```

And this is the output on a Windows Server 2012R2 DHCP server:

```
PS C:\> Add-DHCPServerv6Scope -Prefix 2001:db8:cafe:10:: -name test1-ipv6 -state Active

PS C:\> Add-DHCPServerv6ExclusionRange -Prefix 2001:db8:cafe:10:: -StartRange 2001:db8:cafe:10::1
-EndRange 2001:db8:cafe:10::256
```

You will want to confirm that the scope state after creating it. To see all the scopes on the DHCP server use the Get-DHCPServerv6Scope cmdlet. The output on a Windows Server 2012R2 Server shows

```
PS C:\> Get-DHCPServerv6Scope | Format-List *

Prefix                : 2001:db8:cafe:10::
Description           :
Name                  : test1-ipv6
Preference            : 0
PreferredLifetime     : 8.00:00:00
PrefixLength          : 64
State                 : Active
T1                    : 4.00:00:00
T2                    : 6.09:36:00
ValidLifetime         : 12.00:00:00
PSComputerName        :
CimClass              : ROOT/Microsoft/Windows/DHCP:DhcpServerv6Scope
CimInstanceProperties : {Description, Name, Preference, PreferredLifetime...}
CimSystemProperties   : Microsoft.Management.Infrastructure.CimSystemProperties
```

As you can see, the scope is active and the name of the scope is also displayed. If you have a lot of scopes on the DHCP server (and you likely will) it will be easier to request the specific scope or prefix you are looking for explicitly. You can do this with the -Prefix parameter. The following shows that output (formatted to fit the page) on the same server:

```
PS C:\> Get-DhcpServerv6Scope -Prefix 2001:db8:cafe:10::

Prefix              PrefixLength  Name        State   PreferredLifeTime  ValidLifeTime
------              ------------  ----        -----   -----------------  -------------
2001:db8:cafe:10::  64            test1-ipv6  Active  8.00:00:00         12.00:00:00
```

At this point you will have an active DHCPv6 scope available on the DHCP server.

DHCPv6 Scope Options

Regardless of whether you do DHCPv6 stateful or stateless you will want to set up options on the DHCP server to provide basic network information to DHCP clients. Specifically, you will likely want to provide DNS and NTP information. For IPv6 you can do this with the following PowerShell cmdlets:

```
Set-DhcpServerv6OptionValue -OptionId <#> -value <parameter value>
```

Once you have set up them you can confirm they are set up with the following PowerShell cmdlets:

```
Get-DhcpServerv6OptionValue -OptionId <#>
```

To set up the DNS Recursive Resolver IPv6 address with Googles public IPv6 server, for example, you would use the following PowerShell cmdlet snippet:

```
Set-DhcpServerv6OptionValue -OptionId 23 -value 2001:4860:4860::8888
```

The following shows executing these on a Windows Server 2012R2 DHCP server. The output is modified to fit on the page.

```
PS C:\> Set-DhcpServerv6OptionValue -OptionId 23 -value 2001:4860:4860::8888

PS C:\> Get-DhcpServerv6OptionValue -OptionId 23

OptionId  Name              Type         VendorClass UserClass Value
--------  ----              ----         ----------- --------- -----
23        DNS Recursive Nam... IPv6Address                     {2001:4860:4860::8888}
```

Changing the Windows Client DHCP Settings

There may be times you want to control some aspects of how client DHCPv6 settings work within your environment. You can control these behaviors on Windows Server 2012, Windows Server 2012R2, Windows 8, and Windows 8.1 with the following PowerShell cmdlets:

```
Set-NetIPInterface
Stop-Service
```

If you need to shut off the DHCP client behavior on only a single interface you will use

```
Set-NetIPInterface -InterfaceIndex <#> -Dhcp Disabled
```

If you do not want the DHCP client service to run at all you can shut it off completely (for all interfaces) with the following PowerShell cmdlet:

```
 Stop-Service Dhcp -Confirm:$false
```

If you need the DHCP client behavior to survive a reboot you should disable the DHCP client service on the Windows host. That will prevent the Windows host from running a DHCP client process. It is safe to do this on statically assigned servers and hosts but you will need to make sure you provide DNS resolver IP addresses and other information as the host will not be able to obtain those from the DHCP server. If you want control something like RouterDiscovery through DHCP you would use an example PowerShell like the following:

```
Set-NetIPInterface -InterfaceIndex 15 -AddressFamily IPv6 -RouterDiscovery ControlledByDHCP
```

Some of these options can also be done on Windows Server 2008, Windows Server 2008R2, Windows Vista, and Windows 7 but via the GUI. Unfortunately the netsh command for client DHCP is designed to provide debugging information only and therefore is limited in configuration capabilities.

The list is not huge in terms of client DHCP settings, but you should have enough options in the Set-NetIPInterface cmdlet to perform the functions you need to match what you are doing with DHCP for IPv4 today.

Operationally Managing DHCPv6

PowerShell has a wide variety of DHCP specific cmdlets once you install the DHCP role on Windows Server 2012 and 2012R2. To see all the cmdlets available use Get-Command -Module DHCPServer which will display every cmdlet associated with the DHCP module. The specific cmdlets that impact IPv6 are

```
Add-DhcpServerv6Class
Add-DhcpServerv6ExclusionRange
Add-DhcpServerv6Lease
Add-DhcpServerv6OptionDefinition
Add-DhcpServerv6Reservation
Add-DhcpServerv6Scope

Get-DhcpServerv6Class
Get-DhcpServerv6DnsSetting
Get-DhcpServerv6ExclusionRange
Get-DhcpServerv6FreeIPAddress
Get-DhcpServerv6Lease
Get-DhcpServerv6OptionDefinition
Get-DhcpServerv6OptionValue
Get-DhcpServerv6Reservation
Get-DhcpServerv6Scope
Get-DhcpServerv6ScopeStatistics
Get-DhcpServerv6StatelessStatistics
Get-DhcpServerv6StatelessStore
Get-DhcpServerv6Statistics

Remove-DhcpServerv6Class
Remove-DhcpServerv6ExclusionRange
Remove-DhcpServerv6Lease
Remove-DhcpServerv6OptionDefinition
Remove-DhcpServerv6OptionValue
Remove-DhcpServerv6Reservation
Remove-DhcpServerv6Scope

Set-DhcpServerv6Binding
Set-DhcpServerv6Class
Set-DhcpServerv6DnsSetting
Set-DhcpServerv6OptionDefinition
Set-DhcpServerv6OptionValue
Set-DhcpServerv6Reservation
Set-DhcpServerv6Scope
Set-DhcpServerv6StatelessStore
```

While there are a lot of specific IPv6 DHCP PowerShell cmdlets, it is unlikely you will use them all. I will review some of the more common cmdlets you might use in operating your DHCPv6 scopes that we have not already covered in this chapter. They would be

```
Add-DhcpServerv6Reservation
Get-DhcpServerv6DnsSetting
Get-DhcpServerv6ExclusionRange
Get-DhcpServerv6Reservation
Remove-DhcpServerv6ExclusionRange
Remove-DhcpServerv6Lease
Remove-DhcpServerv6Reservation
Remove-DhcpServerv6Scope
Set-DhcpServerv6DnsSetting
Set-DhcpServerv6Reservation
```

It is relatively easy to tell what most of the PowerShell cmdlets do: for instance, the Add-DhcpServerv6Reservation cmdlet will set up a specific DHCPv6 IPv6 address reservation based on the DUID. The Remove-DhcpServerv6Reservation cmdlet will remove the reservation. If you need to modify or change it you use the Set-DhcpServerv6Reservation cmdlet and you can view the reservation with the Get-DhcpServerv6Reservation cmdlet.

The Get-DhcpServerv6DnsSetting cmdlet will display the DNS setting that the DHCP server is providing and you can narrow that down to specific scopes or system wide. The Set-DhcpServerv6DnsSetting cmdlet will allow you to set DNS settings globally or specifically for a scope.

It is possible to review the IPv6 scope exclusion ranges you have set up. To do this you use the Get-DhcpServerv6ExclusionRange cmdlet and to remove them use the Remove-DhcpServerv6ExclusionRange cmdlet.

As we noted earlier you can view a DHCP server scope leases on an existing server.

```
PS C:\> Get-DhcpServerv6Lease -Prefix 2001:db8:cafe:10::

IPAddress              ClientDuid            HostName        LeaseExpiryTime
---------              ----------            --------        ---------------
2001:db8:cafe:10:...   00-01-00-01-19-d5...  Surface-Spud    12/19/2013 12:43:08 PM
```

To remove that scope you would use the Remove-DhcpServerv6Lease cmdlet, so, for example:

```
PS C:\> Remove-DhcpServerv6Lease -Prefix 2001:db8:cafe:10::
PS C:\> Get-DhcpServerv6Lease -Prefix 2001:db8:cafe:10::
```

This particular cmdlet does not use the -confirm parameter so if you execute it the leases will be deleted for that prefix; therefore, use this cmdlet with caution. Let's quickly set up a DHCPv6 scope reservation based on a client device that has already obtained an IPv6 address from the DHCPv6 server. We can see on the Windows 8.1 client that it obtained an IPv6 address (some formatting options were included in the PowerShell to make it easier to focus on the information I want).

```
PS C:\> Get-NetIPAddress -AddressFamily IPv6 -InterfaceIndex 19 | select
ifIndex,IPAddress,SuffixOrigin | ft –AutoSize

ifIndex IPAddress                           SuffixOrigin
------- ---------                           ------------
     19 fe80::65bc:3073:4cf:f7aa%19         Link
     19 2001:db8:cafe:10:37b4:d165:e0a3:ad40  Dhcp
```

On the DHCPv6 server we can see the lease in that specific scope too.

```
PS C:\> Get-DhcpServerv6Lease -Prefix 2001:db8:cafe:10:: | fl
IPAddress        : 2001:db8:cafe:10:37b4:d165:e0a3:ad40
Prefix           : 2001:db8:cafe:10::
ClientDuid       : 00-01-00-01-19-d5-12-ed-00-00-00-00-00-00
Iaid             : 251678806
HostName         : Surface-Spud
LeaseExpiryTime  : 12/19/2013 12:43:08 PM
AddressType      : IANA
Description      :
```

Let's remove the lease from the DHCPv6 scope and create a new reservation and confirm the reservation is in place.

```
PS C:\> Remove-DhcpServerv6Lease -Prefix 2001:db8:cafe:10::

PS C:\> Get-DhcpServerv6Lease -Prefix 2001:db8:cafe:10:: | fl

PS C:\>
PS C:\> Add-DhcpServerv6Reservation -Prefix 2001:db8:cafe:10:: -IPAddress
2001:db8:cafe:10:b:b:b:b -ClientDuid 0001000119d512ed000000000000 -Iaid 251678806
-name test-spud

PS C:\> Get-DhcpServerv6Lease -Prefix 2001:db8:cafe:10:: | fl
IPAddress        : 2001:db8:cafe:10:b:b:b:b
Prefix           : 2001:db8:cafe:10::
ClientDuid       : 00-01-00-01-19-d5-12-ed-00-00-00-00-00-00
Iaid             : 251678806
HostName         :
LeaseExpiryTime  :
AddressType      : IANA
Description      :
```

We can simply disable and enable the interface on the Windows 8.1 client and the DHCPv6 client request will kick off again. Alternately, you could use the ipconfig /renew6 command to kick off the DHCPv6 request process.

```
PS C:\> Disable-NetAdapter -Name "VMware Network Adapter VMnet6" -Confirm:$false

PS C:\> Enable-NetAdapter -Name "VMware Network Adapter VMnet6" -Confirm:$false
Now let's check on the DHCPv6 server to confirm the reservation was used for that client.
PS C:\> Get-DhcpServerv6Lease -Prefix 2001:db8:cafe:10:: | fl
IPAddress        : 2001:db8:cafe:10:b:b:b:b
Prefix           : 2001:db8:cafe:10::
ClientDuid       : 00-01-00-01-19-d5-12-ed-00-00-00-00-00-00
Iaid             : 251678806
HostName         : Surface-Spud
LeaseExpiryTime  :
AddressType      : IANA
Description      :
```

And then we can confirm the Windows 8.1 client received the IPv6 address we specified.

```
PS C:\> Get-NetIPAddress -AddressFamily IPv6 -InterfaceIndex 19 | select
ifIndex,IPAddress,SuffixOrigin | ft -AutoSize

ifIndex IPAddress                    SuffixOrigin
------- ---------                    ------------
     19 fe80::65bc:3073:4cf:f7aa%19      Link
     19 2001:db8:cafe:10:b:b:b:b         Dhcp
```

Figure 9-8 shows the properties of the same reservation via the DHCPv6 server GUI.

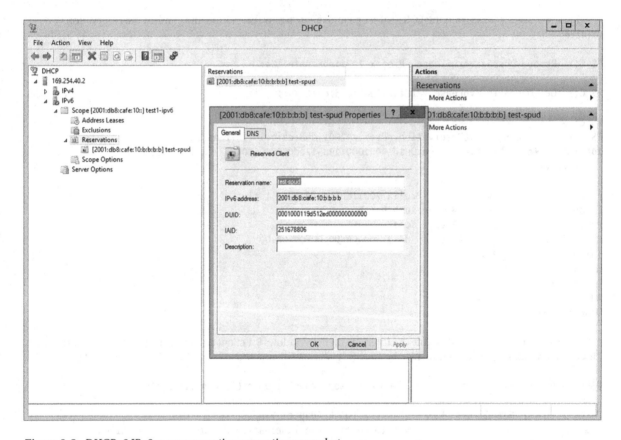

Figure 9-8. *DHCPv6 IPv6 scope reservation properties screenshot*

Notice that the actual hostname of the Windows client is not in the reservation properties. The reservation name displayed is the one we set in the PowerShell cmdlets earlier. If you want the hostname of the client, the PowerShell output for the Get-DhcpServerv6Lease command does display that. It is also possible to set DHCPv6 options modification for a specific reservation, but I do not advise doing that as it requires a lot of additional operational work to maintain.

Finally, Figure 9-9 shows how to add a new IPv6 reservation via the DHCPv6 server GUI.

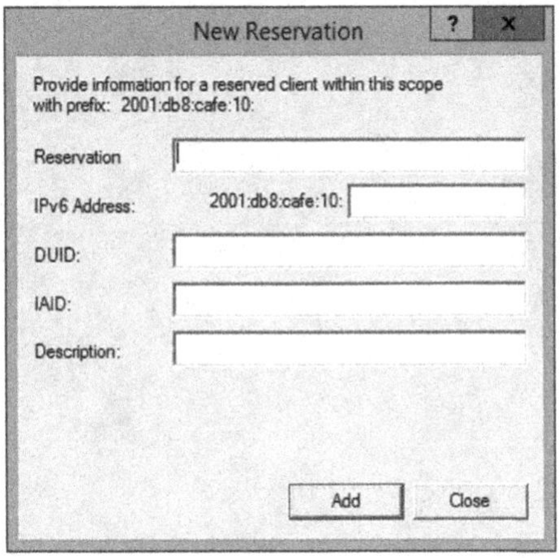

Figure 9-9. *DHCPv6 IPv6 scope new reserveration screenshot*

Other Address Allocation Methods

There are other methods for providing IP addresses to hosts. Specifically, you can also provide IPv6 addresses via SLAAC and static assignments. Chapter 3 covers both of these methods. SLAAC will be more common in home environments or in some guest networks (for instance, wireless). Static IPv6 assignments will be more common in data centers for servers, routers, switches, and other key critical network infrastructure.

I will again recommend a DNS, DHCP, IP Address Management (DDI) solution to help keep all this information in a central and organized place. Keeping track of static IPv6 address information is difficult and prone to error, even when doing cut and paste. In addition, if you are using something like Microsoft Excel to store IPv4 information today it is more difficult to keep sorted lists of IPv6 addresses due to the fact they have HEX values in the address and a delimiter that Excel wants to use to divide the information into different cells if you are importing data. Excel is not an ideal management method.

DHCPv6 Challenges

There are some challenges you will face when running DHCP that will likely revolve around rogue DHCP servers, misconfigured DHCP relays, or missing DHCP relays. These problems are not unique to IPv6, but some challenges are unique to IPv6 due to how the protocol works.

For instance, mismatching RA flag values on the same VLAN (virtual local area network) or subnet will cause problems. They could cause client hosts to behave differently or to even flop back and forth (which is likely a worse behavior than just having hosts stay one way or the other). You will need to coordinate with your network team (if you have one) so that the RA flag values are the same for the appropriate IPv6 prefix. This means also having matching DHCPv6 relay settings so your DHCP traffic is not going to different resources. Unless you have a highly available and distributed DDI solution (for instance an Infoblox solution) you will likely want to keep the DHCP relay configuration simple so it is easier to troubleshoot if there is a problem.

Finally, we should address the issue of cloning virtual machines and duplicating host OS images for client deployment. Without the proper steps you could end up with duplicate DUIDs on several hosts. You need to insure you utilize sysprep to avoid this problem. Chapter 7 covers in more detail what you need to do to resolve this potential problem. Remember, a DUID is used for reservations and for logging purposes in DHCPv6. The function of the DUID in DHCPv6 is like a MAC address in IPv4 reservations in DHCP. A duplicate MAC address would cause the same issue for DHCP, so save yourself from a headache and insure the DUID is unique for all your hosts.

■ ■ ■

## CHAPTER 10

Miscellaneous IPv6

Among the biggest challenges with IPv6 is understanding the impacts it can have in situations in which you would not normally think a network protocol would change behavior or change what is happening. IPv6 can become frustrating, unexpectedly impactful, and, at its worst, operationally disruptive. While it is not uncommon to make regular network changes for things like Ethernet ports, virtual local area networks (VLANs), and even IPv4 network configurations, IPv6 is not well understood by many and therefore can be a mystery to those trying to work with it. The wrong configuration option or setting could have an impact that was never intended. With IPv6 being enabled and for all practical purposes preferred in the Windows operating system (OS), much greater challenges than anticipated can arise.

One of the goals of this book was to make you more operationally efficient with IPv6 and to make you feel more comfortable working with it. Only with practice can you feel comfortable using something and IPv6 is no exception. In this chapter I hope to cover some miscellaneous IPv6 topics that I have found to be impactful while running a Windows environment but which don't fit explicitly in one of the previous chapters. Thus, there is no particular order or logic for their listing in this chapter. I just hope they are useful to you in case you run into them in the future. With that, let's cover the first one, which is NCSI.

NCSI on Windows

I covered NCSI in Chapter 3 but as a quick summary Network Connection Status Indicator is the method that Windows utilizes for several Internet detection functions. One of them is to determine if you can access the IPv6 Internet. It does this by first attempting to resolve `ipv6.msftncsi.com` (which only has an AAAA record published, no A record). Once it has the IPv6 address it will attempt to connect to that IPv6 address using http. One of the IPv6 addresses the Windows host has in use will be preferred in the prefix policy table and will be the source traffic. If none of the global unicast addresses or ULA (unique local addresses) are able to connect, then the Windows host will fall back to IPv4. The exception is if the Windows host attempts to connect to the URL (uniform resource locator) and gets back a capture portal or some other http notification. When it gets this response Windows indicates you have "Limited" connectivity. If it can detect that it is Internet proxy that does a redirection for login it will launch your default browser to bring the page up.

At this point Windows will have determined if you have a working IPv6 implementation for getting out to the public IPv6 Internet. But what if you are only running IPv6 for your lab? NCSI will fail and Windows will no longer use IPv6, which likely isn't the configuration that you wanted.

Impact of NCSI

If you don't understand how NCSI impacts Windows 7 with the IPv6 readiness update (`http://support.microsoft.com/kb/2750841`), Windows 8, Windows 8.1, Windows Server 2008R2 with the IPv6 readiness update, Windows Server 2012, and Windows Server 2012R2 then you will have problems getting IPv6 to work properly. Global unicast and ULA will both be impacted by NCSI behavior and there are a couple of use cases where I have found I needed to get IPv6 working with global unicast or ULA but with NO public IPv6 access.

The first example case occurs when you are trying to deploy a lab with no public IPv6 Internet access for the purpose of testing application behavior with IPv6. You need IPv6 working to study the impact on applications; there is no requirement to communicate with the Internet at all (IPv4 or IPv6) but NCSI will prevent IPv6 from working.

The second example occurs when you are utilizing ULA for internal use of IPv6 but you have not deployed global unicast addresses to allow permitted hosts to reach external resources via IPv6.

How to Work Around NCSI

It is appropriate to work around NCSI when you need to test IPv6 in your lab, but you do not have public IPv6 access or are doing a limited test. Thus, how do you go about modifying NCSI to allow you to test IPv6 without your Windows servers and clients falling back to using IPv4 because they think IPv6 is not functioning?

There are two ways to fake out NCSI. The first is to set up a temporary web server with a routable IPv6 address in your lab. Publish in your internal DNS (Domain Name System) an AAAA record for `ipv6.msftncsi.com` and then put the IPv6 address of your internal web server in for that AAAA record. On that web server build out the default web server response page to return a simple text file that has the following content:

```
Microsoft NCSI
```

The name of the file should be `ncsi.txt` so the complete URL will be

```
http://ipv6.msftncsi.com/ncsi.txt
```

Once you have the web server, DNS entry, and text file built out, the Windows clients that are using the internal DNS will resolve to your internal web server and get back the correct content, which means that the Windows client will have passed the NCSI test.

The other option is to modify the URL that the Windows client uses to test for NCSI. This allows you to specify a URL other than the `ipv6.msftncsi.com`. For instance, you can use PowerShell on a Windows host named Howfunky to do this with the following cmdlet to set it to `ipv6.ncsi.example.com`.

```
Set-NCSIPolicyConfiguration -CorporateWebsiteProbeURL http://ipv6.ncsi.example.com
-PolicyStore Howfunky
```

You can confirm that the settings worked by using the Get-NCSIPolicyConfiguration PowerShell cmdlet. As shown, it lists the NCSI parameters the host is currently using.

```
PS C:\> Get-NCSIPolicyConfiguration
Description                    : NCSI Configuration
CorporateDNSProbeHostAddress   :
CorporateDNSProbeHostName      :
CorporateSitePrefixList        :
CorporateWebsiteProbeURL       : http://ipv6.ncsi.example.com
DomainLocationDeterminationURL :
```

If you need to reset the default configuration of Windows on the client you can simply execute the following PowerShell cmdlet:

```
Reset-NCSIPolicyConfiguration -PolicyStore Howfunky
```

Using these simple methods you can enable lab testing of IPv6 without requiring external IPv6 Internet access. It likely is easier to take the first approach involving the web server if you do not plan to modify Windows clients in your test environment, or if there are too many instances of the clients to make it worthwhile to modify the clients in any way. If your lab will be relatively stable and the clients you are testing are fewer in number it may be easier to quickly do the PowerShell cmdlets. Regardless of the method you choose you will need to set up a web server to host the NCSI text file. There is no requirement that the web server be running Microsoft IIS (Internet Information Services) on the Windows server; it will work just fine on Linux, OSX, or some other OS running Apache, for instance. But, given that this book is all about running IPv6 on Windows I recommend you set it up on Windows Server 2012 R2 with IIS.

Prefix Policy Table

While there is RFC 3484 and its update RFC 6724 to define the default behavior of hosts with regard to how they should build out their prefix policy table there are times when you may need to modify the prefix policy table to do what you need for your environment. While I don't think this is something you will do very often it may come up (especially for lab and testing situations) and it is something you will want in your tool belt, just in case. What is unusual about modifying the prefix policy table is that traditionally routing decisions were often confined to the role of a networking team.

The RFC specifies that this flexibility is something that should be accommodated and Microsoft has included this in Windows. Unfortunately, Microsoft has not updated the PowerShell cmdlets to support anything beyond looking up what is in the prefix policy table. You can do that with the following cmdlet:

```
Get-NetPrefixPolicy
```

Some example output from a Windows 8.1 host for the Get-NetPrefixPolicy PowerShell cmdlet is

```
PS C:\> Get-NetPrefixPolicy
```

Prefix	Precedence	Label
3ffe::/16	1	12
fec0::/10	1	11
::/96	1	3
fc00::/7	3	13
2001::/32	5	5
2002::/16	30	2
::ffff:0:0/96	35	4
::/0	40	1
::1/128	50	0

There are also netsh commands to do the same but also to add, remove, and change existing prefix policy table entries. These commands are

```
netsh interface ipv6 show prefixpolicies
netsh interface ipv6 add prefixpolicy <prefix> <precedence> <label>
netsh interface ipv6 set prefixpolicy <prefix> <precedence> <label>
netsh interface ipv6 remove prefixpolicy <prefix> <precedence> <label>
```

As you can see, besides the prefix itself (to define what IPv6 prefix to match against) the commands also include a precedence and label. The precedence is an integer that the Windows host uses to order the prefix lists based on destination. The lower the value, the less preferred that destination address to use is for the host.

The label is an integer that the Windows host uses to order the source preference based on a destination prefix. It is not something that you will commonly modify, but be aware it does play a role after the precedence in determining matches for behavior.

Now let's take a moment to clarify the differences that happened between RFC 3484 and 6724 and the impact those have on the prefix policy table. Table 10-1 summarizes the updates in RFC 7624 for the prefix policy table.

Table 10-1. RFC 6724 vs. RFC 3484 Prefix Policy Table

IPv6 Prefix Range	RFC 3484 Precedence	RFC 6724 Precedence
3ffe::/16	40	1
fec0::/10	40	1
fc00::/7	40	3
::/96	20	1
::ffff:0:0/96	10	35

It likely is not obvious, but the goal for the update was to de-preference some IPv6 prefix ranges. Specifically the old 6Bone range of 3ffe::/16 is no longer used and neither is the site-local prefix of fec0::/10 nor the IPv4 compatible address range of ::/96, so all are set to a precedence of 1. This is the least desirable setting and so this makes sense because those prefixes are no longer in use.

Notice that ULA's prefix of fc00::/7 was moved lower below tunneling options like 6to4 and Teredo. Overall, these are good changes; however, they result in inconsistent behavior between Windows OS versions. Those that conform to RFC 6724 are Windows 8, Windows 8.1, Windows Server 2012, and Windows Server 2012 R2. All previous versions of Windows will conform to RFC 3484 and will therefore require you to apply a new prefix policy table to change them to match RFC 6724. You can do that with the following netsh commands:

```
netsh int ipv6 add prefixpolicy 3ffe::/16 1 12 store=persistent
netsh int ipv6 add prefixpolicy fec0::/10 1 11 store=persistent
netsh int ipv6 add prefixpolicy fc00::/8 4 13 store=persistent
netsh int ipv6 add prefixpolicy fd00::/8 3 14 store=persistent
netsh int ipv6 add prefixpolicy ::/96 1 3 store=persistent
netsh int ipv6 add prefixpolicy ::ffff:0:0/96 35 4 store=persistent
```

You will notice that Windows 7 and Vista will require that you build two entries for the ULA address space. For some reason the netsh command will not accept the fc00::/7 prefix. The reality is you will only need to apply the fd00::/8 prefix entry. The fc00::/8 is reserved and unallocated and should not be used on any IPv6 network today. This may change in the future, but it is unlikely to happen anytime soon.

You can find more resources on netsh and prefix policy modification at the following TechNet article:

```
http://technet.microsoft.com/en-us/library/cc740203%28v=WS.10%29.aspx#BKMK_5
```

Best practices for modifying the prefix policy table on Windows hosts is to leverage Group Policy to push out the appropriate netsh commands. You can filter your client and server devices so you only push changes to hosts that actually require any prefix updates.

NPTv6 and NAT66

There is an ongoing debate in the IPv6 community about Network Address Translation (NAT) and what (if any) role it should have in the brave new world of IPv6. A little bit of history of how NAT came about should help frame the debate a little and so humor me as I cover how NAT became so commonly used in IPv4.

NAT was first defined in RFC 1631 (`http://tools.ietf.org/html/rfc1631`) and was brought about because of a dismaying trend that network operators were noticing in the early 1990s. The depletion of IPv4 was happening at an alarming rate that would bring about the early end to IPv4 addresses and the IPv4 routing table was growing more rapidly than routers at the time could handle. To address both these problems two solutions came about. First was Classless Inter-Domain Routing (CIDR), which moved the previous IPv4 addressing allocations away from the classful A (/8), B (/16), and C (/24) blocks to a more efficient allocation based on bit boundaries. CIDR was first introduced in 1993 and was the first step taken to slow the rapid consumption of the IPv4 address space.

The second step taken was the introduction of NAT. NAT was brought about to reduce the rate of consumption of IPv4 until a better next-generation IP could be developed. That protocol was first called IPng and is now known as IPv6. NAT was first introduced in 1994 to help reduce the consumption of IPv4 addresses by overloading public IPv4 addresses. If you review RFC 1631 it is interesting to note that the authors do not consider security to be an advantage of implementing NAT. In fact, the negative section lists the following:

"It hides the identity of hosts. While this has the benefit of privacy, it is generally a negative effect."

So, even the original authors of NAT knew that the long-term impact on security would be negative. The reason is obvious; if you have hosts behind NAT attacking another network they can act by hiding behind NAT and reduce the effectiveness of easily identifying who they are explicitly. This only benefits the attacker in these situations.

So, where does this leave the debate of NAT and IPv6? NAT was introduced to provide a solution for IP address depletion. We needed to slow the consumption of IPv4 addresses so we could have time to develop a new networking protocol with more address space. We now have that new protocol, IPv6, which is a nearly limitless address space. So do we need NAT when we do not need to conserve IP address space anymore? The answer is more complicated than you might think and the IPv6 community reflects this. Let's dig into the first NAT solution for IPv6 that actually has some valid use cases, NPTv6.

NPTv6

Network Prefix Translation for IPv6 (NPTv6) is defined in RFC 6296 (`http://tools.ietf.org/html/rfc6296`) and is designed to allow one IPv6 prefix to be translated to a different IPv6 prefix of the same prefix size. It is an IPv6-to-IPv6 translation solution and is designed to be stateless in function.

NPTv6 addresses some potential common use cases for NAT and IPv6, specifically the use of ULA on hosts that need to connect to something on the IPv6 Internet and also the case of non-BGP multi-homing. These are covered in more detail in the RFC along with some other example use cases in section 2 of the RFC.

Remember that NPTv6 requires that the two IPv6 prefixes be identical, so if you are utilizing a /48 internally for ULA then you will need a /48 for the external IPv6 global unicast prefix in order to run NPTv6. One of the advantages of doing the one-for-one matching is that only the leftmost 48 bits in this example have to be changed. The rightmost 80 bits remain the same no matter what. Depending on the size of the prefix this will change obviously so a /64 will only translate the leftmost 64 bits, but you get the picture of how it works. This simple concept allows NPTv6 to be stateless. In other words, the router or firewall that is performing this function at the edge of the network does not have to keep any state information about the IP flow. It may still be performing some sort of Stateful Packet Inspection (SPI) but it does not have to keep a NAT table at all. It simply transforms the address as it ingresses an interface and does the reverse on the other interface it needs to forward the traffic too.

For those who are architecting an IPv6 network, your prefix matching can be subsets. For example, you may have a /48 prefix for a site but only one /64 out of that /48 actually needs to get prefix translated, which means you only need a /64 to do the prefix translation. If you expand the network beyond the one /64 already doing NPTv6 then you will need to allocate another /64(s) to match the newly expanded network. You can continue to grow the NPTv6 definitions this way or you can simply do a /48-to-/48 matching as noted previously.

There really are some legitimate use cases for NPTv6; however, at this time I am not aware of any commercially supported implementation of NPTv6. I do expect to see it released as a feature from the majority of network manufacturers.

NAT66

Unlike NPTv6, NAT66 requires the network edge device to be stateful. It functions in the same fashion as NAT44 but simply does it for IPv6 instead of IPv4. This means that the devices that perform NAT66 have to keep track of state information.

One of the advantages of NAT66 is that you do not require matching IPv6 prefix sizes in order for it to work in theory. I am not sure that this is as big an advantage as one would like it to be given the relative ease it is to get appropriately sized IPv6 prefixes.

There are NAT66 implementations in existence today from Cisco, Juniper, and others. They function as expected but will have all the same downsides as NAT44, such as breaking many IP transport protocols and requiring many applications to have to do a lot of extra work to determine if a NAT is happening between two hosts or not.

NAT66 also requires application-specific fixes just as NAT44 does. This means that applications that embed IPv6 information in the protocol have to be manipulated by the NAT66 device. This is the same for NPTv6 as it also is changing the IPv6 source and/or destination information to match the new prefix it is translating. The efficiencies gained from NPTv6 are the fact that no state information has to be kept.

Carrier Grade NAT

So, how is Carrier Grade NAT (CGN) different from NPTv6 and NAT66? Both NPTv6 and NAT66 are IPv6-to-IPv6 solutions. CGN was designed to stretch out the lifetime of IPv4 even further. If we first started with CIDR and then NAT44 we are now expanding NAT even further than we ever intended. CGN basically goes to the next logical step to perform NAT within a carrier's network resulting in NAT444 and potentially in some cases NAT4444.

Unfortunately, CGN also exasperates some of the problems we have with NAT44 today as it adds yet another level of NAT into the IPv4 solution, resulting in a typical NAT444 solution.

This means that a CGN solution not only requires lots of devices to maintain state throughout the network but also requires an extensive amount of logging so that lawful intercept requirements by law enforcement can be met. There are some interesting solutions that are developing now to try to help reduce this requirement but none are mature enough to go over in detail at this time.

Figure 10-1 shows a typical service provider network with Customer Premise Equipment (CPE) and its standard IPv4 network deployment today.

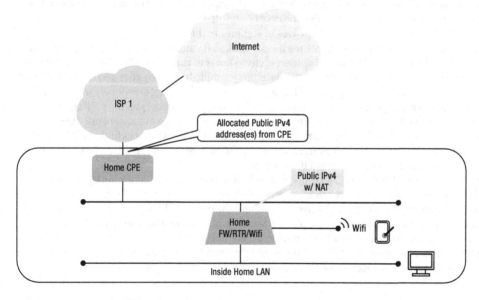

Figure 10-1. *A typical home Internet service*

With the implementation of CGN the carrier network transitions to one that looks like Figure 10-2, where the CPE is no longer provided a public IPv4 address but instead is using an RFC 1918 IPv4 private address. The NAT function to the public IP address it uses happens back in the service provider network.

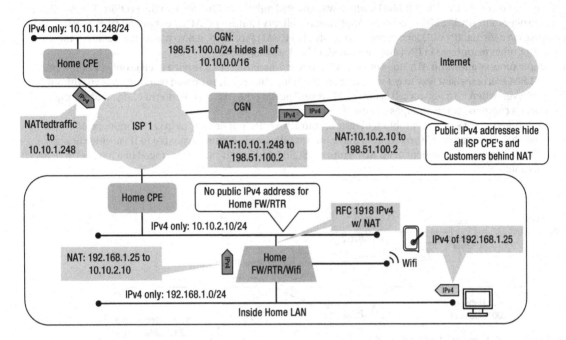

Figure 10-2. *Home Internet service with CGN*

There are several things that are not desirable with CGN. First, as a customer you no longer have a public IPv4 address on your device. This limits your ability to host services like VPN (virtual private network) back to your home. It requires that you subscribe or use a service that proxies the connection. Also, if you use gaming consoles like Xbox and wish to host or provide peer-to-peer gaming sessions it is no longer possible except on your own LAN (local area network). Xbox One leverages IPv6 and Teredo to get around some of these limitations, but it does not solve the problem for older gaming consoles and for other console platforms.

Because CGN is sharing a single IPv4 address across multiple customers and is making use of Port Address Translation (PAT) to overload the number of IPv4 network addresses to unique PAT requests, a resource constraint occurs. For both TCP (Transmission Control Protocol) and UDP (User Datagram Protocol) there are 65,536 total ports available per transport layer protocol. TCP is the most commonly used (for HTTP, SMTP, etc.) and if you share a single IPv4 address among enough customers you can run out of TCP ports. This causes some unexpected behavior like Google Maps not building out the complete web page, resulting in blank areas on the map. This is due to how many TCP sockets are opened at the same time to load the web page. If the service provider CGN does not have enough ports available then the session request never happens or times out.

If you do plan on leveraging CGN or if your company has to work with it you should understand some of its operational impacts. A good starting point is the RFC draft (http://tools.ietf.org/html/draft-nishizuka-cgn-deployment-considerations-01) on CGN Deployment Considerations which was last updated in September 2013.

As a final thought, CGN is likely to become a more common solution for service providers until their IPv6 deployments are completed and they see significant traffic (above 10%) on IPv6. For many service providers, investing in CGN is about preserving IPv4 resources. They only have to do this due to the lack of adoption of IPv6. We all win the more quickly we adopt and use IPv6 as our primary (and eventually only) networking protocol.

SLB64

There are other transition technologies available to allow IPv6 hosts to connect to IPv4 resources. One of the easiest to leverage is Server Load Balancer 6 to 4 (SLB64), which was covered quickly in Chapter 4, in the section "HA–Application Delivery Controllers and IPv6." SLB64 allows an Application Delivery Controller (ADC) to have an IPv6 interface that it can advertise via a Virtual IP (VIP) for a service, typically HTTP, SMTP, or DNS. It also has a connection to the internal DMZ or other resources via IPv4 and can translate back and forth.

This simple process allows an ADC to provide IPv6 services when the actual service itself is only available on an IPv4 server. SLB64 is an excellent way to get web, mail, and other public services up and working on IPv6 without fully deploying IPv6 everywhere in a network. It is designed around putting the ADC at the Internet Edge and setting up the specific services a company wants to expose to the IPv6 Internet.

SLB64 solutions do not solve the problem of testing your IPv6 VIPs, nor do they help with a more rapid deployment of IPv6. They can help if you want to make internal IPv4-only content available to IPv6-only clients. Figure 10-3 shows a typical deployment of an ADC running SLB64 and how it can be leveraged in a long-term IPv6 transition solution.

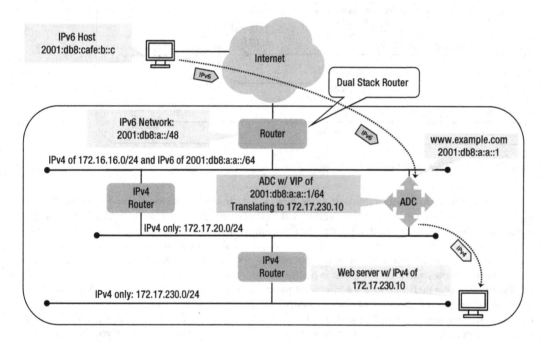

Figure 10-3. *ADC running SLB64*

Formats for IPv6

Because there are so many ways to express IPv6 addresses, one of the challenges you will encounter is how to search for IPv6 addresses in logs, databases, and any other location where IPv6 addresses might be kept. IPv4 has been around a long time and the operational model for how to store IPv4 addresses and how to look for them was established and standardized a long time ago. In fact, for many today, consideration about how an IPv4 address should be stored doesn't even come up anymore.

With IPv6 we need to revisit this discussion. Because there are multiple ways to express IPv6 addresses, there are naturally challenges with selecting the correct format to display, store, and search for addresses. Remember, two different requirements that have to be met: (1) a universal way to display or represent an address to users and (2) a way to store and compare addresses to allow for efficient use of regular expressions and search matches. Unfortunately, these two requirements don't result in a single method, so let's review what each provides.

Because presenting an IPv6 address to users is a universal issue, RFC 5952 (`http://tools.ietf.org/html/rfc5952`) defines recommendations for IPv6 address text representation; it really is an RFC about displaying IPv6 addresses.

To simplify displaying an IPv6 address, just realize that a standard address format per the RFC should meet the following requirements:

- Leading zeros must be suppressed.

- A 16-bit field of all zeros (i.e., `:0000:`) must be represented as a single zero (i.e., `:0:`).

- Shorten as MUCH as possible.

- Do not use double colons to shorten a single 16-bit field (quibble), just use a zero (so `:0:` not `::`).

- The longest run of consecutive zeros must be shortened with a double colon; however, if there are two or more equal-length zero segments the leftmost or "first" of them should be shortened. You should always try to keep "shortening" in the prefix portion of an address if possible.

- Prefer lowercase for "a" through "f" in the address.

- Square brackets should be put around IPv6 addresses if a port needs to be displayed (i.e., `[2001:db8::1]80` for port 80).

For search, log files, and any other method that may require comparing or matching against an IPv6 address we need to take a different approach. Specifically, if you plan to support searching, storing, or managing IPv6 addresses then I recommend you conform to the fully enumerated IPv6 address format (a full 128-bit value) unless you have a very good reason not to do so. Alternately, make obvious zero compression while still keeping the total number of quibbles consistent. For example, `2001:0db8:cafe:000a:6023:59cd:7eff:0ba0` would be shortened to `2001:db8:cafe:a:6023:59cd:7eff:ba0`.

While the difference may seem minor we are still fully expressing the address with all quibbles having a value and simply removing leading zeros. In cases where a lot of leading zeros are being compressed (such as in link-local) you still will want to have all eight quibbles present, so, for example, the typical link-local address on a Windows host would be expressed as `fe80::540c:3394:3b89:3cbd%10`.

If you were logging this value it would likely make more sense to do so as `fe80:0:0:0:540c:3394:3b89:3cbd`.

The next natural question to ask is should the ZoneID (ScopeID) be stored with the IPv6 address. This really depends on how you plan on using the IPv6 address later. If it will be for the purpose of modifying the prefix policy table or the routing table you will want to store that information. Otherwise, as a general rule you will not need it.

I think it makes sense to mention that you will likely run into a wide variety of formats and methods for storing IPv6 addresses. As the adoption of IPv6 becomes more aggressive the standardization of formatting for the IPv6 address will happen. Don't be shocked if you have to spend some time and energy reformatting IPv6 addresses or doing more complex regular express syntax in order to actually get a match to work properly. It is just part of the transition costs of moving to IPv6.

Common Tools That Support IPv6

I often get questions about what commands support IPv6 or if there are new commands for IPv6 in general for Windows. The great news about Windows since Vista and Server 2008 is that all common commands you would use with IPv4 work with IPv6 and might even have IPv6 switches or parameter support. Following is a brief list of some of the commands that work with IPv6:

- Ping

- Tracert

- Nslookup
- Ipconfig
- Route
- Pathping
- Netstat

In case you didn't notice in the rest of the book, there are numerous networking PowerShell cmdlets and most of them support IPv6 parameter values. There is a small subset that are IPv4 only or IPv6 only. When at all possible I have used PowerShell to perform functional tasks. There are also netsh commands available and those have been updated to support IPv6 also. Both the PowerShell and netsh command lists are too long to list here, but if there is a command that is missing in IPv6 you should open a support ticket with Microsoft (unless it is an IPv4-only command!) because Windows by design should fully function and support both IPv4 and IPv6.

It is important to note that native Microsoft Windows commands are not the only ones that support IPv6 as input and output values. Common utilities and tools like dig, iperf, and wireshark all work as expected on Windows (after they are installed) and will take IPv6 parameter values if appropriate.

Other IPv6 Transition Technologies

In addition to the built-in native transition services in Windows (6to4, ISATAP, and Teredo), some other transition technologies should be mentioned. All three mentioned here are for a Windows server. Depending on the server OS (operating system) version they may or may not be available.

IP-HTTPS

Microsoft introduced IP-HTTPS for DirectAccess (DA) with Windows Server 2008R2. Microsoft leveraged SSL/TLS (Secure Sockets Layer/Transport Layer Security) and the fact that almost every firewall allows access to a remote IP address on port 443 to build a new tunnel method for a DA client to connect to a DA server. If you think of IP-HTTPS as an SSL client VPN solution (it is not one but close enough) you would not be far off the mark. In fact, you can even do SSL offloading with an ADC if you want for Windows 7 clients with a Windows Server 2012 DA deployment. Unfortunately, Windows 8 clients use NULL encryption, so offloading is not an advantage in that case. Having IP-HTTPS available gave more flexibility in the deployment of DA servers in networks and provided a well-accepted method for remote access, allowing easier adoption of DA as a solution.

NAT64/DNS64

NAT64/DNS64, which allows an IPv6 client to establish a connection to an IPv4 resource, was added to Windows Server 2012. Before Windows Server 2012, to obtain the NAT64/DNS64 functionality you needed to run Forefront UAG. Thankfully Microsoft decided to integrate these services directly into the server OS and give system administrators an easy tool to help with IPv6 transition. Unfortunately, NAT64/DNS64 does not give you IPv4-to-IPv6 capabilities, which limits its usefulness for things like manage-out for Windows clients. You can find more details about NAT64/DNS64 in Chapter 4.

PortProxy

PortProxy is an application-layer gateway that has been available in the Windows server since Windows Server 2003. You would utilize a dual-stacked server and run the PortProxy service on that host in order to proxy IPv6-to-IPv4 or IPv4-to-IPv6 sessions. It can also be used to proxy IPv6 to IPv6 or IPv4 to IPv4 since it is a simple application proxy service. It is commonly used for apps that cannot natively support IPv6. It is sometimes leveraged in DA deployments to allow the DA clients to connect to IPv4-only resources that have no IPv6 support, even if the server itself may support IPv6. One of the limitations of PortProxy is that it only supports TCP and only has netsh commands. You can find more details about PortProxy on the TechNet web site at http://technet.microsoft.com/en-us/library/cc786629%28v=ws.10%29.aspx.

You can find the PortProxy netsh commands found at http://technet.microsoft.com/en-us/library/cc776297%28v=WS.10%29.aspx.

There are other IPv6 transition technologies available; however, these are the additional ones that you should be aware of for the Windows server. The Windows client OS does not have these as an option.

Order of Interfaces in Windows

One of the challenges with deploying IPv6 is understanding the order in which interfaces are used by Windows. Obviously this can vary depending on several factors. Those would be

- Windows OS version

- RFC 3484 vs. 6724

- Public or private IPv4 addresses on a Windows host

- Global unicast or ULA on a Windows host

- Prefix policy table overwrite

As a general rule of thumb it is easiest to have an ordered list to follow and simply know that there may be exceptions from time to time. The ordered list with most preferred listed first is

1. Native IPv6

2. 6to4

3. ISATAP

4. IPv4

5. Teredo

You can use the flow diagram in Chapter 4 for RFC 6724 to determine source and destination address selection; however, this will only apply to Windows Server 2012 and 2012 R2 along with Windows 8 and 8.1. There are other considerations for how RFC 3484 impacts destination selection. For instance, Windows Vista and Server 2008 on will not honor DNS round robin by default unless a registry key is modified. This is due to how Windows uses RFC 3484 vs. what DNS round robin tells the OS to do. More details can be found at the following Microsoft support article: http://support.microsoft.com/kb/968920.

Also note that Windows has de-preferenced Teredo in the prefix policy table since Windows Vista and Server 2008. Some other OSs did not do this and followed strict RFC 3484 standards. RFC 6724 changed the preference of Teredo formally, but many OS manufacturers (including Microsoft) had been doing this for years prior to RFC 6724 even coming out.

Do Binding Orders Matter?

You would think that the binding order questions would have an obvious answer. Unfortunately, the binding order status keeps changing over time. Let's start with where Microsoft would like to see this and where Microsoft is with it now.

In the long term, Microsoft will remove the dependency on binding orders completely, and to a great extent this has gone away in the OS entirely. There may be some cases where products or services will tell you to change the binding order for a service, but in reality they have no good reason to do so; it is just what they have always done. Because Microsoft is trying to move away from having the binding order be a dependency in how the OS behaves you may want to test to see if this requirement is a real one or if someone is simply repeating steps from older documentation.

For the most part in Windows 8.1 and Server 2012 R2 you should not have to manage or deal with the binding order. In fact, on the client side, you should not have to touch it at all and it should have little to no impact on the behavior of the OS. For Windows Server 2012 R2, depending on the service you are deploying, there may be cases where the product group will tell you to modify the binding order in its deployment recommendations guides. This is typically due to the order that the OS is choosing to look up DNS name resolution based on binding orders for DNS IP resolver lists. For instance, you will see this recommendation from the cluster team in its deployment guides.

Today, it is typical to modify the binding order via the graphical user interface (GUI). You do this by right-clicking the network interface display in the task bar and selecting "Open the Network and Sharing Center." From there you can press the Alt key and the pop-up menu will prompt you; you will select the Advanced menu option, as shown in Figure 10-4, and then Advanced Settings.

Figure 10-4. *Network Connections, Advanced, Advanced Settings Window*

■ **Tip** If you do not press the Alt key from the Network Connections window the Advanced menu option will never appear in the window. Make sure you hit the Alt key when that window is active or you will spend a lot of time being frustrated when you can't find the Advanced Settings option!

This will bring up the Adapter and Bindings window where you can actually modify the binding order for each interface connection. If you have cluster interfaces, this is where you can move them to the top of the list so the DNS name resolution process works as expected. Figure 10-5 shows the window to modify the binding order.

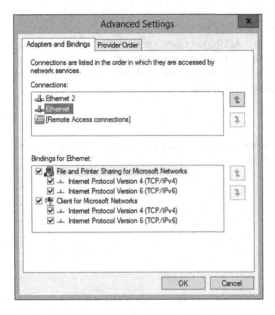

Figure 10-5. *Adapters and Bindings advanced settings*

While a binding order is not an IPv6-specific issue, it is so common that I felt it was important to cover, at least quickly, how to do this, as you can control whether IPv4 or IPv6 is listed first or second on an interface. As I mentioned earlier, this should not impact how the OS behaves for the majority of services, but there may be rare cases where you will have to deal with it. I imagine Microsoft will want this dependency to go away entirely, but for now you will need to know about it.

IPAM in Windows

One of the biggest mistakes I see people make when deploying IPv6 is the lack of a management system for their IPv6 addresses. While getting a small lab operational is relatively easy, a production deployment of IPv6 will quickly grow beyond the limits of most IP address management systems used previously. These were typically spreadsheets, scraps of paper, or a quick review of the DHCP server and routing table to see what was in use on a network. With IPv6 the world of address management becomes a much more serious issue.

I think this becomes more obvious when trying to deal with the total IPv6 addresses available in a single /64 prefix. As noted in Chapter 3, with 2^{64} addresses available it is not possible to store all the IPv6 addresses in a standard spreadsheet, and it would not be an efficient way of doing things even if you could. Just imagine trying to search for a hostname or IPv6 address in a spreadsheet that large—it would take forever.

Because it is very unlikely that you will use anywhere near the usable address space in a /64, it makes much more sense to have a dynamic system that only keeps track of actual in-use IPv6 addresses. With this in mind, Microsoft has provided a specific tool to meet this requirement: IP Address Management (IPAM). The IPAM solution from Microsoft is good enough, but I recommend companies to evaluate if that is really all they require. There are DNS, DHCP, and IPAM (DDI) solutions available from companies like Infoblox, SolarWinds, and others, and often these provided enhanced functionality above and beyond what Microsoft provides in its solution. With that being said, Microsoft's

IPAM solution is available for free and is integrated into the OS platform. My best practice recommendation is to run some sort of IPAM, so at a minimum you should run that.

To install the IPAM role on a Windows Server 2012 R2 host you can use the following PowerShell cmdlet:

```
Install-WindowsFeature IPAM -IncludeManagementTools
```

Microsoft recommends you install the IPAM role on a server that is AD joined since it will be able to pull information from other AD services. If you do not do this, then you are not gaining some of the advantages of the IPAM service so do make sure your Windows server is AD joined. After the role is installed you need to actually set up the database and roles, so issue the following PowerShell cmdlet to set all that up:

```
Invoke-IpamServerProvisioning -Confirm:$false -Force
```

Once that is done you can now leverage the IPAM role with PowerShell or with the GUI client that Server Manager makes available. Figure 10-6 shows the Server Manager IPAM role installed.

Figure 10-6. *Server Manager IPAM role*

You will have to install the client separately if you are managing IPAM remotely; there is a link available in Server Manager to do this if, when you did the PowerShell cmdlet, you left off the -IncludeManagementTools parameter. Figure 10-7 shows the link for the IPAM client installation wizard.

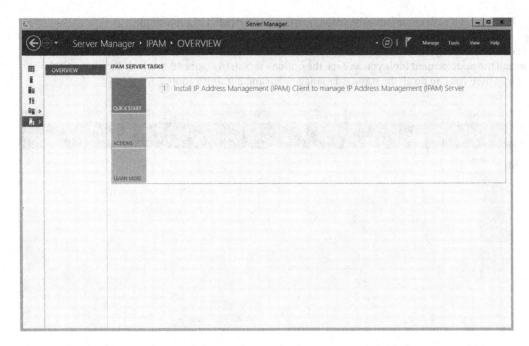

Figure 10-7. IPAM client install wizard launch

When you launch the link it brings up the installation wizard for the IPAM client as shown in Figure 10-8.

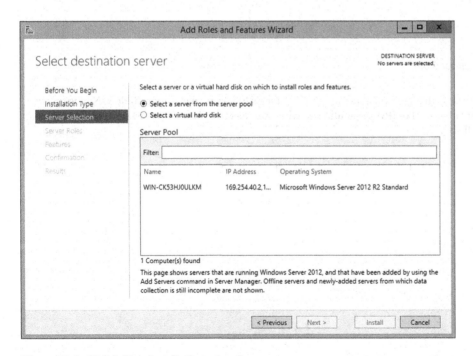

Figure 10-8. IPAM client installation wizard

Personally I have found it easier to remove the IPAM service and to install it again with the
-IncludeManagementTools parameter as I have seen problems with getting the roles and features set up separately
with the wizard later. Your mileage may vary.

If you did install the management tools you will see the options shown in Figure 10-9, which shows the IPAM
Overview page. From here you can do all the standard management and administration.

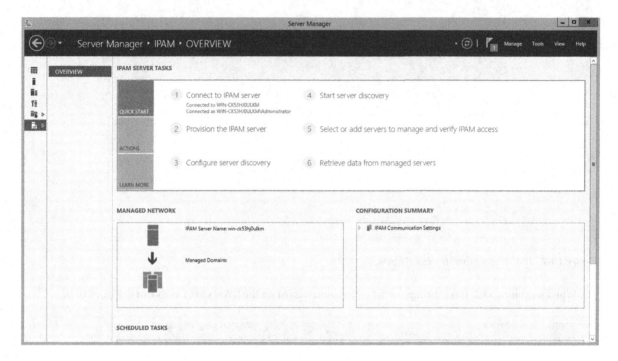

Figure 10-9. *IPAM Overview window*

Figure 10-10 shows the tasks that are available from the IP Address Blocks management window. Notice that you
can perform these tasks for either IPv4 or IPv6 depending on what you select. All functional tasks you could complete
can be done via PowerShell also.

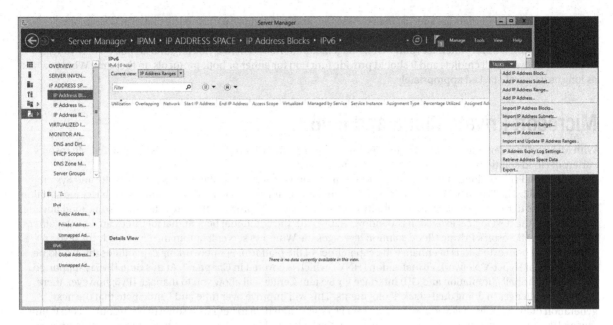

Figure 10-10. *IPAM options*

The list of PowerShell cmdlets for IPAM is pretty extensive. A shorter list of those you might find useful includes

```
Add-IpamAddress
Add-IpamBlock
Add-IpamRange
Add-IpamSubnet
Export-IpamAddress
Export-IpamRange
Export-IpamSubnet
Find-IpamFreeAddress
Get-IpamAddress
Get-IpamBlock
Get-IpamCapability
Get-IpamConfiguration
Get-IpamDatabase
Get-IpamRange
Get-IpamSubnet
Import-IpamAddress
Import-IpamRange
Import-IpamSubnet
Remove-IpamAddress
Remove-IpamBlock
Remove-IpamSubnet
Set-IpamAddress
Set-IpamBlock
Set-IpamConfiguration
Set-IpamSubnet
Update-IpamServer
```

Obviously these cmdlets are specific to the IPAM role and if you utilize a third-party platform (i.e., Infoblox Trinzic IPAM) the interaction between the Windows OS and those platforms will likely be through some other API (application programming interface) and GUI management interface. There is nothing that is specific to IPv6 vs. IPv4 in the IPAM PowerShell cmdlets and it should provide function for either or both protocols on the same Windows host as long as it is dual-stacked appropriately.

Microsoft Private Cloud and IPv6

With Microsoft's recent push of defining its Windows OS as the new Cloud OS platform, it is natural that Microsoft's variety of cloud solutions would support IPv6 in some capacity.

Microsoft Private Cloud encompasses several components—specifically, Windows Server 2012 R2 and System Center 2012 R2. The Private Cloud solution leverages all these components to deliver a unique scalable cloud solution for companies to run on premise with the ability to extend to a service provider that provides Microsoft Cloud hosting. Additionally, the next logical extension is Windows Azure with the additional benefit that all three can work together.

Because Microsoft's Private Cloud solution leverages the Windows server it automatically is ready for IPv6. Microsoft has built extensions to enhance the capabilities of the platform. For networking capabilities this would be the addition of Hyper-V Network Virtualization (HNV), which is covered in Chapter 7. At this time IPv6 is supported and the PowerShell automation and GUI interface for System Center will allow you to manage IPv6; however, there are some challenges in doing dual-stack deployments. This will improve over time and I anticipate that the next generation of Private Cloud development may even leverage more IPv6 to help with some of the resource constraints that an IPv4 network solution presents—in particular, the lack of public IPv4 addresses to allow for unique services, which is not an issue for IPv6.

For now, just realize that Microsoft's Private Cloud solution is fully ready for IPv6 and you should not have any issues with implementing your IPv6 data center solution on top of Microsoft's solution.

Azure and IPv6

Azure today does not support IPv6 in any capacity unless you are setting up IaaS (infrastructure as a service) with a shared service name for virtual machines that are hosted in Azure. Even then, the IPv6 support will only be link-local in nature by default. If you chose to deploy ULA or global unicast you will find that you have no native IPv6 support at all and are unable to connect to public IPv6 resources.

At this time Microsoft has not published any status on when global unicast IPv6 address support will happen in Windows Azure. I would be surprised if Microsoft does not announce some sort of IPv6 support in 2014, but there is no guarantee this will happen. Given that some of the competitors of Azure are already providing IPv6 I would not be shocked to hear that it is on the supported roadmap, but unfortunately I do not have more details to share.

IPv6 and Microsoft Support

Another common comment I hear from many Windows administrators is the following: "I just turn off IPv6 on all my Windows devices. I don't have to worry about IPv6 at all." I get flashes of Star Trek landing parties and this Windows administrator is a red shirt—he is going die in this episode, he just doesn't know it yet!

At this point I'd like to reiterate that even Microsoft says not to turn off IPv6. In fact, since 2008, Microsoft no longer tests its own software in IPv4-only deployments. Think about that. This means that if you turn off IPv6 you are technically running an untested configuration. The consequence of choosing not to run IPv6 is that the burden is on you to validate everything as being operationally supported in an IPv4-only environment. I am pretty sure most companies purchase support from Microsoft exactly so they don't have to do that. For those that don't, believe me, here is the TechNet article for your enjoyment.

http://technet.microsoft.com/en-us/network/cc987595.aspx#EKG

Make no mistake, Microsoft will do everything it can to help support your deployment of its software (within reason). Just be aware that Microsoft may ask you to turn IPv6 back on. So, if your stance is to ignore or turn off IPv6 for as long as possible, Microsoft may cut your dreams a bit short. For this reason alone I recommend to all my friends and colleagues in the industry, learn IPv6. IPv6 is a critical technology you need to know, I hope this book helps you on your journey to learning it.

IPv6 is the future and the future is now.

Index

▨ L

▨ M

Get the eBook for only $10!

Now you can take the weightless companion with you anywhere, anytime. Your purchase of this book entitles you to 3 electronic versions for only $10.

This Apress title will prove so indispensible that you'll want to carry it with you everywhere, which is why we are offering the eBook in 3 formats for only $10 if you have already purchased the print book.

Convenient and fully searchable, the PDF version enables you to easily find and copy code—or perform examples by quickly toggling between instructions and applications. The MOBI format is ideal for your Kindle, while the ePUB can be utilized on a variety of mobile devices.

Go to www.apress.com/promo/tendollars to purchase your companion eBook.

Apress®
THE EXPERT'S VOICE™